Education and Employment:
The DfEE and its Place
in History

Richard Aldrich
David Crook
David Watson

Bedford Way Papers

INSTITUTE OF
EDUCATION
UNIVERSITY OF LONDON

Rt Hon. David Blunkett,
Secretary of State for Education and Employment, 1997–.
By courtesy of David Blunkett and the DfEE.

Spencer Cavendish, 8th Duke of Devonshire,
President of the Board of Education, 1900–1902.
By courtesy of the National Portrait Gallery, London

Rt Hon. John Hodge,
Minister of Labour, 1916–1917.
By courtesy of the National Portrait Gallery, London

First published in 2000 by the Institute of Education, University of London,
20 Bedford Way, London WC1H 0AL

Pursuing Excellence in Education

© Institute of Education, University of London 2000

British Library Cataloguing in Publication Data:
A catalogue record for this publication is available from the British Library

ISBN 0 85473 605 0

Design and Typography by Joan Rose
Cover design by Tim McPhee
Page make-up by Cambridge Photosetting, Cambridge

Production services by
Book Production plc, Cambridge

Printed by Watkiss Studios Ltd, Biggleswade, Beds

Contents

Acknowledgements

Many people have helped in the preparation of this book; we thank them all.

Rt. Hon. David Blunkett MP, Sir Michael Bichard and Sir Tim Lankester allowed us to conduct substantial interviews. We are most grateful to David Blunkett and the DfEE for permission to include his photograph, and to the National Portrait Gallery, London for permission to include the portraits of Spencer Cavendish, Eighth Duke of Devonshire, and Rt. Hon. John Hodge.

Useful feedback was provided by those who attended our seminars at an international vocational workshop in Oslo in August 1997, the annual conference of the History of Education Society at the University of Wales, Swansea, in December 1997, the Institute of Education in July 1998, the Institute of Historical Research in May 1999 and the conference of the British Educational Research Association at the University of Sussex in September 1999.

Patrick Ainley, David Budge, Collin Crooks, Dennis Dean, Peter Gosden, Rodney Lowe, Gary McCulloch, Peter Mortimore, Peter Robinson, Jim Tomlinson, Geoff Whitty, Susan Williams and an anonymous external reader provided information and advice. Averil Aldrich, Christopher Clews and James Thomas assisted in the production of the final manuscript. Deborah Spring and Sarah Jenkin saw the book into print.

Our main debt, however, is to the Nuffield Foundation, whose generous support has been essential to the writing of this book and to the conduct of the research upon which it is based.

Richard Aldrich
David Crook
David Watson
Institute of Education
University of London

Abbreviations

ACAS	Advisory, Conciliation and Arbitration Service
ADT	American District Telegraph
AOC	Association of Colleges
BACIE	British Association for Commercial and Industrial Education
BMA	Bundesministerium für Arbeit und Sozialordnung
BTEC	Business and Technician Education Council
CBI	Confederation of British Industry
CPS	Centre for Policy Studies
CPSA	Civil and Public Services Association
CSE	Certificate of Secondary Education
CTC	City Technology College
DE	Department of Employment
DES	Department of Education and Science
DETR	Department of the Environment, Transport and the Regions
DfE	Department for Education
DfEE	Department for Education and Employment
DoE	Department of the Environment
DPO	Department Planning Organization
DTI	Department of Trade and Industry
EEF	Engineering Employers Federation
EOC	Equal Opportunities Commission
ES	Employment Service
ET	Employment Training
EU	European Union
FE	Further Education
FEFC	Further Education Funding Council
FEU	Further Education Unit
GCE	General Certificate of Education
GCSE	General Certificate of Secondary Education
GDP	Gross Domestic Product
GHQ	General Headquarters
GNVQ	General National Vocational Qualification
GPO	General Post Office
GTC	Government Training Centre
HE	Higher Education
HMI	Her/His Majesty's Inspectorate
HSE/C	Health and Safety Executive/Commission
ICL	International Computer Limited

ICT	Information and Communication Technology
ILA	Individual Learning Account
ILEA	Inner London Education Authority
IMF	International Monetary Fund
ITA	Industrial Training Act
ITB	Industrial Training Board
JIC	Juvenile Instruction Centre
JUC	Juvenile Unemployment Centre
LEA	Local Education Authority
LEC	Local Enterprise Company
MP	Member of Parliament
MSC	Manpower Services Commission
NACEIC	National Advisory Council on Education for Industry and Commerce
NACETT	National Advisory Council for Education and Training Targets
NAFE	Non-Advanced Further Education
NATFHE	National Association of Teachers in Further and Higher Education
NAHT	National Association of Head Teachers
NCE	National Commission on Education
NCVQ	National Council for Vocational Qualifications
NHS	National Health Service
NTI	New Training Initiative
NTO	National Training Organisation
NTTF	National Training Task Force
NUT	National Union of Teachers
NVQ	National Vocational Qualification
OECD	Organization for Economic Co-operation and Development
OFSTED	Office for Standards in Education
PAR	Programme Analysis and Research
PPS	Parliamentary Private Secretary
QCA	Qualifications and Curriculum Authority
RDA	Regional Development Agency
SCAA	School Curriculum and Assessment Authority
SCIP	Schools Council Industry Project
SEAC	School Examinations and Assessment Council
TA	Training Agency
TC	Training Commission
TEC	Training and Enterprise Council
TEED	Training, Enterprise and Education Directorate
TES	*Times Educational Supplement*
TOPS	Training Opportunities Scheme
TRG	Tory Reform Group
TSA	Training Services Agency

TSD	Training Services Division
TUC	Trades Union Congress
TVEI	Technical and Vocational Education Initiative
UfI	University for Industry
UGC	University Grants Committee
USSR	Union of Soviet Socialist Republics
WEA	Workers' Educational Association
WEF	World Economic Forum
WO	Welsh Office
YEO	Youth Employment Officer
YES	Youth Employment Service
YOP	Youth Opportunities Programme
YTS	Youth Training Scheme

1 Introduction

Starting points

The Department for Education and Employment (DfEE) was created in July 1995. In September of that year the DfEE set out its overall aim as being:

> To support economic growth and improve the nation's competitiveness and quality of life by raising standards of educational achievement and skill and by promoting an efficient and flexible labour market.[1]

In November 1995, a DfEE briefing paper entitled *The English Education System: An Overview of Structure and Policy* repeated this aim verbatim, and declared it to be 'the government's principal aim for the education service at all levels and in all forms of learning'.[2]

The creation of the DfEE can be interpreted in many ways. Some of these interpretations are explored in Chapter Two. For example, it might be seen as reward to a minister for political loyalty, or as a cost-cutting administrative measure leading to a 32 per cent reduction of posts at the divisional manager level. To the historian, however, the DfEE, its structures and policies, essentially represent a potentially fundamental cultural change.

Education and employment are two of the most basic and important of human activities. For most of human history, children have been educated with a view to their future employment. In medieval times, education was vocational, social, religious and moral. Much of this education took place in the family, where fathers and mothers prepared sons and daughters for their future occupations and roles in life. This was supplemented by more formal arrangements, for example, in church, in apprenticeship, and in school. Schools might teach rudimentary literacy to many, but extended schooling was a means of vocational preparation for a few.

In the eighteenth century, the decline in the domestic economy was accompanied by a decline in domestic education. In the nineteenth century, education was revolutionized by the rise of the schooled society, a process which removed children from the labour market. At the same time, employment was transformed by industrialization and urbanization. In the early years of the twentieth century, the state's increasing interest in these two areas of education and employment was indicated by the establishment of the Board of Education and the Ministry of Labour. By the end of the twentieth century, however, state-controlled schooling had not only usurped many of the educational functions of family, church and workplace, but had also transformed its traditional purpose. The school curriculum, as confirmed by the Education Reform Act 1988, was organized into subject disciplines. In the United Kingdom, as in the majority of other countries around the world, the academic had taken precedence over the vocational.

For most of the twentieth century, the existence of two separate government ministries seemed to reinforce the gap between education and employment. Of course, some contacts and similarities between the two departments existed, but they also exhibited distinct cultures in terms of ethos and policy. Their fusion in 1995 raised two fundamental questions. Would employment once again become the chief goal of education? Would the new department recognize and support the educational and employment opportunities provided by such factors as the revolution in information and communications technology and the changing nature and location of work?

With such questions in mind, in 1996 two of the authors of this book, Richard Aldrich and David Crook, prepared a proposal for an historical and cultural study of the DfEE. The proposal became reality as a result of generous financial support from the Nuffield Foundation, which allowed David Watson to be recruited as a full-time project officer for some 18 months from September 1997. This book is the major outcome of the project.

We all approach things from different positions. As indicated above, our starting point, as historians, was the belief that the creation of the DfEE marked a potentially important turning point in British, and particularly English, history.[3] A similar sense of historic occasion was apparent amongst some contemporary commentators in 1995. Only a minority of these commentators, however, was probably aware of the origins and histories of the two separate departments, which had begun life as the Board of Education in 1900 and the Ministry of Labour in 1916. From education's perspective the merger was welcomed as a means of ending what were widely perceived as long-standing and damaging educational, social and cultural divisions, divisions reflected in hierarchies of educational institutions and of types of knowledge. These found expression in distinctions between private and public, education and training, academic and vocational. Many employers shared these perceptions, and welcomed in particular the new department's emphasis upon skills and vocational qualifications.

The DfEE, therefore, was hailed as a means of producing a better-educated and trained workforce. It was also seen as a body that would bring to an end the anti-industrial and commercial culture so long associated with the most prestigious of England's schools and universities, and which commentators such as Correlli Barnett and Martin Wiener had identified as being a major cause of Britain's relative economic decline.[4] The work of Barnett and Wiener was enormously influential within political circles including the Thatcher cabinets of the 1980s where, according to John MacGregor (Secretary of State for Education and Science, 1989–1990), it was widely read – an example perhaps of the contribution of historical analysis to current policy-making.[5]

The DfEE's first Secretary of State emphasized the importance of the new department as an enabling structure. In July 1995, at the time of the merger, Gillian Shephard announced to a conference of directors of Training and Enterprise Councils (TECs):

I know structure does not mean policy, but a lack of structure can inhibit policy. I didn't put forward a vision – it's not the way that I work. We have to have a structure to allow the vision and to see how best to use to advantage all these new opportunities.[6]

However, not all comments were favourable, and the constant stream of instrumental initiatives from the DfEE soon aroused the hostility of those critics who feared that the purposes of state education were being redefined in terms of the market economy. Thus, in September 1998, in a sharp attack on the 'National Year of Reading', Libby Purves declared that 'We have now almost entirely reduced education to "training"; we have a government department ominously called Education and Employment as if the sole purpose of the first was the second. It isn't.'[7] Richard Hoggart has described the approach of the DfEE as:

Gradgrind translated into late-twentieth century language; not a word about education 'for the love of God and the relief of man's estate'. Instead, the key word, as the relentless bright initiatives follow one another, is 'vocational'. Which means that every new promotion must be described purely functionally, as marketable, performance-assessable, and financially definable.[8]

At the same time, critics from the employment side were pointing out that good quality education and training were neither a sufficient, nor perhaps in some instances even a necessary, condition of full employment. Highly skilled and well motivated workers in England were being made redundant as a result of such factors as global recession, fall in demand, and a collapse in prices of a range of commodities from oil to micro-chips. These were events over which they, their employers and even the government, appeared to have little, if any, control. By the late 1990s, those very countries of Asia, including Japan, whose educational standards and employment levels had long been held up as models to emulate, were themselves suffering severe economic problems.

International perspectives

The creation of the DfEE was an important episode in British history, but its significance must also be appreciated in an international context. Issues of education (including lifelong learning) and the promotion of active labour market policies (often linked to social security systems) have become major priorities for governments around the globe. There is a widespread, although not necessarily universal, belief that high-quality education and training systems provide a key to national economic prosperity and to social cohesion, although the levels and content of such education and training are matters of debate. As yet, moreover, there is no clear answer as to what kinds of new administrative structures and values, if any, will best serve to promote and support these concerns. For example, in the European Union (EU), uncertainty still exists over whether vocational education should be within the domain of education, employment or welfare policy.[9] This is a key issue and a source of considerable tension between education and training providers. What is clear, however, is that the United Kingdom's Department for Education and Employment represents a unique solution, and one that is being watched with great interest.

A broad shift towards supply side measures in education and employment is visible in almost every member country of the Organization for Economic Co-operation and Development (OECD). Indeed, in the 1980s, the OECD promoted the concept of employability internationally, arguing for a fusion of education and economic policy within the general ambit of human capital theory.[10] This theory, developed in the USA and elsewhere during the 1960s, maintains that education and training which boost individuals' skills are a national economic investment rather than a cost. Thus, the education system is not only a social service, as it was viewed until the late 1950s, but a part of economic policy. In many countries, however, the dominant policy development has been a merger of employment and welfare structures and policies, rather than those of employment and education. In September 1997, the Australian government established a new organization, Centrelink, responsible to the Minister of Social Security, which unified the delivery of the Employment Services, training programmes and social security benefits. The service delivery functions of the former Department of Social Security were separated from the central, policy-development functions.[11] In New Zealand, the Employment Service, the benefit agency, community employment and training schemes have been integrated under a Minister of Social Services, Work and Income. Unemployment benefit will become a 'community wage', paid in return for community work or participation in training schemes.[12] The close co-ordination of employment and social security policy has also been the hallmark of recent German administrative changes. The Federal Ministry of Labour and Social Affairs (Bundesministerium für Arbeit und Sozialordnung [BMA]) is a combined employment and social security department, dealing with basic issues of youth unemployment, vocational training, job creation schemes, labour law, collective bargaining and social security. The BMA's remit includes the 'economic aspects of social policy and social aspects of financial and fiscal policy'.[13]

Concerns and changes, therefore, have been many, but, as Figure 1 indicates, the departmental structure created in the United Kingdom in July 1995 differs from those of other countries.

It would appear that no other country in the developed world has yet created a single department of education and employment. Until recently, Australia had a Department of Employment, Education, Training and Youth Affairs, but also retains a separate Labour department. In October 1998, employment services moved to a new Department of Employment, Workplace Relations and Small Business, leaving a Department of Education, Training and Youth Affairs. In other countries, the traditional separation between departments of education and employment continues, although in countries such as France and Japan superior government committees exist for the purpose of co-ordinating policy across such areas as education, employment and industrial policy.[14]

Terminology

Terms such as 'education and training', 'vocation' and 'employment' are central to this book, and it seems appropriate to attempt some preliminary

	GERMANY	**UNITED STATES OF AMERICA**	**AUSTRALIA**
EMPLOYMENT DEPARTMENT	**FEDERAL MINISTRY OF LABOUR AND SOCIAL AFFAIRS**	**DEPARTMENT OF LABOUR**	**DEPARTMENT OF EMPLOYMENT, WORKPLACE RELATIONS AND SMALL BUSINESS**
EDUCATION DEPARTMENT	**FEDERAL MINISTRY OF EDUCATION, RESEARCH AND TECHNOLOGY**	**DEPARTMENT OF EDUCATION**	**DEPARTMENT OF EDUCATION, TRAINING AND YOUTH AFFAIRS**
	NEW ZEALAND	**JAPAN**	**SOUTH KOREA**
EMPLOYMENT DEPARTMENT	**DEPARTMENT OF LABOUR/ DEPARTMENT OF WORK AND INCOME**	**MINISTRY OF LABOUR**	**MINISTRY OF LABOUR**
EDUCATION DEPARTMENT	**MINISTRY OF EDUCATION**	**MINISTRY OF EDUCATION, SCIENCE, SPORTS AND CULTURE**	**MINISTRY OF EDUCATION**

Figure 1: Government Employment and Education Departments in Six Countries

definitions here, if only to indicate the complexities which surround them. Education has two key properties. The first is that it is concerned with the acquisition of knowledge, skills and values which are generally considered to be worthwhile. For example, to teach someone to be a liar or a thief would be mis-education rather than education. In contrast, one might be trained as a liar or thief. The second is that education allows for participation by the person being educated, both in the process and in the outcomes. The term 'training' also implies the transmission of knowledge, skills and values from one person to another, but without such participation by the trainee. Thus, it is possible to speak of a person being self-educated, but not self-trained. Given the connotations of these two words, it is not surprising that education is often considered to be superior to training.

The term 'vocational' has two widely differing meanings. A vocation may be defined as a call or commitment to a particular occupation. In particular, it was especially applied to service – either to God (for example, as a missionary, priest or nun) or in a caring profession such as medicine or teaching. Vocational education in this sense meant preparation for the exercise of such a vocation. During the nineteenth century, however, the term 'vocational education' also came to be used pejoratively, in contrast to academic or liberal education – education for its own sake and intrinsic worth. Today, vocational education is frequently applied to training for a range of semi-skilled and low-status occupations.

Employment means engagement in work or some other occupation or activity. To be unemployed is to be without work or occupation. Some employment may lead to financial or other rewards; other employment may not. Not all work is necessarily considered as being worthwhile, and some types of work are considered to be more valuable than others. For some people, the most valuable work is that which secures the greatest financial rewards; for others in the caring professions, such as nurses, value may be measured in terms of enhancing the well-being of those in their charge. Some employment is freely chosen and enjoyed; other work is undertaken under duress and brings little reward, either in terms of finance or fulfilment. Throughout history, much of the work undertaken by children and young people has fallen into the latter category.

Cultural perspectives

The purpose of this section is to attempt some definition of the terms 'culture' and 'cultural', and to explain how they are employed in this book.

History and historical perspectives may be taken to include all the dimensions of human existence – political, administrative, economic, social and cultural. The use of the word 'cultural' in such a list would imply artistic or leisure activities, although there would probably be no agreement as to what should be included, while disputes over whether some cultural activities ('high culture') are superior to others have a long history. Yet the term 'cultural' is not restricted to artistic or leisure activities, and has a multiplicity of meanings and connotations. In its broadest anthropological sense, indeed, like the term 'history', it can be applied to every element in the life of a people or nation.

The complexity of cultural definition may be demonstrated further. Perhaps the most common use of the term 'culture' is in respect of a nation, i.e. national culture. Thus, it is a truism to state that the United Kingdom has a culture which is distinct in many respects (for example, language) from those say of Germany or Indonesia. Although the United Kingdom is united, a single state with a single monarchy, each of its four parts – England, Northern Ireland, Scotland and Wales – has a separate history as well as a shared one. Each also has distinctive national, linguistic, religious (and in an artistic sense as used above) cultural identities. They also have distinctive (as well as shared) histories of education and employment. These distinctions are reflected in constitutional and administrative arrangements, for there have long been separate ministers and departments, and now even assemblies, for Northern Ireland, Scotland and Wales, although not for England. The inhabitants of the three smaller countries are proud of their separate identities and also of their shared Celtic heritage and culture, although the term 'Anglo-Saxon' is used widely in a broad cultural sense to describe not only the United Kingdom, but, on occasion, other countries such as Australia and New Zealand which once formed part of the British Empire. Indeed, within any broad culture or group there are separate cultures, based upon a variety of factors, including age, sex, ethnic origin, social class, wealth, and education and employment.

Complexities in national culture are mirrored at other levels. For example, there may be a clear demarcation between the roles and cultures of politicians on the one hand (the members of the two Houses of Parliament) and civil servants on the other. Yet individuals have moved from one category to another, while history provides several examples of civil servants, 'statesmen in disguise' such as James Kay-Shuttleworth and Robert Morant, who have taken leading roles in the determination, as well as the execution, of government policy. The cultures of Westminster and Whitehall are in a constant state of flux, and James Christoph has outlined the ways in which Margaret Thatcher attempted 'to shape the senior British Civil Service into a responsive instrument of policy implementation from the standpoint of her political values'.[15] There can be little doubt that in recent years the work of the Civil Service has become more politicized, for example with the appointment within Education of such advisers as Stuart Sexton under the Conservatives and Michael Barber under Labour. Chris Woodhead, the current Chief Inspector of Schools, has become embroiled in more than one political controversy. Another significant development has been the proliferation of quasi-autonomous non-governmental organizations, quangos, which have frequently been packed with government supporters.[16]

Recent discussions of education and employment have emphasized the role of education as a major culprit as a factor in British economic decline. Such discussions, as in the writings of Barnett and Wiener, have frequently been located within broad cultural frames which can conflate a variety of meanings or levels of culture. For example, Wiener asserted that in the first half of the nineteenth century English culture was characterized by an industrial spirit. He saw the Great Exhibition of 1851 as marking the high water mark of that spirit; subsequent years were notable for its decline. The anti-industry spirit became diffused throughout society and Whitehall, and was reproduced through the educational system. Although such analysis was widely challenged by historians, by the end of the 1950s the notion that the United Kingdom was suffering from serious economic decline had become a common theme in political discourse. 'Declinism', which emphasized subjective or cultural explanations for this condition, became popular at the same time as theories of human capital which internalized skills and education into classical economic theory. Declinist cultural interpretations, however, should not be confined to educational and economic contexts. At the beginning of the twentieth century, a nation which had the largest empire and navy in history had an understandable confidence in its institutions and policies. That confidence was shattered in two World Wars and their aftermaths, and by the end of the 1950s it was clear that the United Kingdom was no longer a major world power.

This perceived culture of decline has been enormously influential. The sequence of four Conservative electoral victories from 1979 was achieved in great measure because Margaret Thatcher and John Major convinced the electorate that theirs was the party which could reverse the decline, by the introduction of a new enterprise culture based upon private rather than public initiatives. Margaret Thatcher, who had herself been Secretary of State for Education (1970–1974), had a very low opinion of the Education department, and was aware of the difficulty of securing radical change. She deplored what she saw as the excessive power of the educational producers, particularly left-wing local education authorities (LEAs) and teachers' unions, and later regretted that her most significant educational reform was delayed until 1988. Similarly, Conservative governments were wary of a Ministry of Labour which had come to be seen as providing a voice for trade unions within Whitehall itself.

This study focuses upon the DfEE and its antecedents, their core responsibilities and areas of interaction. It does not provide comprehensive accounts of the work of the Education and Employment departments throughout the twentieth century. It does not engage in any substantial way with structural and policy analyses proceeding from a sociological perspective.[17] It is concerned, like the cultural studies of Barnett and Wiener, with long-term historical perspectives, but also with a clearer sense of the different uses of the term culture. It recognizes three levels of culture: broad national cultural or intellectual debates, the political and organizational cultures that permeate Whitehall and the body politic as a whole,[18] and the administrative cultures of specific departments and their agencies.[19] These three categories are distinct, although closely interrelated. Policy-makers are influenced, and at times constrained, by broad national debates and by organizational and administrative cultures. Organizational and administrative cultures are affected by political decisions, which may in themselves have organizational connotations. For example, the creation of the DfEE brought about considerable administrative change in the two former departments, but political decisions in 1995 about the reshuffle of ministers were constrained by an organizational imperative – an unwillingness to increase the size of the Cabinet. The role of individual ministers is also important. For example, the status and culture of the Education department under Sir Keith Joseph (1981–1986) differed considerably from what it had been under his predecessor, Mark Carlisle, and what it was to become under his successor, Kenneth Baker.[20] During the 1980s, the status and culture of the Education and Employment departments, their ministers and civil servants, were influenced by powerful political figures such as Michael Heseltine at the Department of the Environment (DoE) and by Margaret Thatcher herself.[21] The role of individuals has also been affected by changes in the media. Politicians have long been aware of the power of the press, and from the inter-War years of the radio; few more so than Churchill. However, the advent of television, the photo opportunity, the 'sound-bite' and the 'spin', have brought about further fundamental cultural changes.

Finally, in this section, having indicated the problems and complexities of the cultural perspective, what of the cultural reputations of the two departments?

In the inter-War period the Board of Education was likened, on occasion, to an Oxford college. Its Oxford-educated senior civil servants, such as Sir Edmund Chambers and Sir Lewis Selby-Bigge, even its eyes and ears, His Majesty's Inspectors (HMIs) such as Dover Wilson, were scholars who continued to engage in research and writing during their time at the Board. During the whole of the twentieth century the Education department was relatively small in the context of government departments. It was a policy and supervisory department; the responsibility for the actual provision of education – in terms of building, teachers and ancillary services – lay with the LEAs. The education service was provided locally, although under central direction.

The Employment department presented a different culture. It was a larger department in terms of staff, with a direct responsibility for delivering a service. As such, it was more accountable for its budget. In the inter-War period, the Ministry of Labour did not exude a collegiate air and its civil servants took an active role in promoting measures to alleviate unemployment, including the development of juvenile instruction centres. By the second half of the twentieth century, senior staff in further education had built up a preference for dealing with an Employment department whose nationwide network of offices were staffed by civil servants who had intelligence and information about job vacancies and skills requirements in particular localities. For most of its existence, the department's core culture was defined as encouraging co-operation between the two sides of industry and avoiding the imposition of settlements by central government. By the 1980s, this culture was beginning to be undermined by the intrusion of neo-liberal ideas concerning the role of the state and of trade unions in industry. Similarly, the emphasis of the Employment Service changed from job finding and placement to benefit-related work.

Although there were differences, there were also many similarities. In common with the rest of Westminster and Whitehall, both departments were headed by white people, nearly all of whom were male. Between 1900 and 1994, all but five of the 46 political heads of the Education department were men, while between 1916 and 1994 there were 37 ministers for Employment, of whom only three were women. During these periods all 16 permanent secretaries at Employment and all but one of the 16 at Education were men. All of the permanent secretaries received knighthoods; the one woman, Mary Smieton, became a dame. While the average length of tenure for a minister in both departments was two years, the average for a permanent secretary was five at Employment and six in Education. Until the 1980s, the general political culture of both departments was shaped by the principles of partnership with local interests and a broadly voluntaristic attitude to their respective clientele. Both departments had internal divisions which allowed for the development of sub-cultures. One clear example of this in Education were the HMI, whose independence on occasion made them a thorn in the flesh of ministers and civil servants alike. Further sub-divisions were complemented by connections between the two departments, so that a common policy or concern might exist between sections of the two departments on a particular issue. Recognition of these former sub divisions and connections is important when considering the success or otherwise of the merger represented by the DfEE, and the extent to which two former separate cultures have continued within it.

Historical perspectives

This section provides two historical perspectives. The first sets out an introductory historical framework. The second provides an explanation of the historical perspectives approach which has determined the organization of this book.

Figure 2 provides a diagrammatic representation of the two departments which began their lives in 1900 and 1916 as the Board of Education and the Ministry of Labour respectively. Further basic information in the shape of the names of the ministers and permanent secretaries throughout this period is provided in the appendices. The origins and early years of both ministries are considered in detail in Chapter Three. Long before the establishment of departments of state, however, governments had exercised power over both education and employment. For example, in 1559 royal injunctions prescribed the use of the *Royal Grammar* in schools and forbade any persons to teach without a Bishop's licence. Another important Elizabethan intervention was the Statute of Artificers 1563. This required written indentures to be drawn up for apprentices, and stated that no person should exercise a craft or trade without serving an apprenticeship of at least seven years and attaining the age of 24.

Direct antecedents in an administrative sense are to be found in the nineteenth century. The Ministry of Labour, established in 1916 during the First World War, may be viewed primarily as the development of one function of an existing department. In 1893 a Labour Department was created in the Board of Trade, and the new Ministry soon took over several responsibilities previously exercised by the Board. On the other hand, the Board of Education was an amalgamation of activities previously exercised by three separate bodies – the Education Department, the

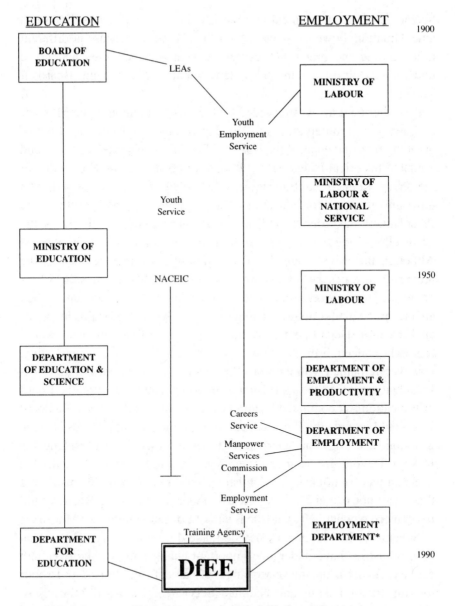

EDUCATION   EMPLOYMENT
                                                    1900

BOARD OF
EDUCATION
                    LEAs
                              MINISTRY OF
                              LABOUR

                    Youth
                    Employment
                    Service

                              MINISTRY OF
          Youth   LABOUR &
          Service   NATIONAL
                               SERVICE

MINISTRY OF
EDUCATION
                                                    1950
                    NACEIC
                              MINISTRY OF
                              LABOUR

DEPARTMENT
OF EDUCATION &   DEPARTMENT OF
SCIENCE   EMPLOYMENT &
                              PRODUCTIVITY

                    Careers
                    Service   DEPARTMENT OF
                    Manpower   EMPLOYMENT
                    Services
                    Commission

                    Employment
                    Service
                                   EMPLOYMENT
          Training Agency   DEPARTMENT*

DEPARTMENT   1990
FOR
EDUCATION   **DfEE**

*From 1988 the Department of Employment was also known as the Employment Department

Figure 2: The Education and Employment departments 1900–1995

Science and Art Department and the Charity Commissioners. Even this amalgamation, however, does not tell the full story, because at different times during the nineteenth century educational activities had come under the aegis of a number of departments, including the Board of Trade.

A further contrast was provided by the fact that although the Ministry of Labour was the epitome of a modern ministry, created at a time of great urgency and change, the Board of Education inherited a curious and outdated historical baggage. Its ultimate forebear was the Committee of the Privy Council on Education, established in 1839 to superintend government grants for education. The Committee, headed by the Lord President of the Council and including such leading ministers as the Chancellor of the Exchequer and the Home Secretary, met only rarely.[22] Although the Privy Council and its committees might be seen as the precursor of a general supervisory ministry, by 1856 the unsatisfactory nature of this device, which had become 'at first an irrelevance, then an anachronism and finally a laughing stock', led to the establishment of an Education Department, together with a Vice-President who would represent education in the House of Commons.[23] Overall responsibility, however, remained with the Lord President, while the duties of the Vice-President included the supervision of imported cattle. In 1899, the Board of Education Act continued this tradition of a supervisory body – a board that would include the President and other ministers. In fact this became a fiction, and with characteristic candour the then Lord President, the Duke of Devonshire, later admitted that he could not remember why the decision had been taken to establish a Board rather than a Ministry, but that it did not matter as it was clearly understood that the Board would never meet. Not until 1944 did the Board of Education become a Ministry.[24]

Several further comments may be made on Figure 2. The first is that both ministries have undergone important changes during the twentieth century. On occasion, the very changes of name, from Ministry of Labour to Ministry of Labour and National Service in 1939 and Ministry of Education to Department of Education and Science in 1964, indicate changes in areas of responsibility and emphasis. Given such changes, and given the variety of administrative arrangements current in other countries, there is every possibility that the DfEE will be subject to further reform, perhaps as a logical result of the development of such programmes as 'Lifelong Learning' or 'Welfare to Work'. The common antecedent of both departments in respect of the Board of Trade, albeit the one major the other minor, reflects the fact that Employment in particular has been strongly connected with government departments with major responsibility for economic policy. In 1996 an Employment Policy Institute report suggested that a Labour government could de-merge Education and Employment, resurrecting the Department for Education (DfE) and creating a new 'powerhouse' Department of Industry, containing economic, trade and training functions.[25] In the following year, Lord McCarthy, former adviser to Labour Employment Secretaries, proposed that there should be a Department of Work.[26] These proposals indicate concerns that the DfEE may not be an appropriate body to develop the long-term economic strategy, including the co-ordinated planning of long-term skills, that the nation requires.

Although proposals have been made for the disaggregation of the Department for Education and Employment, other commentators see the need not only for a greater sense of coherence within that body itself, but also for an organizational culture which demonstrates the ability to connect and co-operate with a wider range of bodies, including those at regional and local levels, and individual schools and firms. The theme of lifelong learning implies the need to co-ordinate enormously complex systems of education and training which have spread through different institutional areas of society and which are overseen by a variety of controlling bodies – central, regional and local. One fundamental example of this need for co-ordination may be seen in respect of the relationship between the DfEE and the TECs. Indeed, comments to the effect that the DfEE represents a merged culture of education and training need to be qualified by the recognition that by the time of the merger in 1995 the training element of the Employment department had been devolved to the TECs. Although the attainment of greater cohesion across the worlds of education and training in the context of lifelong learning may be difficult to achieve, it would appear to be consistent with other moves towards a more unified educational structure and culture: the introduction of a single examination, the General Certificate of Secondary Education (GCSE), at age 16, the establishment of a Qualifications and Curriculum Authority (QCA), the bringing together of academic and vocational qualifications and the end of the binary line in higher education.

Two further introductory comments, therefore, should be made here in respect of the relationship between the two departments and other levels of government, relationships which do not feature prominently in Figure 2. The role of super ministries or co-ordinating committees has already been noted with reference to such countries as France and Japan, but, as the succeeding chapters demonstrate, in the United Kingdom powerful Cabinet committees, on occasion chaired by the Prime Minister of the day, have also exercised supervisory functions over a number of policy areas, including those of education and employment. In October 1998 there were 15 ministerial committees of the Cabinet. The Secretary of State for Education and Employment served on four of these: Economic Affairs, Local Government, Home and Social Affairs, House of Lords Reform.[27] The idea of a 'superministry' has been mooted at various times in the twentieth century as a means of producing and implementing broad developmental policies. The roles of regional and local agencies must also be noted here. These have been reflected on several levels, for example by the existence of separate ministers and legislation for Northern Ireland, Scotland and Wales, by regional authorities, and by bodies such as LEAs which under the Act of 1902 were based principally upon counties and county boroughs.

The historical perspectives approach employed in this book was developed for a previous research project funded by the Leverhulme Trust.[28] It is based upon the belief that to situate ourselves accurately in time is potentially as rewarding as it is difficult. History is the study of human events with particular reference to the dimension of time – past, present and future. Our lives in the present and future are governed to a great extent by what has happened in the past. Each human situation is unique and we cannot predict the future with certainty. Nevertheless, the record of human experience that is usually referred to as 'history' provides a rich store of data which we neglect at our peril. Our understandings of the present and journeys into the future will benefit from possession of accurate maps of the past. The provision of such maps is one of the major tasks of the historian.

Historical study has many purposes, of which the understanding of the past in its own terms is the most important. But history also enables us to be wise before, rather than after, the event. History provides an acquaintance with a much greater range of human events and experiences than would be possible simply by reference to the contemporary world. Thus, it is a most important means of distinguishing between those things that are of permanent value and those that are transitory and ephemeral. In consequence, historical study may lead to a more sophisticated awareness not only of specific themes, for example the relationship between education and employment, but also of the nature of knowledge and of truth.

Previous historical studies have provided accounts of the development of each department as administrative organizations, for example Ince's *The Ministry of Labour and National Service*, written in 1960.[29] However, such studies often lack grounding in the political context of central administration. Others such as Pile's *The Department of Education and Science* or Lawrence's *Power and Politics at the Department of Education and Science* provide a political analysis but refer only obliquely to the social and economic factors underpinning historical change in the departments' functions and roles within Whitehall.[30] While many accounts have proved valuable to the current study, especially Lowe's history of the inter-War Ministry of Labour, *Adjusting to Democracy: The Role of the Ministry of Labour in British Politics, 1916–1939*,[31] as yet none has looked at the development of the two departments and the political and organizational relations between them over the course of the twentieth century.

The organization of this book reflects the historical perspectives approach employed in the Leverhulme project. The major outcome of that research was a book entitled *Education for the Nation*. That volume provided historical perspectives on seven educational themes: access, curriculum, standards and assessment, teaching quality, control, economic performance and consumers. Each chapter was divided into three sections: the contemporary situation, historical perspectives and conclusions drawn from the application of those historical perspectives to the contemporary situation. In this instance, however, the sequence of present, past and future is not employed within the separate chapters but encompasses the whole book. Thus, Chapter Two, which deals with the creation of the DfEE in 1995, is concerned with the present, or very recent past. Four historical chapters follow, in straight chronological sequence, from 1900 until 1995. These provide information and analysis about relationships between the Education and Employment departments throughout the century. Chapter Seven focuses upon developments which in Figure 2 are shown as lying between the two departments. This involves a revisiting of some of the historical period previously covered, but with a special emphasis on further education and employment. The concluding chapter draws out the historical perspectives and provides an assessment of issues currently facing the department.

Notes

1. DfEE press release, 210/95.
2. DfEE, 1995, 1.
3. The direction of education and employment within the United Kingdom is a complex matter, which is further complicated by the current process of devolution of powers to separate assemblies in Northern Ireland, Scotland and Wales. The principal concern of the Department for Education and Employment, and therefore of this book, is with England. Whilst the educational systems in Scotland and England have many similarities, the academic/vocational divide has not been as pronounced in Scotland as it has been in England. The debate in England around this issue, and around the need for institutional change, has been highly political but in Scotland it has had a lower profile. See Howieson et al, 1997.
4. Barnett, 1986; Wiener, 1981.
5. See McCulloch, 1994, 58.
6. *Financial Times*, 15 July 1995.
7. *The Times*, 22 September 1998.

8. *Guardian*, 14 May 1996.
9. Freedland, 1996.
10. Ashton and Green, 1996; Chitty, 1989.
11. See http://www.centrelink.gov.au
12. See the Department of Labour website at http://www.dol.govt.nz
13. See the BMA website at: http://www.bma.de For the Federal Ministry of Education, Science, Research and Technology, see http://www.bmbf.de
14. The Ministry of International Trade and Industry, and the Commissariat General du Plan.
15. Christoph, 1992, 163.
16. Dictionaries offer the alternative definitions of quasi non-governmental organizations and quasi-autonomous national governmental organizations.
17. See, for example, Ball, 1994; Gewirtz and Ozga, 1990; McPherson and Raab, 1988.
18. For organization theory and organizational culture, see Allaire and Firsirotu, 1984; Smircich, 1983; Mercier, 1994.
19. Anechiarico, 1998.
20. Baker, 1993, 161.
21. Young, 1989, 78.
22. Paz, 1976.
23. Bishop, 1971, 24.
24. For a further discussion of this point, see Aldrich and Leighton, 1985, 15–16.
25. Employment Policy Institute, 1996.
26. McCarthy, 1997, 6.
27. *The Times*, 22 October 1998.
28. 'Historical perspectives upon current educational issues', a project funded by the Leverhulme Trust, Ref. 1411. See Aldrich, 1996.
29. Ince, 1960.
30. Pile, 1979; Lawrence 1992.
31. Lowe, 1986.

2 The Creation of the DfEE

Introduction

The creation of the DfEE in July 1995 was welcomed by a broad range of organizations and individuals, from the National Union of Teachers (NUT) to the Confederation of British Industry (CBI). Many people involved in education and its administration saw the possibility of a solution to some of the policy problems associated with the long-standing divisions between academic and vocational qualifications, education and industry. As Michael Bichard, Permanent Secretary of the DfEE, put it, there was 'an unusual degree of support from people who seemed to be in agreement about little else'.[1] The merger united people whose concerns had traditionally been educational underachievement and inequality with those whose focus was national and individual competitiveness. The new DfEE embodied a shared understanding of the need for training and education to be brought under one administrative roof. For Sir Geoffrey Holland, who had served as Director of the Manpower Services Commission (MSC) and Permanent Secretary at Employment, 1989–1993 and Education, 1993–1994, it was 'an historic moment and an historic opportunity'.[2]

Gillian Shephard, the new department's first Secretary of State, declared that 'the merger was entirely welcome to me'.[3] She also claimed that it was:

> widely welcomed ... by absolutely everybody including a number of trade unions and a number of bodies representing employers ... and a number of other groups as well. I think that what has happened is that

employment and education can be seen as a continuum, which it is, in the experience of the individual.[4]

Shephard stated that:

The merger of the two departments gives us a once-in-a-lifetime chance to harness the strengths of Britain's de-regulated, innovative industrial sector to the strengths of our education system. We now have the opportunity to offer young people education, training and jobs that fit together in a single, seamless progression.[5]

The construction of a consensus was being attempted. This is perhaps indicated by the fact that the terms 'continuum' and 'seamless' used by Gillian Shephard to describe the link between education and employment were borrowed from previous, politically divergent merger recommendations, made by the National Commission on Education in 1993 and the Conservative Party's Tory Reform Group in 1994.[6]

Yet the Prime Minister's announcement of the merger also produced shock and concern among some observers, over the abrupt way the new department had been brought into being without a consultation process, and more particularly over the dispersal of the remaining functions of the Department of Employment (DE) across Whitehall. The Labour Party and the Trades Union Congress (TUC) both condemned the effective disappearance of a discrete Employment ministry as a means of 'sweeping unemployment and insecurity under the carpet'.[7] A few days earlier, the Conservative Party had emerged from a bruising leadership election in which John Major had defeated his opponents on the Euro-sceptic right wing. Some critics suspected that the merger, announced as part of a Cabinet re-shuffle, was a matter of expediency rather than the culmination of a carefully developed policy. In the summer of 1995 a rejuvenated Labour opposition was mounting a serious challenge in the increasingly important area of education. Gillian Shephard had redeemed some of the errors of her predecessor, John Patten. New alliances with educational interests would help to consolidate this progress by creating an agreement around the goal of a better educated and skilled workforce. The immediate political context, therefore, prompted doubts as to whether

such an institutional reorganization, a 'shotgun marriage' as one commentator put it,[8] would yield a new coherence in policy to match the
expectations it had aroused. Would structural merger mean the effective
integration of the cultures of education and employment or would absorp-
tion into one department lead to an entrenchment and deepening of existing differences?

In this chapter the formation of the DfEE is examined under four areas:
the reactions of a range of interested organizations; the recent history of
the idea of a merged department; the political process that led to the events
of July 1995; and the relative weight of the two antecedent departments
within the structures of the DfEE. The conclusion summarizes these
points and identifies issues to be examined in the succeeding historical
chapters.

Reactions to the merger

Michael Bichard has said that the merger was extraordinary for three
reasons.[9] First, the speed of the change was unprecedented; no-one in the
old Department for Education (DfE) or DE knew about the Prime Minister's
announcement until an hour before it was made. Most employees of the
two departments either received an e-mail from Gillian Shephard, or a
handwritten letter from the Secretary of State for Employment, Michael
Portillo, after the event. Second, the cultures of the two previous departments were very different. Both had long histories of working in particular ways: the DfE was a hands-off, policy-based administrator, while the
DE was a hands-on, frontline operator. Third, initially, two permanent
secretaries were retained, an unusual practice in Whitehall terms. There
are a number of possible explanations for this, including a concern to
prevent accusations of bias in favour of education or employment.

The speed of change heightened an existing sense of insecurity among
the employees of the new DfEE. Staffing at the DE had already been cut
from 57,000 in 1993 to 50,000 in 1995.[10] Both sets of civil servants
feared that they had been taken over by the other. Michael Portillo immediately wrote to his staff that, 'the good work that you all do will still

need to be done and for many the change may not be very great. But for others the change will bring huge changes and will be quite a shock.'[11] The old DE had been seen as the unions' direct link to government, even as their 'mentor' during previous administrations, and the TUC, as well as Harriet Harman (then Labour spokesperson on employment matters), voiced 'horror' at its demise. John Monks, General Secretary of the TUC, said, 'it's a sad day when the department that is supposed to stick up for the unemployed, the vulnerable and those liable to exploitation will not be represented at the Cabinet table'.[12] At a meeting of the Employment Select Committee held shortly after the announcement, Labour MPs criticized the merger on the grounds that Parliament would not be able to scrutinize the area of unemployment, as it would be fragmented across at least four government departments.

Although the Employment Service and the Training, Enterprise and Education Directorate had been transferred to the DfEE, industrial relations and the Advisory, Conciliation and Arbitration Service (ACAS) had been lost to the Department of Trade and Industry (DTI), on the grounds that the DTI bore the responsibility for 'developing a competitive industrial sector'. The Health and Safety Commission (HSC) and the Health and Safety Executive (HSE) were moved to the Department of the Environment (DoE), while the Central Statistical Office received responsibility for unemployment statistics. Some Labour MPs alleged that the DE had been abolished in order to take the issue of unemployment out of the spotlight before an election.[13] A more fundamental analysis in the *Guardian* by Will Hutton interpreted the lack of prior discussion as reflecting a long-standing Whitehall tradition of secrecy. He argued that it indicated a desire on the part of the Conservatives to return industrial conciliation to the Board of Trade, where it had begun life in 1893, before becoming an independent ministry in 1916 as the price of Labour support for the War Cabinet. Now the 'wheel has turned full circle'.[14]

For Hutton, and for some MPs such as Greville Janner, chair of the now defunct Employment Select Committee, the prime motivation behind the merger was a political one – the abolition of the DE. In contrast, Sir Geoffrey Holland explained that:

The political justification is the belief that a prime concern in employment in this country is the quality of supply of the workforce and, therefore, the bringing together in a powerful operational machine of the
educational and training policies in a lifelong continuum, and that is
relevant to the twenty-first century as well.[15]

Holland was stating an argument which prevailed over objections such as
those of the Select Committee. Quality in the supply of skilled labour
was seen as the key factor in countering unemployment and promoting
productivity. This change of emphasis away from quantity of demand
was attracting a wide range of support within the education and training
worlds. As Bichard explained:

What we must not forget is that the Department [of Employment] also
had a very important labour market function and that must continue to
be given priority in the new department because that too needs to be
linked in to our education system.[16]

Asked whether the objective of the merger was a better way of 'putting
people into jobs', Bichard agreed, and pointed out that the 'centre ground'
of further education, youth and adult training, was 'really the meat of this
merger'.[17] Labour and TUC positions on the neglect of the unemployed
were undermined by this new approach. Government could argue that an
end to the DE meant a *more* effective policy on unemployment as there
would be better co-ordination of training policy and a focus on creating
employment through 'up-skilling' the workforce (and the potential workforce) rather than on the relief of unemployment. Therefore, the merger
can be seen as marking a formal end to a welfare-based labour policy.
Indeed, as has been pointed out, the merger happened one week after the
passage of the Jobseeker's Act which fundamentally changed the status
of the unemployed.[18] As a senior Employment Department official said
in response to suggestions that the Employment Service should have been
transferred to the Department of Social Security, 'the last thing ministers
want is to have job centres and the Jobseeker's Allowance run by the
welfare department'.[19]

A majority of educational organizations favoured the merger. Concerns

about the dispersal of the DE were outweighed by the prospect of greater
parity of esteem between academic education and vocational training.
This historic divide was widely believed both to have crippled the world
of education and 'bedevilled' British economic performance.[20] The new
DfEE would bridge the gulf and, in so doing, provide better opportunities
for unemployed young people. Doug McAvoy of the NUT summed up
the response of many potential critics in the education world:

> Abolition of the Employment Department is to be deplored as a panic
> measure. Nonetheless, the transfer of training to Education has merit.
> The NUT has long argued that the distinction between education and
> training created artificial barriers and resulted in training being given a
> lower status. Bringing education and training together should serve to
> promote vocational education and the development of lifelong educa-
> tion and training as an important facet of the nation's future.[21]

The CBI was more fulsome:

> The CBI welcomes the changes in structure for education and training
> announced today by the government. We have long argued that respon-
> sibility for these two vital areas should be brought closer together. The
> proposed structure will help to provide a clearer focus and more coher-
> ent policy formation.[22]

The National Association of Teachers in Further and Higher Education
(NATFHE):

> welcomed the creation of the new Department for Education and
> Employment; the union has had a long-standing policy that education
> and training should be covered by one government department, to help
> bridge the academic–vocational divide.[23]

Government publicity and media commentary on the merger centred on
the issue of educational and training inadequacies as an explanation for
Britain's relative economic decline. In 1995, the World Economic Forum
(WEF) had reported that the United Kingdom had slipped from fourteenth to eighteenth in the global competitiveness league, let down by
the quality of its education system and workforce. Defects in levels of

productivity and quality in manufacturing and service industries were directly linked to defects in education and training. In this context, merger was seen as a most positive and welcome step. Michael Bichard proclaimed that it was 'something which for the competitiveness of this country is desperately important'.[24]

Former civil servants at the Employment Department confirmed that the national targets for education and training had been the 'critical focus' of all their work. These targets were directly linked to the United Kingdom's future prosperity, and were endorsed in the White Papers on Competitiveness in 1994 and 1995. The 1996 White Paper, *Competitiveness: Creating the Enterprise Centre of Europe*, went further in placing an education system relevant to industry at the centre of the government's plans for the economy. The boldly declared aim of the new DfEE at its inception was 'to support economic growth and improve the nation's competitiveness and quality of life by raising standards of educational achievement and skill and by promoting an efficient and flexible labour market'.[25]

During the 1990s, the Conservatives' former emphasis on skill levels changed to an emphasis on competitiveness, a broader concept which allowed for the combination of cultural and educational factors. This was linked to the important concept of labour flexibility. However, doubts were expressed about the validity of such a direct link between education and economic performance. For example, Peter Robinson, Senior Economist at the Institute for Public Policy Research, has presented data which suggest that while basic levels of literacy and numeracy are necessary for a country to converge on the living standards of the advanced industrial economies, 'any agreement on the links between education and economic growth tends to stop there'.[26] Avis et al argue that, from the time of James Callaghan's Ruskin Speech in 1976, such links have been used to underpin the wider New Right political agenda of deregulation.[27] Merson similarly suggests that the use of education in this way is essentially a political explanation, as opposed to a strictly economic analysis, which allows a shift in balance of power between players in the educational sphere and legitimizes intervention in the curriculum.[28] In the 1990s, however, explanations linking economic decline with low skill levels were complemented by the argument that inadequate education and skills were detrimental and unfair to young people as individuals. According to the *Times Educational Supplement* (*TES*), bridging the academic/vocational divide would create the potential for 'a more coherent system for the sake both of short-changed young people and of the economy'.[29]

The government also claimed that the 'turf wars' between the two departments, 'the long battle between training and qualifications which had been waged by the two ministries', were now at an end. Gillian Shephard said: 'There will be no effort wasted defining departmental differentials. We can get rid of all that and get on with the job.'[30] Exactly how this would be organized was not clear, but merger of the National Council for Vocational Qualifications (NCVQ) and the School Curriculum and Assessment Authority (SCAA) was identified almost immediately as the first offspring of the new department. Exam boards were also enthusiastic. The chairman of the Business and Technician Education Council (BTEC) 'looked forward to very substantial and speedy progress towards such goals' and an end to confusion over funding between Training and Enterprise Councils (TECs) and colleges was anticipated.[31] Directors of TECs had lobbied for a merger on the basis that it would level the playing field between the funding of college-based education and work-based training. The director of public policy at the TEC National Council proclaimed: 'We want to ensure that work is being done to bring down the artificial barriers between vocational training and education.'[32] Euphoria in the world of further education was diminished when allocation of ministerial responsibilities revealed that the sector would not be linked with higher education (HE) under a single minister. The chief executive of the Association for Colleges argued that, 'To give higher education to a minister of state and further education to an under-secretary signals that the esteem in which they have constantly told us they hold further education is no longer reflected in their policies'. The move was an 'unnecessary unstitching' of the new seamless robe.[33] Crucially, further education was not now to be included within the Dearing Review. Some critics argued that once again further education had been placed outside the mainstream of education and that the ideal of lifelong learning had been compromised. Debates at a conference of chief education officers, held in Manchester a few days after the merger announcement, reflected some of the uncertainty. Most participants were reported to favour the title 'Department of Education and *Training*', rather than Employment, and one delegate from the Association of London Government came forward with a rather cynical new logo for the DfEE: crossed sticks of chalk over a UB40 card.[34] Nevertheless, the overall mood was one which regarded merger as 'unexpectedly positive news for education'. In place of the 'Patten nightmare', Gillian Shephard had introduced a return to educational common sense; a major reform, long advocated by key figures in the political parties and Civil Service, in education and industry, had been produced.[35] Justifiable concerns might be expressed from further education colleges and elsewhere but, as the *TES* observed, now that Shephard 'is to preside over a Department of Education and Employment, so much else can fall into place in the unreconstructed post-16 jungle'.[36]

Overall, the merger appeared to signify a higher priority and status for technical and vocational education, a priority which would be of great benefit to many young people as individuals, and to national economic performance. High hopes were generated. But, as Howieson et al have pointed out, the issue of the unification of vocational and academic learning in English education has acquired a *politicized* meaning, and has been strongly associated with critiques of the existing educational system.[37] An examination of the recent history of the idea of merger will provide the context for understanding the nature of the consensus which had been formed.

The idea of a merger

Shortly after the merger announcement, civil servants from the former DfE were at pains to stress that for some time education and training policies had been planned to converge. The two departments had been working closely for some years and a joint agenda was in place, reflected in the *Competitiveness* White Papers of 1994 and 1995 – 'Specifically within the last two years we have been planning policy developments.'[38] On behalf of the Employment department, Michael Bichard reported that the cultures of the two departments had moved together in recent years. Education had become more sensitive to issues of the labour market and the need for vocational training, while Employment had been developing several links with Education. He confirmed that 'the future of the Department of Employment has been a matter of controversy, discussion over many, many years. It was always known that this might happen at some time.'[39] Sir Geoffrey Holland was more specific and declared that merger had been on the cards for 20 years.[40]

From its very foundation in 1916, the need for a separate Employment department had been questioned. Renewed proposals for the transfer of responsibility for training from the Employment to the Education department were made from the early 1960s. One interesting example was the recommendation to transfer training to Education made in 1961 in the Oldfield-Davies Report of the Central Advisory Council for Education (Wales).[41] The report argued that industry's immediate needs, not the long-term, national economic requirement, were determining the supply of skilled workers through the apprenticeship system. This uncompetitive state of affairs could only be remedied by the establishment of craft training as a national responsibility, rather than the private concern of individual firms or workers. The Council proposed the establishment of a National Craft Apprenticeship scheme throughout Britain. This would be administered by the Ministry of Education, rather than by the Ministry of Labour which was wedded to the principle of voluntarism in industrial matters, including apprenticeship. In the event, the Parliamentary Secretary to the Minister of Labour blocked the proposal in the Commons.[42]

In the 1960s, redistribution of responsibilities between Education and Employment and the production of a closer fit between them were discussed, but were precluded by several factors, including the assumptions of many policy-makers. Thus, the Robbins Report of 1963 was criticized from some quarters because its advocacy of a policy of free and equal access to higher education was made with little reference to the educational needs of industry. In 1964, at a British Association for Commercial and Industrial Education (BACIE) conference on the Robbins Report, Sir David (later Lord) Eccles regretted that 'Robbins takes the edge off his conclusions by failing to do justice to the national requirements for certain categories of trained manpower'.[43] In response, the distinguished engineer and scientist, Sir Willis (later Lord) Jackson, explained:

> I agree with regret that the Committee could not have proceeded differently. The simple facts are that we do not know how to assess the forward-looking needs in employment for qualified people at different levels; nor how in a democratic society, to ensure a pattern of supply which would be commensurate in scale and available in time to meet these needs.[44]

One of the most significant features of the Robbins Report was the extent to which its findings were underpinned by research. On the relationship between education and employment requirements, however, the Committee's statistical adviser, Professor (later Sir Claus) Moser, reported:

> I can assure you that the Committee ... spent a great deal of time discussing this, that we reviewed all available data bearing on it in this country, and that we went to great trouble in all our foreign visits to explore knowledge of the subject. But far too little was known about actual needs for qualified manpower, or about ways of forecasting them, for this to serve as the basis of our quantitative arguments.[45]

The Robbins Report may be contrasted with the Percy Report of 1945 and Barlow Report of 1946, which had been required to address issues of higher education with reference to 'the requirements of industry' and 'the development of scientific manpower', respectively. In the 1960s, failure to link educational planning with employment needs caused widespread dismay in industry and commerce. By 1975, this failure implied to some observers, such as the BACIE, that training and higher education had become irrelevant to the needs of the economy: 'The argument ... which comes through with great force is that a slow and stately rate of change, befitting a rich country, is no longer appropriate for an economy fighting for its solvency against increasing internal and external odds.'[46] Cultures had to change – in particular the presupposition of a conflict between democratic free access to education and national efficiency which had been embodied in the Robbins Report.

During the 1970s, pressure for structural reform increased, especially after the criticisms levied at the Department of Education and Science (DES) by the Organization for Economic Co-operation and Development (OECD) in 1975.[47] Growing awareness of the United Kingdom's relative economic decline came to a head with the International Monetary Fund (IMF) crisis of 1976. These events influenced the debate over the purposes of the educational system. In 1978, the MSC paper, *Training for Skill – A Programme of Action*, raised the question of how best to control and supply vocational training. An NUT conference in 1978, 'Young People in Transition', made proposals for joint administrative structures to cover academic and vocational education, while the Engineering Industry Training Board's *Review of Craft Apprenticeship in Engineering* suggested the merger of the first year of craft apprenticeship schemes with the final year of secondary education. This latter proposal was described as 'revolutionary' by one commentator, P.J.C. Perry of BACIE, as it struck at the heart of the traditional separation of education and training for industry.[48] It was quickly 'matched by a series of trial balloons which are beginning to rise from several, ideologically diverse camps'.[49]

One of the most interesting of these 'balloons' was a report of the Conservative Study Group on Youth Policy, *A Time For Youth*, published in June 1978. This contained several arguments which can be seen as precursors of the merger policy of the 1990s, including the establishment of a Department of Education and Training.[50] Alan Haselhurst MP chaired the Group, its secretary was Biddy Passmore (then of the Conservative Research Department). Members included David Hunt MP, Tim Smith MP and representatives from youth and student organizations. The report began by identifying the increasing alienation of youth, particularly 'minorities', and the danger this posed to social stability and democracy, as the most pressing problem for education policy. Unemployment could only get worse; it was a structural problem which required a structural solution. The expectation of commencement of working life needed to be changed from 16 to 18, thereby taking some 1.3 million people out of the job market.[51] This could be achieved by implementing a universal training and opportunities scheme for all 16–18 year olds who were not in full-time education. Trainees would be paid an allowance similar to that under the Youth Opportunities Programme (YOP). Money would be saved on benefits to 16–18 year olds, and the change in the labour market would motivate employers to achieve higher productivity levels. Benefits would include a reduction in the numbers of aimless and restless young people, a better-equipped and motivated workforce, and an improvement in industrial relations. A profound shift in attitudes to work was envisaged:

> It may be said that the acceptance of the training concept at the outset of working life might persuade people to welcome more readily the idea of further training or education at later stages (recurrent education). This would help people to realise what the pattern of working life for them is likely to be, and make it a more welcome prospect to change from one type of job to another requiring quite different skills and training. This kind of flexibility is something which would be of great benefit to the British economy.[52]

The logical development of such changes would be to end the distinction between education and training. A Department of Education and Training should be set up, comprising the existing Education remit plus those functions of the DE which affected training. Duplication of effort would be stopped. The Department of Education and Training would be concerned with administering 'an overall strategy for the school leaver with specific incentives for further education and training. Young people would be offered a series of alternatives under the wider training programme we have proposed.'[53] The new department would also create a shift in ethos in government, particularly within the MSC. The pamphlet criticized the MSC's emphasis on creating jobs, 'when the real value of its programme ought to lie in training and education. A transfer of responsibility from the DE to the DES will give any new structure a more appropriate context.'[54]

Several components of later Conservative thinking on institutional merger can be identified here. There was a move to downgrade the power of the Employment department, and to emphasize the supply of skills rather than the demand for jobs. The issues of lifetime learning, labour flexibility and re-training were raised, as well as a closer association between education and industry. In 1978, before the development of notions of 'post-Fordism' and globalization, these components were presented as responses to structural unemployment and its social costs, not as responses to a perceived change in the underlying organization of work which would necessitate a different conception of the place of education. The pamphlet may be regarded as representing the beginning of Conservative market-oriented thought on education policy, within the context of the late 1970s preoccupation with unemployment and social cohesion. Its proposals for a merged Department of Education and Training began to be taken seriously. Pressure was thereby put upon ministers and civil servants working within older patterns of thought, although underlying assumptions, or cultural values, concerning the separate functions of education and training were not overturned immediately. As one recent analysis of structural change in Whitehall has suggested, major cultural re-orientations take place when external and internal pressures combine to form 'windows of opportunity'.[55] Such a window would not occur for a further 17 years.

During the 1980s, the idea of merger began to acquire a more substantial basis. From the mid-1970s many of the functions of the DE were relocated. For example, in 1974, the ACAS, the Health and Safety Executive and the MSC all became essentially independent bodies. Its unitary structure was lost in favour of the 'Department of Employment Group', later simply the 'Employment Group'.[56] In the 1980s, industrial relations legislation brought strikes and other union activities within the sphere of direct legal sanction. The tripartite approach to training – of government, employers and unions acting in concert – came to an end.[57] In 1983, the Adam Smith Institute argued influentially for a reduction in the powers of the DE and of the MSC, claiming that deregulation would free the labour market and reduce unemployment. In 1987, when the Employment Service became an executive agency, the journal *Training Tomorrow*, edited by Peter Maxted, could claim to identify 'a groundswell of opinion' that education and employment should be merged. The journal stated that a 'new department should be formed which clearly reflects the essential links between education and training'.[58] Events, and arguments, were overtaking existing institutional arrangements.

At the same time, the idea of merger began to gain ground in the educational world, based upon proposals for radical change in the role of government. In 1990, an influential paper by Finegold et al entitled *A British 'Baccalaureate'*, argued that for years policy-making for 16–19 year olds had been plagued by divisions between Employment and Education departments.[59] The authors suggested the creation of a merged Department of Education and Training. This should oversee the amalgamation of the NCVQ and the School Examinations and Assessment Council (SEAC) and assume responsibility for education and training, both of those aged under 19 and of adult workers. Abolition of the DE, which would continue without its training functions, was not seen as a consequence of the reorganization.

Finegold et al maintained that the social requirement that the educational system should help each individual realize his or her true potential was now matched by the economic necessity that innovative capabilities be spread throughout the population. Educational change should structure economic advance, not vice versa, and economic ends would match, not overrule social goals. These ideas were based on the argument of Finegold and Soskice that Britain was trapped in a low-skills equilibrium – a vicious circle of short-term incentives and low expectations in its training systems.[60] The common demand that education should respond to economic change was too narrow and utilitarian a view of the relationship between the two; education should be geared not to present economic needs but to the economic demands of the future. Job-specific adult training was outdated, and education should shape, not merely respond to, economic and social change. Education would best serve the economy if it helped the whole population to develop skills, critical faculties and innovative capacities. For Finegold et al, institutional reform was not based upon devising an administrative solution to unemployment, but upon a developmental vision of the state's role in the economy.

The government's 1991 White Paper, *Education and Training for the 21st Century*, a joint DES/ED/Welsh Office document, placed great emphasis on equal status for academic and vocational education. It declared that: 'Young people should not be limited by out-of-date distinctions between qualifications or institutions.'[61] In 1993 *Learning to Succeed,* the report of the National Commission on Education (NCE), took up this theme, and many of the points raised by Finegold et al. It, too, recommended a Department of Education and Training. Division of responsibilities between the DfE and the DE had inhibited policy-making for 16–19 year olds. A confused array of training opportunities was being run by two departments when, in reality, there existed a continuum between education and training, rather than a sharp distinction. Education and Training Boards, composed predominantly of local councillors, were proposed. These would function as 'purchasers' for the 'providers' of education and training in schools, colleges, etc. The NCE report shared with Finegold et al the idea that work organization had fundamentally changed in a new 'knowledge economy', although it stopped short of embracing the more extreme versions of this view, including those of some US theorists.[62] The idea of a continuum between education and training was dovetailing with the modernizing, vocationalist current in Conservative circles to form a consensus for institutional merger, despite important differences in conception and politics.

The political process of merger

Supporters of vocational education in the Conservative Party were strongest within the Tory Reform Group (TRG), which in 1994 published a pamphlet by Julian Ayer entitled '*The Great Jobs Crisis*'. This recommended the merger of Employment and Education to form a 'Department of Education and Employment'. In 1994 the Group's president was David Hunt, the Employment Secretary. Its patrons were Kenneth Clarke, Michael Heseltine and John Major. Hunt had been Secretary of State for

Wales (1990–1993), where he had enjoyed responsibility for both education and employment policy. When John Major became Prime Minister,
Hunt recommended merger and Major asked for a submission. Hunt con-
sulted with John Patten and a joint submission was put forward. Major
was still considering it when Hunt was appointed Employment Secretary
in 1993: 'John Major told me I could be doing myself out of a job, but he
felt my Welsh experience would be helpful'.[63] Ayer, interviewed for a
review of his pamphlet, claimed that Heseltine 'is very close to all of us',
and although Cabinet ministers had not seen the pamphlet in draft, 'copies
have floated around'.[64] The pamphlet contained many suggestions which
subsequently were put into practice, and can be seen as a blueprint for the
eventual 1995 merger. *'The Great Jobs Crisis'* began, as did the 1978
paper, *A Time for Youth*, with the threat to the nation posed by structural
unemployment, quoting David Hunt that 'the social and cultural costs
will be high – incalculably high'. Structural unemployment and the resultant 'underclass' were the stated political targets, but this pamphlet also
embraced ideas of globalization and an improvement in the link between
education and industry for the sake of competitiveness. In common with
proposals for merger which had been influenced by thinking from the
Labour side of the political spectrum, the TRG now acknowledged that
the economic and occupational background had changed – 'the future
belongs to the multi-skilled'.[65] Lifelong education needed to become a
concrete policy – 'the link between education and work has to be seamless'.[66] In December 1993, the European Commission had heard from
senior industrialists that the loss of European competitiveness in world
markets was underestimated. The 'only card to play' was commercial
quality and innovation. These required a skilled workforce and better
links between education and industry. Fifteen years of Conservative
governments had established good principles of reform, but these were
not sufficient: 'education for work should be given priority over liberal
academic study for its own sake'.[67]

According to Ayer, a new DfEE would be a strategic department; re-
launched TECs, with powers over local education as well as training,
would deliver its policies. The NCVQ and SEAC would be merged and,

crucially, General Certificate of Education (GCE) A-levels would be abolished. A new qualification incorporating General National Vocational Qualifications (GNVQs) would be introduced. The DfEE would operate in parallel with the DE, but 'not much of the current DE will survive'. As proved to be the case in 1995, the Health and Safety Commission 'will continue on its journey around Whitehall Departments and will not join the new Dept, along with ACAS'.[68] The attack on the DE was justified by serious allegations of malpractice: one should not get 'misty eyed' about the fate of the DE as DE staff used 'Spanish working practices'. DE accounts contained errors, while statistics on the success of Training Agency (TA) initiatives had been manipulated.[69] Finally, the shift to a new managerial culture was anticipated. One chapter was entitled 'Education and training to be depoliticised'; decisions should be taken for managerial rather than party political reasons, as was the case in the armed forces, police or the National Health Service.[70] One major point of difference from the NCE proposal concerned local accountability on the TECs or local boards. TECs would exclude councillors, and thus neutralize the political process at local level.[71]

The combination of personalities and policies reflected in the pamphlet's arguments lends some support to the view, advanced for example by Will Hutton, that the motives for merger were essentially political. The department with links to trade unions would be downgraded. This would demonstrate to the Conservative right that the government was anti-corporatist and anti-statist, and obviate the need to admit John Redwood or any of his supporters to the Cabinet.[72] Conservative antipathy towards the DE (the issue which, according to Geoffrey Holland, had delayed the implementation of the idea of merger) was increased by the furore surrounding the closure of coal pits in 1992. In 1995, when examining Michael Bichard's views on the merger, members of the Commons' Employment Select Committee suggested that the pit closures revealed the Department as a 'Department of Unemployment', in that it had not acted until 'the end of the day'. It was seen to be working to an old union-influenced, welfare agenda. Bichard replied that the lesson of the pit closures was the necessity for concentrating on 'skills supply ... creating employment through a flexible competitive labour market rather than concentrating on, focusing on the unemployed'.[73] Several newspapers suggested that Michael Heseltine, who had been responsible for the pit closures, was arguing in this vein and pushed the merger through in order to undermine Portillo and split the Thatcherites. The restructuring of Cabinet Committees after the Tory leadership election brought the DfEE within Heseltine's ambit.[74]

These immediate political factors may have played a role in the timing of the merger, but divisions in Conservative ranks can be seen as reflecting a wider problem in relation to education policy. The TRG pamphlet argued against those on the right of the Conservative Party who wanted to perpetuate the split between vocational and academic qualifications, and to maintain A-levels as the traditional guarantor of standards. They had adopted a self-fulfilling position – the intellectual content of vocational qualifications had been stripped out, and then A-levels were defended as the intellectual 'gold standard'. The 1991 White Paper, *Education and Training for the 21st Century*, had fiercely criticized the lack of equal status between academic and vocational qualifications, but had also defended A-levels and sixth forms as providing 'a foundation for entry to higher education and for the acquisition of professional skills'.[75] According to Denis Lawton, the preservation of A-levels is a classic example of the maintenance of Conservative values of class and tradition in education policy.[76] In 1994, he argued that the creation of a merged Education and Employment department would make the Conservative position on A-levels much weaker. Merger, therefore, would not take place, the distinction between education and training being too deeply ingrained. With the benefit of hindsight, it is clear that this analysis underestimated divisions in Conservative ideology, and that traditionalism was in conflict with a modernizing Europhile current.[77]

For example, Avis et al argued that Conservative educational reforms were based on contradictory aims: to modernize for the global economy and to preserve the culture and values of Britain as a nation state. These contradictions emerged most clearly over Europe. As Marquand observed: 'free market Tories are ... impaled on a contradiction. They are for the sovereign market and they are also for the sovereign state. They cannot have it both at once.'[78] The paradox at the heart of the drive to modernize education for the challenge of the global economy was that it was accompanied by an attempt to use education to maintain a national identity and value system against the political Left. Education was the key to participation in the global economy, and an institution for the preservation of the values of the nation state. In the late 1980s, the modernizers lost ground to the neo-conservative cultural traditionalists who saw the Education Reform Act 1988 as an opportunity to press for a more nationalistic curriculum.[79] In the event, however, merger kept both the Adam Smith Institute and the TRG reasonably happy. Shephard retained A-levels as the 'gold standard', but reformed the qualifications system in ways which Portillo and Redwood would have opposed – by creating one internal DfEE directorate and a single qualifications authority.[80] The introduction of nursery vouchers, a move advocated by those on the right of the Conservative party, but subsequently criticized by Shephard in a leaked memo,[81] was announced on the same day as the merger. Later in 1995, the TRG returned to the fray with a new paper which again called for A-levels to be abolished.[82] By then Shephard had performed a skilful balancing act.

Fusion or subordination?

Was the merger a subordination of the traditional values of Education to the ethos of Employment? Was Employment dissolved into Education or was there a genuine fusion of the two? The above outline of the progression of ideas and political processes associated with merger suggests that there is no easy answer. The two departments differed considerably in size. Some 2,500 staff at the Education department were vastly outnumbered by the 50,000 in Employment. Civil servants from both departments feared that they had been subsumed into the other, but Bichard maintained an even-handedness, claiming that the 'rhetoric about lifelong learning could be translated into practical action, while education was exposed to the realities of the labour market'.[83]

The *TES* declared that Employment had surprisingly been 'submerged' into Education.[84] In the Budget of November 1995, Education seemed to have gained by receiving money from cuts in the TECs' allocation for the 'Training for Work' scheme.[85] While senior positions in the new department's structure were evenly spread between former DfE and DE employees, Sir Tim Lankester eventually lost out to Michael Bichard as Permanent Secretary. Lower down the hierarchy, former Employment staff felt that they had been taken over, especially at the Sheffield-based training division (the former MSC). Four under-secretaries in Sheffield retired, but in other areas there was a mixture of appointments. Former DfE people stayed in charge of schools, but Roger Dawe, a hybrid having spent time in both departments, took over further and higher education. Lifetime learning and employment was run by Nick Stuart, another hybrid, and former Employment people were placed in charge of strategy, international and analytical services, personnel and finance. John Hedger, formerly of the DfE, assumed responsibility for TECs and the careers service. Some in the TECs feared that work-based training would suffer in favour of college-based courses, and that the £700 million budget for the youth training scheme would be reduced. The basic concern, however, was 'that the academically oriented Education Department, which is smaller will impose its culture on the Dept of Employment, which has been largely concerned with the labour market and work-based training'.[86]

Anxieties were also expressed from the Education side. Ted Wragg was one of those who wondered whether 'the employment tail would wag the education dog'.[87] Some commentators feared that the culture of Education would be limited and diminished. New aims and objectives and a new set of values which emphasized the employment dimensions of education were soon drawn up. A concentration on the traditional Whitehall value of 'quality of process', something for which the DfE had been famous (or infamous), would have to be complemented by a focus on outcomes and standards. A new orientation towards the Department's clients would be encouraged. Michael Bichard spelled out the new agenda:

We were convinced that focusing only on objectives and structures would not deliver a successful merger. These things were important but we needed to be even more concerned with values, behaviour, processes and ... the development of our people.[88]

Draft proposals, designed to move the old Education department in the direction of the former Employment department's 'competitiveness', were drawn up. A new management culture of planning and anticipating, rather than reacting and responding, to events would be encouraged. The opening of Education to the realities of the labour market was a clear consequence of the merger, and involved the adoption of market philosophy inside the Whitehall machine itself. It was less clear whether such a change of culture would take root. As Bichard acknowledged, no change of structure would of itself produce a fundamental change in the ethos of education.

Conclusion

In this chapter, application of immediate historical perspectives to the events of 1995 has enabled the following picture to emerge. Initial reactions to the creation of the DfEE were broadly favourable. There was much support for an initiative which promised to bridge historic divisions between academic and vocational education, and to increase the mutual awareness of education and the world of work. The promotion of greater opportunities for young people, and of national economic efficiency, were widely welcomed. This vision of combined social and economic benefits helped to create a consensus for institutional merger, despite important differences in conception and politics between its supporters. Of course, the merger must be located within the immediate context of Conservative Party politics in the summer of 1995, but the origins of such a merger can be traced back at least as far as the debates and discussions of the 1970s, including those prompted by the speech of the Labour Prime Minister, James Callaghan, at Ruskin College in October 1976. The focus on improvements in training and other supply-side measures as a means of dealing with unemployment and skill shortages attracted a wide range of support within the worlds of education and employment. Changes of emphasis have occurred since the advent to power of a Labour government in May 1997, but several continuities with Conservative policies for the merged department are also apparent. Indeed, Gordon Brown has characterized the connection between employment and education in terms similar to those of Gillian Shephard: 'It is the mutually reinforcing concept of education and employment opportunity together that offers opportunity to individuals throughout their lives.'[89]

In the following chapters, longer historical perspectives are applied to such issues as the cultural divides between academic and vocational education and between the worlds of education and work, 'turf wars' between the departments, and the extent to which 'a skilled labour force, a high level of investment and a stable economy are consequences, as much as causes, of a nation's productivity performance'.[90]

Notes

1. Bichard, 1996, 22.
2. *Times Educational Supplement (TES)*, 14 July 1995.
3. Ribbins and Sherratt, 1997, 211.
4. House of Commons Employment Committee. Session 1995–96, HC 125. Scrutiny session. London: HMSO. Minutes of Evidence, 19/12/95, qs 162–165.
5. *TES*, 21 July 1995.
6. National Commission on Education, 1993; Ayer, 1994.
7. *The Times*, 6 July 1995, quoted in Jones, 1996, 138.
8. *TES*, 1 December 1995.
9. Bichard, 1996.
10. *Civil Service Statistics 1996*. London: Government Statistical Office.
11. *Financial Times*, 6 July 1995.
12. *Guardian*, 6 July 1995. Although unemployment had recently declined, both in terms of numbers and as a political issue.
13. House of Commons Employment Committee. Session 1995–96, HC 99-ii. *The Work of TECs*. London: HMSO. Minutes of Evidence, 9 January 1996, q. 1320.
14. *Guardian*, 15 July 1995.
15. House of Commons Employment Committee. Session 1995–96, HC 99-ii. *The Work of TECs*. London: HMSO. Minutes of Evidence, 9 January 1996, q. 1319.
16. House of Commons Employment Committee. Session 1994–95, HC 458-ii. *The*

Work of the Employment Department. London: HMSO. Minutes of Evidence, 11 July 1995, q. 176.

17. House of Commons Employment Committee. Session 1994–95, HC 458-ii. London: HMSO. *The Work of the Employment Department*. Minutes of Evidence, 11 July 1995, q. 242.
18. Jones, 1996, 149.
19. *Financial Times*, 6 July 1995.
20. *Guardian*, 15 July 1995.
21. NUT press release, 5 July 1995.
22. CBI press release, 5 July 1995.
23. *Lecturer*, October 1995.
24. House of Commons Employment Committee. Session 1994–95, HC 458-ii. *The Work of the Employment Department*. London: HMSO. Minutes of Evidence, 11 July 1995, q. 200.
25. DfEE press release, 210/95.
26. Robinson, 1998, 59. See also Robinson, 1997.
27. Avis et al, 1996. In October 1976 the then Prime Minister, James Callaghan, made a speech at Ruskin College, Oxford. Callaghan favoured a 'basic curriculum with universal standards' and saw the goal of education as equipping 'children to the best of their ability for a lively constructive place in society and also to fit them to do a job of work'. The speech led to a 'Great Debate' on education. See Gordon, Aldrich and Dean, 1991, 94–97.
28. Merson, 1995.
29. *TES*, 21 July 1995.
30. Ayer, 1994, 50
31. Ayer, 1994, 50.
32. *TES*, 21 July 1995.
33. *TES*, 14 July 1995.
34. *TES*, 14 July 1995. An Unemployment Benefit form number 40 provided proof of being unemployed.
35. *TES*, 7 July 1995.
36. *TES*, 7 July 1995.
37. Howieson et al, 1997.
38. House of Commons Education Committee. Session 1994–95, HC 649. *Education and Training for 14 to 19 year olds*. London: HMSO. Minutes of Evidence, 12 July 1995, q. 2.
39. House of Commons Employment Committee. Session 1994–95, HC 458-ii. *The Work of the Employment Department*. London: HMSO. Minutes of Evidence, 11 July 1995, q. 174.

40. House of Commons Employment Committee. Session 1995–96, HC 99-ii. *The Work of TECs*. London: HMSO. Minutes of Evidence, 9 January 1996, q. 1273.
41. See the extract in Maclure, 1969, 268–273.
42. Perry, 1984, 69.
43. Perry, 1984, 27.
44. Perry, 1984, 27.
45. Perry, 1984, 27.
46. Perry, 1984, 27.
47. OECD, 1975.
48. Perry, 1984, 68.
49. Perry, 1984, 68.
50. Conservative Party Study Group on Youth Policy, 1978.
51. Conservative Party Study Group on Youth Policy, 1978, 20.
52. Conservative Party Study Group on Youth Policy, 1978, 22–23.
53. Conservative Party Study Group on Youth Policy, 1978, 28.
54. Conservative Party Study Group on Youth Policy, 1978, 28.
55. Richards and Smith, 1997.
56. For an account of historical changes to the structure of the Employment department, see Crooks, 1993.
57. See Employment Policy Institute, 1996; King, 1995.
58. Maxted, 1995, 5–6.
59. Finegold et al, 1990.
60. Finegold and Soskice, 1988.
61. DES/ED/WO, 1991, 24.
62. See, for example, Blakely, 1997.
63. Thatcher, 1996, 25.
64. *TES*, 20 May 1994.
65. Ayer, 1994, 11.
66. Ayer, 1994, 11.
67. Ayer, 1994, 2.
68. Ayer, 1994, 40.
69. Ayer, 1994, 44.
70. Ayer, 1994, 50.
71. Ayer, 1994, 50.
72. *Guardian*, 15 July 1995.
73. House of Commons Employment Committee. Session 1994–95, HC 458-ii. *The Work of the Employment Department*. London: HMSO. Minutes of Evidence, 11 July 1995, q. 243.
74. *TES*, 28 July 1995.

75. DES/ED/WO, 1991, 25.
76. Lawton, 1994, 136.
77. Hickox and Moore, 1995.
78. Quoted in Avis et al, 1996, 6.
79. Ball, 1994.
80. *TES*, 27 September 1995.
81. *TES*, 22 September 1995.
82. Marshall, 1995.
83. Bichard, 1996, 22.
84. *TES*, 7 July 1995.
85. Jones, 1996, 151.
86. *Financial Times*, 15 July 1995, quoted in Jones, 1996, 151.
87. *TES*, 1 December 1995.
88. Bichard, 1996, 23.
89. Layard, 1997, ix.
90. *The Times*, 3 November 1998.

3 'Adjusting Education to Industry', 1900–1928

Introduction

The creation of the DfEE in 1995 was widely considered to be a new response to old problems. As Chapter Two has shown, these problems were perceived to flow from several long-standing divisions: between academic and vocational education, between education, training and industrial policy, between education for social equality and education for economic efficiency, between the very worlds of education and work and, ultimately, between the government departments responsible for these two areas. The merger of the Education department and Employment department, it was believed, would bridge these several divides. In this, the first of the book's historical chapters, these perceived divisions will be examined during the period from the foundation of the Board of Education in 1900 until the publication of the second report of the Malcolm Committee's investigations into the relations between education and industry in 1928. Some of the questions posed here are fundamental, and will reappear in subsequent chapters. For example, to what extent and for what reasons were the Board of Education and the Ministry of Labour acting in isolation from or in concert with each other? How did prevailing economic and social doctrines affect policies for education and employment?

The chapter is divided into five sections. The first deals with the general theme of national efficiency and its promotion by central government; the second and third with developments in the two departments. The fourth section is concerned with the key area of youth employment. Finally, some conclusions are drawn.

The first three decades of the twentieth century were characterized by great change: from the confidence and imperial trappings of the Edwardian era, through the mass destruction of lives and futures in the First World War, to the disillusionment of recession and financial stringency in the 1920s. Contradictions abound. On the one hand, Whitehall was pervaded by a broad political culture of *laissez-faire*, reflected both in the separation of education and employment, and of academic and vocational education. On the other, the period witnessed a notable growth in state intervention, both in education and employment, as components of the emerging Welfare State. According to Rodney Lowe, the historian of the inter-War Ministry of Labour, this 'silent revolution' provided the central contradiction of the 1920s. Governments were forced by economic crises and social unrest to develop interventionist economic and social policies, yet, ultimately, they remained anchored in *laissez-faire*, class-bound ideology.[1] In consequence, while levels of debate about issues of education and youth employment reached new heights, the relevant government departments were denied the political weight and resources to resolve them. This chapter examines this contradiction in the context of the institutional and cultural development of the Education and Employment departments. The Board of Education was itself an amalgam of three antecedent organizations, the Education Department, the Science and Art Department and the Charity Commissioners, each with its own internal culture and orientation towards employment issues. The Ministry of Labour emerged from the Board of Trade bearing the imprint of that department's distinctive history. While differences and discrepancies existed – indeed, a separate Employment department did not appear until 1916 – it is also apparent that there was a more complex and dynamic relationship between them than is usually acknowledged.

National efficiency and the role of central government

As Jose Harris has observed, in the first 20 years of the twentieth century an intense local culture continued to be a major strand in British social and political life.[2] In particular, the different traditions of the four nations and the municipal culture and civic pride of many provincial cities remained strong. Throughout this period, the preservation of local autonomy and customs was seen as the foremost feature of the British national character – 'in marked contrast to the centralization, rationality and legalistic uniformity imposed on continental countries by the legacy of the two Napoleons'.[3] Yet while localism occupied a powerful place in British social and political development, in the 1900s a shift to the metropolis began. The structure and location of wealth changed; money moved away from local manufacturing towards international finance. New social problems emerged which proved to be beyond the scope of local administration and finance to resolve. In particular, unemployment became 'a powerful, though inadvertent, catalyst for the assumption of new responsibilities by a reluctant central government'.[4] Government departments with responsibility for dealing with these new problems began to learn new ways of working, and of relating to their constituencies. In so doing, their particular cultures began to diverge from the traditional political culture of *laissez-faire*.

The role and ethos of central government were contested within a general debate over the state of the nation stimulated by the recruitment, condition and performance of Britain's armed services in the Boer War.[5] In the course of this debate, the notion of 'national efficiency' was closely related to perceptions of German (and Japanese) military and economic superiority. The German administrative structure of effective, centrally-organized welfare, education and industrial systems was admired by many, while in some quarters the British stress on personal liberty and local autonomy came to be seen as a problem, rather than as a national virtue. Anxiety over the country's social and economic organization generated a 'political movement for modernization' consisting of an alliance of Fabians, Liberals and tariff reformers identified with Joseph Chamberlain.[6] Members of this movement argued that imperial decline stemmed from the failure to keep abreast of the modernized competition. National efficiency, they believed, should be promoted by administrative reform and by state support for industry in the shape of increased resources for technical education. The events of the First World War sharpened both the criticisms of Britain's institutions and comparisons with Germany, and the improvement of technical education was widely seen as an appropriate solution to the problem of relative economic decline. A variety of reconstruction proposals were put forward, including those leading to the Education Act 1918 which raised the school-leaving age to 14. Fabian concern with administrative efficiency found expression within the influential Committee into the Machinery of Government chaired by R.B. Haldane. In contrast, many industrialists, newspaper editors and local politicians believed that a return to pre-war commercial normalcy was required. After 1920, their views won the day, and although there was some strengthening of vocational elements in elementary education, deflationary economic policies stymied the proposed expansion of technical education.[7]

In 1901 a series of popular journalistic articles, which alleged apathy in the face of US enterprise and energy, was published in book form as *The American Invader*.[8] The failures of the army in the Boer War were linked both to the education system in general and to the lack of a mental training in scientific method in particular. British society was portrayed as amateurish and decadent, descriptions which caught the public mood. In this prevailing climate of self-criticism and a search for new solutions to national deficiencies, Sidney and Beatrice Webb's arguments in favour of state socialism found fertile soil, even within the Board of Education. The Webbs developed the notion of the 'National Minimum', a standard of life below which no-one should fall. This should be provided by education, sanitation, leisure and wages. The National Minimum forged a clear link between national efficiency on the one hand and the socialist programme of raising the quality of life of the poor on the other.[9] Various measures, including the Labour Exchanges Act 1909 and the Unemployment and Health Insurance Act 1911, could be seen as improving the conditions of workers and the efficiency of labour. It appeared that reforms emanating from central government could effect the reconciliation of socialism and national efficiency. The programme of the movement for national and imperial efficiency included educational, training and scientific dimensions which were diametrically opposed to the leisured and cultured Liberalism of the Victorian period.[10] It displayed a disregard for individual liberty, and a functional approach to educational policy and to state schools.

The Webbs' ideas on education, and the notion of a new link between educational systems and economic efficiency, however, were not egalitarian. The image of the ladder often appeared in their writings and schools were 'agencies for the sifting of the talent necessary for the effective running of the meritocratic state'.[11] Education was not even the 'free opening of all avenues to individual ability'; instead 'the whole body of citizens were to be trained in accordance with their particular aptitudes and capacities for the service of the community'.[12] A belief in a limited pool of talent was implied in these views. It was not until the 1930s that the Webbs, under the influence of their visit to the Union of Soviet Socialist Republics (USSR), developed an enthusiasm for common schooling.

Although such new economic and political ideas had little immediate impact on policy, they exercised a diffuse influence on the 'wider climate of economic and political culture'.[13] On the outside, high politics still 'glistened with the patina of aristocratic power' but underneath a new dimension of political activity, unconnected with economic wealth, was being formed.[14] The rise of the Labour Party was associated not only with the introduction of a new politics based upon social class, but also with the espousal of a moral, public-service approach to educational and social policy which transcended class. This duality within the Labour Party reflected two different, yet complementary, ideas about the role of government. One viewed the state as an agent of social reform; the other, a strand of neo-classical theory, suggested that all governments could usefully undertake public works as complementing the free market.[15]

In the early years of the twentieth century, these issues aroused considerable, and often heated, debate. For example, following his criticism of the British bias against government the neo-liberal economist, Alfred Marshall, was accused of exhibiting 'tendencies to socialism'.[16] Marshall was no enthusiast for government intervention, but he re-stated the classical economists' attitude to state functions, such as education, as providing a moral framework for the functioning of the market. In this sense education debates were dominated not by the content of the secular curriculum, which might directly link the economic effects of education with its delivery, but by the moral and religious questions which impinged upon questions of youth and work. Thus, while it is true to say that the economic effects of education were not the dominant element in policy-making, some economic historians suggest that the classical bent of grammar and public school curricula has been exaggerated or misunderstood. In these years, natural sciences and engineering did grow in importance, while technical education for the working and lower middle classes made substantial, if uneven, progress.[17] The purposes of state-provided education were essentially to teach the members of the working classes how to be moral and how to improve their basic conditions of life. These purposes would have an economic outcome inasmuch as they promoted habits of punctuality, obedience and hard work, but education policy in this period cannot be regarded as having any clear connection to national competitiveness.

Newton and Porter argue that although ideas drawn from the movement for national efficiency permeated the political process, they did not significantly shift policy-making away from *laissez-faire* principles, as the movement never had a mass political base.[18] Policy-makers had expected that Germany would emerge from the First World War as a militarily defeated, but still economically strong, state. This did not happen, and the strategy of constructing a post-War anti-German economic alliance was replaced by one designed to rebuild the conditions of the pre-War liberal economy. So, while the Treasury lost its central role in the control of government expenditure during the course of the War, and traditional liberalism was replaced by a patriotic nationalism on a popular basis, it ended the conflict in a strengthened position. Nevertheless, the War led to a crisis in the ideas underpinning the state and reshaped the concept of efficiency.[19] Prior to the War it was widely assumed that private enterprise was an efficient system in its own terms, even if the distribution of wealth was unjust. Assumptions changed during the War, so that in 1920 Sidney Webb could write that 'it was one of the unexpected discoveries of the Great War that the system of capitalist profit-making as a method of producing commodities and services, habitually fell so enormously short of the maximum efficiency of which it was capable'.[20] Efficiency was seen to involve a much greater role for the government. The Federation of British Industries, formed in response to the wartime alliance of government and unions, called for a Ministry of Commerce or Industry to press British interests abroad. Such developments were politically significant, but interventionist ideas did not gain ascendancy in economic policy. Labour, even though its supporters were producing a variety of arguments for reforming the economic status quo, could not offer a significant challenge to this restored hegemony of liberal economic policy.[21]

As Colls has written, in the period between 1900 and 1920, 'a capacious liberalism remained the dominant force within the political culture'. In subsequent years, however, a more 'visceral' idea of the state emerged, so that 'after 1920 the resources of English polity are seen to reside less in a diverse civil freedom and more in a corporate national efficiency'.[22] This involved a renewed debate over the significance of vocational education and about the links between education and industry. In 1919, H.A.L. Fisher, President of the Board of Education, stated: 'I have always felt that the great problem for the next years is to bring the world of business and the world of education into clear connection.'[23] In 1927, Sir David Milne-Watson, an industrialist and member of the Malcolm Committee, argued that in the nineteenth century industry had abdicated its position as the 'special patron of education', which the merchant community' had established in relation to the grammar and public schools in earlier periods.[24] Throughout the 1920s, the ideological ground shifted further in these directions taking the form, for example, of the progressive Conservatism of Boothby and Macmillan, together with currents such as Mosley's protectionism and other advocates of expansionary plans within the Labour Party. These forces represented a new political synthesis in which an active approach to industrial efficiency was much to the fore.[25] Keynes' attempts to settle the debate, however, by arguing that '*laissez-faire* was dead' did not have sufficient political force to be successful. At the same time as this synthesis was forming in the 1920s, Conservative

fears about the growth of socialism and about the political role of education as an instrument of socialism were at their highest point.[26] In addition,
while the report of the 1927 Balfour Committee might argue that 'the
problem of creating and maintaining skill is one of the crucial problems
of industry', industry's employers were often indifferent.[27] Improvements
in education and training were neglected by business as long as economic
performance was reasonably good.[28]

In the 1920s, pressure towards greater intervention by the state was
accompanied by the growth of the idea of social democracy, which
emphasized the role of education in enabling individuals, particularly
workers, to participate more effectively in political, social and economic
life. In the United States of America, John Dewey wrote that industrialization and the democratic transformation of society required a democratic
transformation of education. Like the Fabians, Dewey supported changes
in schooling to enable people to adapt to changes in living and working
conditions.[29] Unlike the Fabians, he was against the idea of education
for economic efficiency. In Britain, R.H. Tawney was the key figure in
educational theory and political journalism. Tawney was central to the
Labour Party's new Advisory Committee on Education established in
1918, and his *Secondary Education for All,* published in 1922, 'became
the axis around which the party's approach to education revolved' up to
and including the 1944 Act.[30] For Tawney, it was morally inexcusable
that education, along with the rest of society, was divided by class. He
argued that his position was neither essentially Christian nor party political, but a humanist one based on the belief that 'the whole fabric and
mechanism of social institutions' should be a means to the 'perfection of
individual human beings'.[31] Tawney criticized the tendency in modern
society to separate economics from social philosophy, and sought to re-
introduce a cultural evaluation or moral critique of economic progress.
As Chapter Four shows, Tawney also theorized a new, positive connection
between economic efficiency and equality. Fifty years later, it was this
element in his thought that would both provoke the wrath of neo-liberal
Conservative writers and inspire the leaders of the Labour Party to a new
fusion of economic and social goals. During the first 30 years of the

century, however, such ideas, and new pressures on the state to intervene, were battling against traditional *laissez-faire*, political cultures. This confused situation led to different outcomes for the Education and Employment departments, as they sought to define both their own roles and their relationships with each other.

Modernizers and traditionalists at the Board of Education

The Board of Education Act 1899 abolished the former departments of Education and Science and Art and the educational role of the Charity Commissioners. The new Board, which was nominally composed of a president and other principal ministers, had three branches – Elementary, Secondary and Technical – but only one permanent secretary. A Consultative Committee was set up to advise the Board and to frame regulations for a teachers' register, while Her Majesty's Inspectorate (HMI), established in 1839, reported on the state of schools. During the Edwardian era, distinctions between political and administrative careers were often blurred. For example, the Board of Education's first permanent secretary, Sir George Kekewich (1900–1903) became a Liberal MP at the election of 1906.[32] Until the end of the First World War the Board of Education appointed its officers by nomination, rather than by orthodox Civil Service recruitment procedures. Nomination, according to the department's annual report for 1950, 'enriched the work of administration with a leaven of scholarship and humanity which was in the best tradition of public life'.[33] Others have called it a system of patronage, which produced an elitist outlook and an education system that reflected the class-bound and anti-practical educational backgrounds of its senior civil servants.[34] Sidney Webb, the leading national efficiency modernizer of the time, believed that successive presidents of the Board of Education had bowed down before their civil servants and the Treasury: 'It is in the classrooms of these schools that the future battles of the Empire for commercial prosperity are being already lost.'[35] A strong education minister was needed and the question of education was bound up with administrative reform.

In *The Education Muddle and the Way Out*, written in 1901 following the establishment of the Board of Education and widely read in Whitehall in the period preceding the Education Act 1902, the Webbs argued that it was necessary to get rid of the 'arbitrary separation' of elementary and technical education. At the Board of Education, the pamphlet claimed, there was no proper internal organization. Instead there was a 'merely mechanical concentration of existing departments under a single roof'. Real unity between different types of education was needed, and the Board should have powers of inspection over every kind and grade of education, for example all primary and secondary schooling. Internally, there should be a geographical organizational basis. The Board should have powers to fine a Local Education Authority (LEA) and to appoint Commissioners in its place should the LEA fail to provide the minimum level of education. Nevertheless, the tension between such a strengthening of the centre and the continuing power of localism was clearly at work within the Webbs' thinking: 'our birthright of local self-government' should not be given up for a 'pottage of bureaucratic administration'.[36] In 1918, Sir Robert Morant (Permanent Secretary at the Board of Education 1903–1911), became a member of Haldane's Machinery of Government Committee which scrutinized the administrative efficiency of government departments. While the Committee regarded the Board as a good example of the application of the principle of concentrating responsibility for a specific service in the hands of a single department, it noted that LEAs had to obtain the approval of the Local Government Board, not the Board of Education, to raise loans, for example for building new schools. This lent some sensitivity to the Board's relations with the LEAs, and the Report stressed the need for the Board to ensure that these relations were 'close and cordial'.[37] Tensions arose because of uncertainty over the distribution of decision-making powers between them following the 1902 Act, and the Board sought to tilt the balance of power away from the LEAs. These attempts to transfer power to the centre existed concurrently with an overall financial squeeze and consequent attempts by the Board to devolve burdensome administrative detail to the LEAs. By the time of the First World War, however, the LEAs' autonomy was well

established. For example, the Board's plans to abolish the Part III authorities, which had responsibility only for elementary education, were
abandoned in the face of their opposition and that of the Association of
Education Committees.[38] In 1919, the Board lost responsibility for making university grants to the University Grants Committee (UGC) and, in
1922, a reorganization of its structure along territorial lines placed greater
emphasis on links with the LEAs.

During this process of change, important questions were raised concerning the status of the Education department, and the nature of youth
employment as an educational or an industrial issue. The Education Act
1918, introduced by the Liberal President of the Board of Education,
H.A.L. Fisher, was 'not only an immediate product of the years of War
but also the culmination of decades of reform proposals, and a pledge for
the future'.[39] The latter dimension led to the imposition of new restrictions on child labour, including the ending of employment of children
under 12 and the extension of continuation schooling to 14–16 year olds.
However, the demand for national efficiency during the War steered
educational opinion in many LEAs towards practical and vocational
elementary schooling and towards a general contraction in spending on
other forms of education. This was in opposition to what they regarded
as the Board's imposition of a policy of expansion. During and after the
War, some LEAs exerted their independence to promote vocational and
practical curricula in elementary schools.[40] The Board of Education took
the approach of refusing to relax regulations on child labour, but of leaving decisions on implementation to the LEAs. When too many exemptions
were granted by particular LEAs, the Board's attempts to shame them
into a more progressive attitude failed to have an effect. In 1916, Sir
Lewis Amherst Selby-Bigge (Permanent Secretary, 1911–1925) wrote to
the President of the Board, Lord Crewe: 'We shall never stand in proper
relation to LEAs till we reform our Elementary grant system, paying block
grants over the whole area (not school by school) and having a corresponding power to reduce this block grant if the LEA fails in its duty'.[41]

Technical education was included under the remit of the Board of
Education, and represented by a separate branch which oversaw the work

of technical and continuation schools and other elements of post-elementary education. Under the terms of the Education (Choice of Employment) Act 1910, the Board assumed responsibility for juvenile unemployment centres, although these were handed over to the Ministry of Labour in 1927. But the Board of Education faced a difficult task in establishing its status and role in Whitehall within the economic sphere, not least because education was widely regarded as a matter of consumption rather than investment in economic terms. By 1921 recession and social unrest induced various sectors of the press to accuse the Coalition government of extravagance, an accusation which led to the formation of the Geddes Committee. The Geddes 'axe', inspired by the principles of *laissez-faire*, fell on many of the government's spending proposals, and education suffered badly with an £18 million cut recommended from its budget of £50 million. After a campaign by educationists, the LEAs, trade unions and Labour and Liberal politicians, this was reduced to £6.5 million, but the Board's inter-War status was badly affected.[42]

In this period, the Board of Education clearly experienced the contradictory pressures at work within all new Whitehall departments. According to Doyle, the years to 1920 were 'marked by a sequence of strategies to combine traditions of aristocratic cultural mystique with utilitarian programmes of industrial and social administration'.[43] Strategies of this sort linked the groups making up the movement for national efficiency. As Colls argues:

> Lloyd George's massive extensions of state collectivism in welfare were tied to imperial defence: old age pensions went with Dreadnoughts, healthier mothers went with stronger soldiers, 'soft' state merged with 'hard' state.[44]

A revitalized political leadership was at stake and traditional modes of cultural authority were re-worked to govern a class-divided, industrial society. This combination of methods was manifest during the early years of the Board: 'The foundation of the Board of Education signalled the acceptance within the official culture of a need for policies that would co-ordinate an efficient and fully national system of education.'[45] Yet while the 'liberal education' of the 1902 Act created a sense of a common culture in the country at large, it also allowed for an education differentiated along class and gender lines.[46] There was a tension between the utilitarian needs of business and the 're-invigoration of a cultural leadership', and the resultant strategy involved an attempt to reconcile 'practical utility, patriotism and the human ideal in education'.[47] Contrary to many accounts, therefore, the Board was not simply attempting to preserve the primacy of a liberal education system. Relationships between education and the economy cannot simply be explained in terms of a conflict between an academic status quo and a progressive modernism, in which the former was victorious. On the contrary, civil servants and some politicians made genuine attempts to redefine and develop such relationships.

The most influential and controversial figure in the Board's early days was Sir Robert Morant, former tutor to the Crown Prince of Siam and architect of the Education Act 1902. According to some historians, he laid the foundations for the later domination of the grammar school ethos, with its classics and arts bias, which blocked the country's development of technical education and contributed to its economic decline.[48] Morant's reforming zeal, however, embraced several elements, including the promotion of national efficiency. In 1898, he wrote an article on Swiss education, arguing that English education needed:

> a really expert Central Authority for the whole of our National Education, a localized 'guidance of brains', which will watch, consider and advise upon *all* our national arrangements of all grades, of every type, *as one whole*. (Emphasis as original.)[49]

This centralized approach to the administration of education attracted Fabian and other supporters, and the 1902 Act laid the basis for a national system of secondary schools, albeit under LEA control. As Permanent Secretary (1903–1911), Morant was responsible for implementing the Act and, while initially unsympathetic to technical and vocational education, he later turned his attention to these areas. In 1909, he instigated an investigation into the possibility of promoting commercial education, and in 1910 technical and further education were replanned. Morant's departure in 1911 delayed the implementation of these schemes, but he supported the notion of continuing education as a means of widening the education of workers, and also encouraged the development of the Workers' Educational Association (WEA). Morant was eager to develop the social welfare aspects of education such as nursery schools, and brought into being the School Medical Service in 1907. The classic tradition of public school and Oxbridge backgrounds persisted (all five permanent secretaries in this period were Oxford men) but these officials were dedicated to the construction of a national system of education, a system which involved a more complex relationship with the worlds of industry and employment than is often recognized.

Similar comments may be made about many of the political heads of this period. By the late 1920s, according to Lord Eustace Percy (President, 1924–1929), the pattern of administration and authority established by Morant had become outgrown.[50] Morant's aim of a highly centralized system had been undermined by the growth of the LEAs' power. Percy developed a system of dealing with the LEAs by 'indirect rule', and thought that the elementary school system should be geared to further and technical education in a continuous, graduated development parallel to that which existed between secondary schools and universities.

Some senior officials at the Board of Education regarded Percy as weak, both in his dealings with the LEAs and with the Ministry of Labour. They viewed his willingness to co-operate with suspicion and dismay. Nevertheless, Percy was prepared to argue against those educational reformers who thought that education should merely sustain existing social values rather than create new ones, and against those who aimed simply to preserve the liberal professions rather than to stimulate technological advance. Percy was the foremost Conservative educationist to relate technical education to social goals. He adapted the arguments of the US vocationalists and tried to cajole and coerce industrial and commercial concerns into influencing the secondary schools of the twentieth century. Industry and commerce had played little enough part in the reforms of education carried out in 1870 and 1902, but in the post-War world they should be ready for such intervention. In 1928 Percy contributed a preface to a Board of Education pamphlet entitled *Education for Industry and Commerce*. In it, he maintained that the time had come for the industrial and commercial professions to make a substantial contribution to the nature and standards of education, similar to that performed by the liberal professions in previous centuries.[51]

Simon argues that the Board's doctrine consisted solely of a concern with cost-cutting and an aim 'to provide for the mass of the working class what was thought to be good for them', whilst maintaining the academic secondary school.[52] This is an accurate assessment of the clear bias within the Board, but Simon's judgement that this doctrine presented a 'blank front to the concept of economic growth', and to the question of how education could contribute to it, must be qualified. Percy's ideas contained a particular view of how education could serve industry, not a rejection of education's role in economic performance. Within these ideas, economic and social questions did not stand in a simple 'either/or' relation to each other. Industrial efficiency was closely associated with the moral education and discipline of young workers.

The educational system over which the Board of Education presided in this period, and the internal culture of the department, can be seen as a balance of tensions, rather than as a simple partnership with the LEAs. These tensions involved pressure towards central control in the name of national efficiency, pressure towards cost-cutting in the interests of national solvency, and a battle of ideas with other government departments and LEAs over areas of responsibility. These areas were particularly contested in respect of relations with industry and the administrative control of policies for youth employment (and unemployment). Battles with other departments, and with LEAs, were carried on in the knowledge that the Board of Education was a small department, with 2,000 members of staff, whose responsibilities extended to policy and planning rather than to implementation.

During this period, the Board of Education's general policy was to preserve the social status quo, a policy reinforced by financial stringency; strict economy was the watchword. Yet it also responded positively to pressures for administrative intervention in matters previously seen as the preserve of private responsibility, and this extension of powers became an accepted feature of its central administration. Nevertheless, the *laissez-faire* approach of governments condemned the Education department, along with other providers of what were regarded as social services, to political weakness. The presidency might carry Cabinet rank, but it was often seen as little more than a staging post in the careers of ambitious ministers. It was this weakness, rather than any anti-industrial bias or cultural incompatibility with the Employment department, that was the major factor in causing the Board to retreat from its interventionist ideas concerning the links between education and industry, and which led to conflicts with the Ministry of Labour.

The Ministry of Labour: a social or economic department?

The Ministry of Labour was a wartime creation, established under the provisions of the New Ministries and Secretaries Act 1916. In the following year, it assumed responsibility for industrial conciliation, labour exchanges and trade boards, industrial relations, employment statistics, and elements of national insurance, responsibilities previously exercised by the Board of Trade. According to Rodney Lowe, 'the creation of the Ministry had a certain air of inevitability about it',[53] and indeed the devolution of the Board of Trade's functions was accepted as inevitable by its officials. There was an irresistible political impetus, heightened immediately by labour demands during the War, but proceeding originally from the increased power of the labour movement and from the widely accepted need to improve living and working conditions for the mass of the population. Many other countries had created labour ministries before the War and, since 1892, a series of Royal Commissions and Parliamentary Bills had called for a similar establishment in Britain.

The growth of the Labour Department of the Board of Trade, created in 1893 by Hubert Llewellyn Smith, had added administrative momentum. The Department was the 'prototype of a modern ministry'.[54] It examined the causes of unemployment, the use of manpower and the condition of the labour market; it compiled statistics on strikes and lock-outs; it undertook a census of wages. Llewellyn Smith began the tradition whereby civil servants intervened in disputes between capital and labour, and in the improvement of the conditions of the workforce, an approach very much in tune with the 'New Liberalism' of the Edwardian era. The first Permanent Secretary of the Ministry, Sir David Shackleton, had been a Labour MP (1902–1910) and President of the TUC (1908–1909).[55] Nevertheless, despite these roots in the political growth of labour, there were different views on what a Ministry of Labour could and should do. While union leaders such as Ben Tillett and politicians such as Keir Hardie described it as a potential remedy for unemployment, and the TUC championed it as means of nationalization, there was opposition from other members of the labour movement, on the grounds that it threatened the traditional independence of the trade unions. Within the labour movement there was ambivalence over the role of the state, and divisions existed over the value of some welfare services, including employment exchanges.

Churchill also opposed the new creation:

> I do not myself hold with such a Ministry. Arbitration and Conciliation are the functions of an impartial department like the Board of Trade. *Factories* are well managed by the Home Office. Labour *policy* belongs to the Government. (Emphasis as original.)[56]

In contrast, some of the new ministry's earliest advocates had envisaged a development and further co-ordination of the economic services of the Board of Trade. For example, the Webbs had argued for a 'national authority for unemployment', in order to predict economic downturns and implement contra-cyclical public works. The 'Athenaeum' group of Liberal reformers, anticipating the 1968 change of name to the Department of Employment and Productivity,[57] called for a 'Ministry of Labour and Industry' committed to the promotion of industrial efficiency. Llewellyn Smith approved of such an extension of title and role, maintaining that a comprehensive ministry would be less likely to become a pressure group for labour.[58] This conception, however, was countered by the Haldane Committee, which recommended the creation of a Ministry of Employment. Such a title, it was maintained, would reflect the guiding principle of concentration of the functions of government according to the nature of the services provided. The Committee rejected the concept of a comprehensive Ministry of Industry, with responsibility ranging across such areas as the stimulation of production, the employment of labour, and technical and vocational education. Such a ministry would lead to unacceptable degrees of overlap with the work of existing departments.[59]

These debates clearly anticipated the discussions that arose in 1995 around the merger of the Employment and Education departments. Rodney Lowe has posed the crucial question: would the pre-War Board of Trade, as a comprehensive 'Ministry of Labour and Industry' with a dual responsibility for economic and social policies, have been the most effective instrument for dealing with the mass unemployment that was to come?

> The Board's dismemberment consigned 'employment policy' to a departmental limbo and a series of expedients had to be improvised ... in order to satisfy the most basic requirement that 'national problems were actually being faced and thought out in advance on a basis of fact'. They were by no means wholly successful. Was, therefore, the necessary restructuring and rationalization of British industry delayed by the prior need to restructure and rationalize Whitehall?[60]

Nevertheless, during the 1920s, the Ministry of Labour did assume further functions. Responsibilities for youth employment were transferred from the Board of Education, for the training and employment of the disabled from the Ministry of Pensions, and for the supervision of regulations concerning the registration of trade unions, carried out by the Registrar of Friendly Societies, from the Home Office. The bulk of the work, however, was concerned with unemployment, including responsibility for payment of the 'dole' and the creation of special schemes of public works for the unemployed, administered through the Unemployment Grants Committee. In 1922, in common with the Board of Education, the Ministry of Labour came under attack by the Geddes Committee; indeed, the Committee even recommended its abolition. Its low status within the established Whitehall machinery was reinforced by Lloyd George, who described it as political 'chaff'.[61] The growth of the Ministry of Labour after the First World War, however, convinced many civil servants that abolition was impossible, and no serious consideration was given to the Geddes' recommendation. Its sheer size and the volume of work undertaken through the employment exchanges, including payment of benefits, convinced the Treasury that it could not be abolished.

During the inter-War period, the Ministry of Labour became one of the largest government departments in terms of complement, second only to the General Post Office (GPO). In 1932, its budget reached £78.62 million, one-fifth of total public expenditure. Thus, in an administrative sense, the new ministry was transformed from a minor government department into what one Treasury official described as a 'bloody soviet'.[62] It also struggled hard to win the acceptance of employers, many of whom remained hostile on the grounds that its social service role actually contributed towards depression and unemployment, while even the 'TUC remained curiously ambivalent', at least until after the General Strike of 1926.[63]

The Ministry of Labour soon came to be seen as a social services department – concerned with the consumption, rather than the creation, of wealth. While the Labour Department of the Board of Trade had been an economic department, the new Ministry's responsibilities, especially as a consequence of the National Insurance Act 1911, became largely social. After the War, the Board of Trade dealt with the economic aspect of unemployment (the stimulation of trade) and the Ministry of Labour dealt with the social aspect (relieving distress). In presenting evidence to the Geddes Committee, Ministry of Labour officials justified their department by the fact that its work was no longer related to the Board of Trade, but to 'the Poor Law side of the Ministry of Health and the factory side of the Home Office'.[64] This role ensured its survival. In the 1920s it was reorganized under Treasury control into a standard Civil Service ministry, with a staffing structure and organization finalized by 1924. Three major policy-making departments were established: General, Employment and Insurance, and Industrial Relations. There were three service departments (Establishments, Finance and Solicitors) and two temporary ones for

Appointments and Training and Civil Liabilities. The Training department subsequently became permanent, and in 1929 two new departments were formed: one for Employment and Training the other for Unemployment Insurance. These changes reflected major changes in Ministry policy – the recognition of unemployment as a long-term problem and a corresponding permanent commitment to retraining and relocating unemployed workers.

Any development of the Ministry's role as an instrument of economic policy, however, was hampered by the Treasury's insistence on limiting its intelligence and statistics functions to those of routine administration. Senior officials at the Treasury, and in the Finance department within the Ministry of Labour, did not favour the interventionist stance associated with some of the new ministries. The Ministry's own officials were not advocates of radical change; their general policy was an orthodox one of restricting government expenditure and 'guarding against the demoralization of the workforce'.[65] Nevertheless, the Ministry's leading civil servants in this period – Harold Butler, Wilfred Eady, Frederick Leggett and Humbert Wolfe – presided over a redefinition of the role of the state in labour administration, by developing the policy of self-government in industry. In 1960 Sir Godfrey Ince (Permanent Secretary, 1944–1956) declared that this policy, 'has been followed by successive governments in this country for over half a century and … has resulted in our industrial relations system being the admiration of the world'.[66] Other leading civil servants included F.N. Tribe, the mentor of many junior administrators, and the official who played a leading role in defining the Ministry's relations with the Board of Education, and with the wider educational world. The Accountant General, F.G. Bowers, was a significant figure in debates over economic policy. A religious man and firm believer in self-help, Bowers nevertheless supported the expansion of training as a cost-effective means of restoring self-respect to the unemployed. He criticized the Treasury for failing to recognize the investment dimensions of training, and its potential for reducing the real cost of unemployment benefit in depressed areas.[67]

Despite the presence of these civil servants, the Ministry of Labour in this period has usually been portrayed as a mechanical provider of in-adequate benefit under weak ministerial leadership.[68] The first two Ministers, J. Hodge and G.H. Roberts, both represented the old, and increasingly outdated, methods and values of the pre-War labour move-ment. Sir Montague Barlow, a businessman and reformer acceptable to the labour movement, held the post in the Conservative government (1922–1924), but carried little weight in Cabinet. Similarly, Sir Arthur Steel-Maitland (Minister, 1924–1929) had industrial experience and credentials as a social reformer. His collaboration with Lord Eustace Percy, President of the Board of Education, to establish a unified youth employment and training policy is considered in the next section. The overall impression he gave, however, was one of indecisiveness. His successor, Margaret Bondfield, had worked her way up from the shop floor, but nevertheless was attacked by the TUC and the *Daily Herald* over the appointment of the Royal Commission on Unemployment Insur-ance in 1931: 'Her political position ... was hopeless from the start.'[69] Other Ministers were often criticized for giving no real lead. The mixture of lowly status but administrative importance was well expressed in 1927 by a future Minister of Labour, Oliver Stanley, who published, with Boothby and Macmillan, an influential statement of the 'middle-way', *Industry and State – A Conservative View.* They argued that 'clearly there would be no place for a Ministry of Labour under a system of *laissez faire*', but that, in the depression of the inter-War years, such a Ministry had become necessary because of the need to 'correlate economic facts and social aspirations'.[70]

In common with the Board of Education, the Ministry became squeezed between the Treasury's economic orthodoxy on the one hand and the local authorities on the other, for both had a significant interest in un-employment policy. Peter Jenkins has described how the Ministry of Labour also faced a 'dilemma of impartiality': 'the Ministry operated in the manner of an embassy to a foreign power – the working classes. As with embassies, it was never entirely clear whether its first loyalty lay with the power it represented or the power to which it was accredited.'[71] Yet, despite this uncertain identity and status, the Ministry's influence increased in Cabinet, and during the Second World War it became a major department. As Lowe has maintained:

> In economic as in social policy the Ministry of Labour had acted as an irresistible magnet for new responsibilities, as the state, through an irresistible combination of democratic electoral pressure and mass unemployment, was obliged to intervene more widely in the economy.[72]

It was to grow rapidly in importance during the Second World War. Throughout the post-War era, the Ministry of Labour was a key department on the 'home front', until the onset of economic crisis and world recession in the 1970s shifted government policy away from corporatism and traditional methods of dealing with industrial relations. The question of its abolition would not be raised again until the 1990s.

Contest and co-operation: the youth employment service

During the first 30 years of the twentieth century, relationships between the Board of Education, the LEAs and the Ministry of Labour were in a formative stage. Co-operation and conflict existed simultaneously. The two central departments attempted to work out a *modus operandi* based, in Lord Eustace Percy's words, on 'adjusting education to industry', but at the local level dealings over juvenile employment policy verged upon 'almost a state of hostilities'.[73] These issues were given an urgency by the largely unwelcome expansion in the demand for child labour arising from the First World War. Juvenile jobs were invariably unskilled, or at best semi-skilled, and there was general agreement that such wartime work was a danger to children's physical and moral welfare. Serious unemployment among juveniles and unrest over wage reductions for returning adult workers was anticipated after the War. A Ministry of Reconstruction Report, *Juvenile Employment During the War and After*, issued in 1918, suggested that 'only measures designed to break the shock of transition can prevent it from being disastrous'.[74] The Report's proposals included: the raising of the school-leaving age and the ending of exemptions; the extension of juvenile employment committees; educational provision and benefit payments for unemployed juveniles. After the War, the Departmental Committee on Juvenile Education in Relation to Employment recommended that the school-leaving age be raised to 14 (the 1918 Act made this law), while the Board of Education and the Ministry of Labour both urged the strengthening of juvenile advisory work.

From the beginning of the twentieth century, this area of policy (i.e. the guidance, placing and supervision of young workers in their first jobs, and their post-school education and training) had been a site of disputed control between the Education and Employment departments and the LEAs. In the years between the Education Act 1902 and the Education (Choice of Employment) Act 1910, a movement developed for the provision of advice to children about employment, a movement which stemmed both from the 'educational side' and from the 'employment side'.[75] Following the Labour Exchanges Act 1909, juvenile advisory services had been established under the auspices of the Board of Trade. Many educationists, however, criticized the exchanges' work and, in particular, the lack of consideration given to issues of education and training. In consequence, the Board of Education came under pressure to secure legislation to enable LEAs to deal with juvenile employment. The government urged co-operation between LEAs and the exchanges, and called for a balance of power between industry and education. The Education (Choice of Employment) Act 1910 gave LEAs the power to provide information and advice on employment for children up to 17 years of age. Thus, there existed the 'strange spectacle' of two government departments being given virtually the same powers over the provision of the same service.[76] In 1911 a Joint Memorandum issued by the two Boards classified and distributed the work between the education authorities and the exchanges. Nevertheless, the competing claims of continuation education on the one hand and paid employment on the other, coupled with the fact that the local authority officers and the exchange officers were paid at different rates and owed their loyalties to two different departments, soon resulted in conflict. To save costs the two officers were often housed in the same building, and examples of contradictory advice to the same child were soon being noised abroad. By 1920, according to Spurley

Hey, Director of Education for Manchester, no-one seriously believed that any real co-operation existed at the local level between officials of the Board of Education and the Ministry of Labour.[77]

In 1921, the Cabinet set up the Chelmsford Committee to deal with the dispute between the two departments. In effect, Lord Chelmsford acted as a single arbitrator, aided by 'assessors' from the Board, the Ministry and the Treasury. He argued that the problem had arisen because the two types of committee dealing with the work – the exchanges' juvenile advisory committees and the LEAs' juvenile employment committees – approached the matter either from an exclusively industrial point of view or from an exclusively educational one. In his opinion, neither interest was paramount, and as the problem was local, the solution should be local as well. Chelmsford, therefore, proposed that LEAs should be given first option of exercising their powers under the Education (Choice of Employment) Act; if they did not choose to do so, the work would fall to the exchanges. In consequence, the choices of LEAs determined whether control in a particular area was assumed by the Board or the Ministry, a solution which left undecided the question of basic responsibility at central government level.[78] The administrative confusion thus generated in Whitehall remained a continuing source of 'friction and delay'.[79] The problem was given added urgency by the high levels of unemployment. As Selby-Bigge, Permanent Secretary at the Board of Education, noted early in 1923; 'Of course, at the present time there is some irony in the use of the expression "choice of employment". There is so little employment that there is no choice.'[80] Only about 20 per cent of school leavers were using the service. This figure confirmed concerns at the central government level about the lack of contacts between juvenile workers and the state.

By 1925, a series of bitter disputes between some LEAs and local offices of the Ministry of Labour prompted the Cabinet to set up a fully constituted Committee under Mr (later Sir) Dougal Malcolm, charged with settling the issue of central responsibility. The determination of policy on youth employment and unemployment was a matter of urgency, and the Committee's importance was such that Churchill argued that a

Cabinet Committee should appoint its members as well as its terms of reference. Three options presented themselves: compulsory attendance at unemployment centres (the Board of Education's favoured option), raising the school-leaving age (the LEAs' option), and lowering the age at which unemployment insurance was applicable (the Ministry of Labour's option).

Each of these options presented potential problems for the government, and for the three protagonists. Central and local authorities in education, moreover, were not necessarily of one mind. For example, in May 1925 Lord Eustace Percy wrote to Sir Philip Cunliffe-Lister MP: 'We are under quite enough pressure at the present moment to raise the school-leaving age and so forth and the result of any really practical inquiry must be to damp down this agitation by showing the serious difficulties in the way of any such proposal.'[81] At the same time, the Board was clearly worried that lowering the insurance age would suggest to educationists that the influence of the Ministry of Labour over young people was being extended, and it warned against the 'prospect of antagonising the LEAs, the teachers and that rather wider public opinion which is growing up about educational matters'. In a memo prepared for representatives of employers and trade unions, the Board attempted to formulate an even-handed public position: 'for every young person employment should be both continuous with education and a continuation of education'.[82] The strength of this conciliatory and co-operative approach was further demonstrated when Percy privately joined forces with Sir Arthur Steel-Maitland, the Minister of Labour, to write a memorandum for the Cabinet. This suggested linking the arguments around education and industry to legislation which would introduce compulsory instruction at juvenile unemployment centres:

> Such a bill will not, however, be accepted by public opinion as sufficient to meet the problem and it may, therefore, excite opposition unless it is brought into relation with a more comprehensive enquiry into the whole problem of the adjustment between education and the requirements of industry.[83]

The Malcolm Committee was eventually asked to 'inquire into and advise upon the public system of education in England and Wales in relation to the requirements of trade and industry, with particular reference to the adequacy of the arrangements for enabling young persons to enter into and retain suitable employment'.[84]

The Committee's Report considered the central argument concerning the precedence of the national industrial interest over local interests, and recommended the transfer of central control to the Ministry of Labour.[85] Local control was left divided between LEAs and Ministry of Labour offices. The LEAs, however, were extremely reluctant to give up their favoured position resulting from the Chelmsford Report. Indeed, their opposition to the proposed transfer of power was such that the Ministry of Labour was forced to give an undertaking that local authorities would be able to develop the work in line with their own local educational policies. On the other hand, the Board of Education, together with the rest of the government, was keen to 'adjust education to industry' as Eustace Percy had initially thought the terms of reference of the Committee should be. In agreeing with the Board and the government, Malcolm recommended the establishment of permanent juvenile unemployment centres and a system of 'working certificates' which would make possible the public supervision of 14–16 year olds. The Unemployment Insurance Act 1935 subsequently gave the Minister of Labour powers to compel unemployed juveniles to attend 'an authorised course of instruction', and to require employers to notify the local office or juvenile employment bureau when a juvenile left employment. These measures formally settled the questions of departmental demarcation, and the relative claims of educationists and industrialists, with respect to the employment of young people. It is important to note, however, that ministers and senior civil servants saw the question of demarcation primarily as a means of clarifying the blurred links between education and industry for the purpose of bringing the two spheres into a clear relationship, not to separate them. The regulation of youth employment was the policy arena in which this process occurred.

Conclusion

Pressures towards change, and change itself, produced contradictory effects within both departments. For example, the key ministers and senior civil servants involved in the early period of the Board of Education and Ministry of Labour – Beveridge, Morant, Percy and Llewellyn Smith – can be seen as embodiments of the tensions between an old political culture of *laissez-faire* and the need for modern, national solutions to problems of competitiveness and the growth of democracy. The process which Jose Harris sees as representing the continuity of aristocratic influence – the appointments of Beveridge, Morant and Llewellyn Smith by means of personal contacts with aristocratic politicians – had an ironic outcome in that by the end of the 1920s these senior civil servants were hailed as representatives of the modernizing movement. They were appointed through aristocratic patronage, but served as modernizing officials.

According to Harold Perkin, while early collectivist legislation (such as the inspection of factories, poor relief, public health) was merely a series of attempts to provide a framework of law for the continued dominance of individualism, nevertheless the free market was under attack from 'men such as Beveridge and Keynes, Morant, Llewellyn Smith … whose analyses of poverty, unemployment and education played a central role in the origins of the welfare state'.[86] The shift to interventionism was very gradual, and sometimes politicians and civil servants could move in both directions at once – promoting intervention in some areas, withdrawal in others. In education, intervention could take place in order to protect, rather than reduce, the private sector and local voluntary effort. But the sheer complexity of modern urban and industrial processes led to the expansion and modernization of Whitehall, at the same time as the ideological or cultural attachment to the more *laissez-faire* public doctrines of the mid-Victorian era still held sway.

This chapter has shown how the Board of Education and the Ministry of Labour began to diverge from the traditional political culture of *laissez-faire* as they developed new ways of working and of relating to their constituencies. The Board began to try to find a means of relating education to employment, at the same time as attempting to preserve the educational status quo, while the Ministry attempted to find an economic role for itself. Co-operation at ministerial level increased in areas of overlap such as youth employment. Both the Board and Ministry, however, failed to assert themselves as central departments of state. Their political weaknesses caused conflict in the localities between themselves, as well as with the LEAs. The Board declined during a period of financial stringency; the Ministry grew as it took on more and more of the social function of dealing with unemployment. Chapter Four shows how the two departments continued in a dynamic relationship of conflict and co-operation. By the end of the Second World War, however, their functions were more defined and they had acquired a greater presence, both at Westminster and in the country at large.

Notes

1. Lowe, 1986.
2. Harris, 1994, 148.
3. Harris, 1994, 17.
4. Harris, 1994, 21.
5. Newton and Porter, 1988, 3.
6. Newton and Porter, 1988, 1.
7. Parker, 1995, 252.
8. Tomlinson, 1994, 36.
9. Tomlinson, 1994, 54.
10. Tomlinson, 1994, 10.
11. Tomlinson, 1994, 28–29.
12. Speech by S. Webb, quoted in Tomlinson, 1994, 30–31.
13. Harris, 1990, 393, quoted in Tomlinson, 1994, 16.
14. Harris, 1994, 194.
15. Harris, 1990, 13.
16. Harris, 1990, 14.
17. See Pollard, 1989, 170.
18. Newton and Porter, 1988, 2.
19. Tomlinson, 1994, 189.
20. Quoted in Tomlinson, 1994, 189.

21. Tomlinson, 1994, 82.
22. Colls, 1986, 29, 30.
23. Reeder, 1979, 122.
24. Milne-Watson, 1927.
25. Tomlinson, 1994, 87.
26. Carr and Hartnett, 1996, 93.
27. Balfour, 1927.
28. Evans and Wiseman, 1984, 138.
29. Reeder, 1979, 117.
30. Wright, 1987, 24.
31. Wright, 1987, 43.
32. Hennessy, 1989, 54.
33. Ministry of Education, 1951, 2.
34. Simon, 1974, 282.
35. Speech by S. Webb, quoted in Brennan, 1975, 80.
36. Brennan, 1975, 70.
37. Haldane, 1918, 52–57.
38. Gordon, Aldrich and Dean, 1991, 49.
39. Gordon, Aldrich and Dean, 1991, 49.
40. Parker, 1995, 254.
41. Quoted in Parker, 1995, 247.
42. Gordon, Aldrich and Dean, 1991, 51.
43. Doyle, 1986, 90.
44. Colls, 1986, 52.
45. Doyle, 1986, 96.
46. Doyle, 1986, 97.
47. Doyle, 1986, 104.
48. Gordon, Aldrich and Dean, 1991, 20–21, 279–281.
49. Quoted in Gordon, Aldrich and Dean, 1991, 18.
50. Simon, 1974, 315.
51. Percy, 1928.
52. Simon, 1974, 320.
53. Lowe, 1986, 15.
54. Hennessy, 1989, 53.
55. Hennessy, 1989, 749.
56. Quoted in Hennessy, 1989, 15.
57. Lowe, 1986, 17, footnote.
58. Lowe, 1986, 18.
59. Haldane, 1918, 43–50.

60. Lowe, 1986, 196.
61. Lowe, 1986, 37.
62. Lowe, 1986, 11–12.
63. Lowe, 1986, 26.
64. Lowe, 1986, 132.
65. Lowe, 1986, 187.
66. Ince, 1960, 204.
67. Lowe, 1986, 71–72.
68. Lowe, 1986, 238–250.
69. Lowe, 1986, 34.
70. Lowe, 1986, 38.
71. Lowe, 1986, 39.
72. Lowe, 1986, 237.
73. Public Record Office (PRO) ED 24/1354; Malcolm Committee Papers. Minute paper, 'Relations with the Ministry of Labour', 25 April 1925.
74. Heginbotham, 1951, 43.
75. Heginbotham, 1951, 3.
76. PRO LAB 19/112; Report following discussions on the juvenile employment service. 'Notes on the relations between the Ministry of Labour and the local education authorities', 1944, para. 1.
77. Heginbotham, 1951, 22, 67.
78. PRO ED 24/1273; Chelmsford Enquiry, 1921–23. 'Juvenile Employment Enquiry' (n.d.).
79. Heginbotham, 1951, 81.
80. PRO ED 24/1273; Chelmsford Enquiry. Minute, Selby-Bigge to President, 5 January 1923.
81. PRO ED 24/1354; Malcolm Committee papers. Letter, Eustace Percy to Sir Philip Cunliffe-Lister, 18 May 1925.
82. PRO ED 24/1354; Malcolm Committee papers. 'Draft memo for consideration by representatives of employers' and workers' organizations in regard to juvenile employment' (n.d.).
83. PRO ED 24/1354; Malcolm Committee papers. Memorandum by the President of the Board of Education and the Minister of Labour, 6 May 1925.
84. Heginbotham, 1951, 80.
85. Malcolm, 1928.
86. Perkin, 1992, 36.

4 Contrasting Fortunes, 1928–1944

Introduction

As the previous chapter has shown, in the first three decades of the twentieth century the fledgling Education and Employment departments formally operated within strictly separated spheres of interest. This accorded with the dominant Whitehall culture but, as pressures to intervene in social and economic life increased, issues about the appropriate relationships between the two departments arose. These relationships occurred in different ways and at different levels. Conflict frequently occurred at the lower levels of the two departments, and between the LEAs and both departments. At a senior level, however, genuine attempts were made to bring the Board of Education and the Ministry of Labour, and the areas of policy for which they had responsibility, into a creative partnership. Such a partnership would remove the potential for turf wars and provide the means of dealing more effectively with crucial policy problems. Prominent among these were the issues of youth unemployment and the nature and suitability of vocational education and training.

This chapter examines how distinctive departmental cultures developed during the 1930s and the Second World War, cultures which depended in part upon a clearer definition of their respective functions and roles. Three broad periods can be identified. For the first 10 years economic crisis caused the Board of Education to retreat into Whitehall. In sharp contrast, the Ministry of Labour flowed out into the localities, recruiting an army of clerks for assessing and paying benefit claims. The initial phases of the Second World War brought about a further retrenchment at the Board of Education, while the Ministry continued to expand as it organized the massive registration programmes through its employment exchanges. During the War, however, both departments made preparations to undertake a larger role in national life: the Board as an arm of the movement for greater social welfare and the Ministry as a serious economic department of state. In these years, a political and administrative culture of increased state intervention gained ground in Whitehall. This was aided by the temporary eclipse of Treasury power. Opportunities arose for those who desired a comprehensive and co-ordinated involvement of the state in the economic and social life of the country. Staff of both departments gained in confidence. Visions, and in some instances detailed plans, of the growth of their influence in the post-War world began to emerge.

Democracy, planning and equality

Following the slump of 1929, widespread doubts arose about the ability of the market system to recover by its own devices. During the next decade, there was a general agreement in political and intellectual circles on the need for some type of planning – a consensus that stretched from Communists to Conservatives. The *laissez-faire* doctrines of the early 1930s countenanced reductions in wages in order to restrict imports. These were to be challenged by policies based upon public ownership and tariffs, policies designed to reduce the probability of social conflict. These years witnessed an 'intellectual groundswell' in favour of the use of state power. For example, Ernest Bevin's view of the role of government revolved around the suppression of what he saw as the unproductive and unjust role of bankers and financiers, and an enhancement of the positive role of 'Science, Management and Labour'.[1] The consensus around the state co-ordination of industrial change meshed with a cultural concept of science promoted by many of the progressive movements and politics of the day. Radical scientists, such as J.D. Bernal, P.M.S. Blackett and J.B.S. Haldane, together with C.P. Snow, whose ideas are discussed in Chapter Five, saw science as the hope of a world brought to the brink of chaos, war and mass unemployment by the traditional elites. This view became bound up with the notion of meritocracy, as opposed to the traditional literary culture of the existing hierarchy. Planning, and the example of the USSR, were influential among one part of a 'science and society' movement which claimed that scientists needed to play more of a role in society. Established rulers and politicians, it was argued, were working to antiquated philosophies that were hopelessly out of touch with the modern world.[2]

At a time of economic crisis, R.H. Tawney's work was influential within this tendency to link rationalism and morality.[3] During the 1980s, Tawney was to be maligned by the intellectual right wing as the prime exponent of 'cultural bias', an anti-industrial ruralism which sapped the nation's competitive resources in the inter-War years.[4] Tawney justified the privileging of equality over efficiency and was a leading exponent of the tradition of welfarism which has been blamed for damaging Britain's economic competitiveness.[5] Today he is lauded by the left, for example by Gordon Brown, for having reconciled equality and efficiency. His *Equality*, written during the period of the 1929–1931 Labour government, emphasized not only the moral defects of social inequality but also its liabilities in an economic sense.[6] Social inequality misdirected production towards unessential goods and failed to educate the population in the characteristics necessary for productive activity. Inequality sustained vested interests which held back economic reconstruction and produced a class struggle that precluded co-operative activity and a common culture: 'Whatever the ends which these features of our society may serve, economic efficiency is certainly not among them.'[7] The intellectual opposition to this influential justification of state-sponsored egalitarianism was provided by conservatives such as F.R. Leavis and the Scrutiny movement who, influenced by Spengler's *Decline of the West*, made impassioned pleas for the preservation of the classical liberal tradition and for the importance of 'minority culture'.[8] For Leavis the national tradition was rooted in the organic, homogeneous rural community which provided the basis of elite literary culture; a common culture was impossible because standards depended on a cultivated minority. Tawney's response was potentially contradictory. He hoped that a common culture would grow, but he also hoped that 'existing standards of excellence' would be preserved.[9] This uneasy relationship between equality and standards was not simply a personal one. It stemmed from a situation in which the notion of equality was construed in a climate of unexamined assumptions about inherent individual differences. These assumptions would underpin policies on the structures of schooling and youth employment throughout the 1930s and the Second World War.

The Education department during the 1930s

In the 1930s, the perceived failures of the education system in relation to industry became a central subject for debate. The Spens Report in 1938 alleged that the Act of 1902 had cast secondary education in a grammar school mould, to the detriment of technical and practical studies. Low standards in mathematics and an overly academic curriculum were among the targets for widespread criticism.[10] The Board of Education was seen as requiring a more vocational approach. Pressures increased for the provision of more secondary schools and the raising of the school-leaving age. In 1936, Oliver Stanley (President of the Board of Education, 1935–1937, and a former Minister of Labour) introduced a Bill to raise the school-leaving age to 15 with effect from 1 September 1939. Considerable controversy, however, centred on the 'beneficial exemptions' clause, which allowed children who had obtained worthwhile employment to leave school after their fourteenth birthday. The operation of the Act was postponed by the outbreak of War. The Spens Report went further in recommending an expansion of secondary education, with greater parity of staffing and treatment between the different types of schools and increased provision of technical schools. It also envisaged the raising of the school-leaving age to 16. During the 1930s, however, in spite of these and other pressures for reform, there were few changes in the structure of the educational system. The basic conservatism among the Board of Education's officials was reinforced by strict economic constraints. The Board retreated into Whitehall while the backgrounds of its officials came under greater scrutiny.

Their commitment to a state secondary school system which privileged a small elite educated in a traditional liberal manner received criticism from Tawney and others who argued that the class bias perpetuated by the Board and its civil servants was both unjust and inefficient. Some 60 per cent of the 179 administrative class officials who worked at the Board of Education between 1919 and 1939 were educated at Oxford or Cambridge.[11] Savage argues that the Board displayed an 'exaggeration of the elitist tendencies of the English Civil Service almost to the point of caricature'.[12]

Liberal and elitist attitudes among civil servants, however, did not imply their rejection of any link between education and economic efficiency, rather a particular and conservative view of such a relationship. In the 1930s, this view was challenged by the emergence of an 'idealist' intellectual framework for social policy which led many to believe that the state should take ultimate responsibility for education and welfare, in particular youth welfare.[13] The Board of Education was aware of such arguments and 'live to the challenge posed by the falling birth rate'.[14] While the Oxbridge culture of its officials and their adherence to divisive social attitudes cannot be in doubt, they acknowledged the need to improve education for the purposes of employment. Although this did not lead to any significant modification of grammar school curricula for vocational purposes, the Board did make some attempts to promote technical education. For example, in 1930 a major report was published about education in the West Midlands, an area of particular industrial importance. Efforts were made to implement its recommendations for improving staffing and facilities for day-release technical courses and full-time vocational education.[15] Officials of the Board's technical branch urged the need for more co-operation between the local authorities in organizing specialist courses in order to reduce duplication.

Sir Charles Trevelyan (President of the Board, 1929–1931) campaigned in the district in an attempt to persuade local authorities to act on the report's findings. Trevelyan urged closer relations between schools and businesses, and the report noted favourably the acceptance by Local Education Authorities (LEAs) of employers on the advisory or management committees of technical colleges. The persistent efforts of Trevelyan and the Board's senior officials met with some apathy although not antagonism from the local authorities. Eventually, in 1935, the West Midlands Advisory Council for Further Education was set up as an administrative means of achieving the Board's desired aim of the rationalization and centralization of courses.[16] This ministerial lead, and shared concerns with the Ministry of Labour, suggests that the Board was attempting to relate education to industry, within the changing circumstances of Britain in the 1930s, even if it could not exert sufficient pressure on either the government or employers to increase funding or access to day-release study for young workers. Keith Burgess has argued that:

> The Board's difficulties were not rooted either in any lack of determination on its part or in its subordination to an anti-industrial and anti-technological ideology. Rather the Board's problems sprang first from its relative impotence in relation to the local authorities and other departments of government, and secondly from the reluctance of industrial and commercial interests to support its claims to scarce resources.[17]

These difficulties, compounded by the widespread emphasis upon academic subjects in public and grammar schools and the absence of any consistent human capital theory, proved to be a 'powerful obstacle to policy innovation', and the West Midlands initiative was not repeated. Much of Trevelyan's energy as President of the Board was devoted to an unsuccessful attempt to raise the school-leaving age. Although the Education Act 1936 presaged both a relaxation of capital expenditure and a leaving age of 15, rearmament, Munich and the outbreak of War itself in the following year brought hopes of educational expansion to an end.[18]

The Employment department during the 1930s

The very economic conditions that led to a general contraction in the Board of Education's activities and a reduction in its staffing, necessitated an expansion at the Ministry of Labour. There was an explosion of unemployment work and an army of clerks was recruited to administer benefit payments. The Ministry of Labour became the second largest inter-War department after the General Post Office (GPO). By 1939, it had 30,000 employees, compared to 7,000 at the Ministry of Health, 5,000 at the Board of Trade and a mere 2,000 at the Board of Education.[19]

During this period, over half of the Ministry of Labour's employees were temporary clerks working in local offices. Nevertheless, Rodney Lowe has argued that the Ministry was not the 'drudge' that Bullock and others have thought it to be. Its political and administrative importance grew in the 1930s, before the comprehensive employment policies of the Second World War.[20] Promotion of officials at the Ministry, as opposed to the Board, was seen to depend more on ability than educational background and they generally displayed a more active approach to policy. Savage concluded that the 'distancing of the professional ethos of Ministry of Labour officials from their social origins lent their views the authority of objectivity and neutrality'.[21] Its officials were the obvious choice to plan and staff the Unemployment Assistance Boards and Special Areas Commissions, while their statistical expertise brought attention to the department as a focus for experiments in uncharted areas of policy. In the prevailing atmosphere of depression and political sensitivity, however, little success was achieved in implementing innovative policies. Orthodox economic ideas continued to dominate within the department.

An example of innovative thinking occurred in 1931 when the Ministry, concerned by a projected shortfall in juvenile labour, produced a scheme which was intended to predict the labour needs in certain sectors. The most tangible results of this initiative, which continued through the 1930s, were the Juvenile Instruction Centres (JICs) and Juvenile Unemployment Centres (JUCs). Nevertheless, as one contemporary writer acknowledged, these were established on the 'shifting sands of unemployment', not on the economic needs of industry.[22] Some 1.5 million unemployed young people passed through these centres, but their levels of training were low.[23] This emphasis on managing the effects of unemployment foreshadowed the later concentration of training policy on social or ameliorative issues rather than on the forward planning of labour requirements.[24]

Ministers found themselves under pressure from such traditional views. Margaret Bondfield was Minister of Labour in the 1929–1931 Labour government and the first woman appointed to a Cabinet post. Bondfield had worked her way up from the shop floor, through the Independent Labour Party and the National Federation of Women Workers.[25] She came under attack after appearing to renege on promises regarding increasing staffing at the Ministry, some critics protesting that she was being 'led' by senior officials who were the 'power behind the throne'.[26] These civil servants opposed a scheme for using the unemployment insurance fund to aid industry and alleviate unemployment, informing Bondfield that it was unacceptable to use public money to subsidize employment.[27] Other schemes were rejected by officials on the grounds of cost. The prevailing ethos was opposed to state intervention in the economy and the imposition of extra costs on industry. Senior civil servants held a conception of the Ministry as an active department, but argued that intervention to ease unemployment should be restricted to the promotion of the free movement and supply of labour, by way of training and transference schemes, thereby oiling the workings of the labour market.

War, efficiency and the Civil Service

During the Second World War, Tawney and other social critics became more forthright in their claims for the beneficial effects of social equality on economic efficiency. Tawney declared that 'While the case against inequality on grounds of justice appears to me as convincing as it always was, the case for it on grounds of national unity and strength seems to me more convincing.'[28] In wartime conditions, the themes of economic efficiency and national unity were closely connected. Class privileges were a positive danger to a country beset by threats of invasion and the demands of total war. Waste was inexcusable and the efficiency of the war effort depended on a new planned approach to the economy, which in turn depended on technical prowess and educational expansion. By the middle stage of the War, a consensus had emerged about the nature of and necessity for educational reform. Mass observation reports showed not only that many people saw the need for education to become more accessible and democratic, but also that they wanted it to become more relevant to the real world, less academic and out of touch with political and social realities. One respondent advised that:

> Education should be more closely linked with everyday life so that 'school' and 'home' will not be held in contrast and so that there will be no such event as 'leaving school'. No boy should dream of burning his exercise books the week before he draws his first week's pay.[29]

In some quarters, it was still proclaimed that education for all would deprive the country of manual workers and educate the lower orders out of their place in society. In contrast, R.A. Butler (President of the Board and Minister of Education, 1941–1945) argued: 'To the question "who will do the work if everyone is educated" the only reply is that education will oil the wheels of industry and will bring a new efficiency, the fruit of modern knowledge, to aid the ancient skill of farm and field.'[30] This shift towards a more active economic and social policy, both during and after the War, was acknowledged in Whitehall. In a note written in 1941 the Board of Education's Deputy Secretary, Sir Robert Wood, stated:

> There are straws to be found in Cabinet papers and elsewhere which indicate the way the wind is blowing, and we may assume that responsibility for the direction of the nation's effort in the immediate post-War years will remain in the hands of a National Government prepared to face radical changes in our social and economic system and contemplating not merely restoration or a return to normality, but reconstruction in a very real sense.[31]

This radical democratic mood was linked to criticism of the elitism of the Civil Service. Demands for administrative reform were driven by a widespread sense of its obsolescence and inability to act with due speed in an emergency. These were days of constant criticism of Whitehall, and instances of inefficiency and nepotism were widely reported in the popular press.[32] Concern was reflected within the House of Commons. MPs alleged that 'senior Civil Service posts were occupied by people so trained in peacetime Treasury methods as to be unable to give the most efficient service in wartime when quite other methods were required' and that 'the country was absolutely "fed up" with the stagnation within the Civil Service'.[33] At the same time, patronage scandals were reported when large numbers of temporary workers, many of them relatives of civil servants, were appointed without recourse to the employment exchanges. The call for businessmen to enter public administration was one manifestation of this unease, although only Beaverbrook stands out as an example of commercial new blood.

There were demands for a Ministry of Production (or Commerce) to co-ordinate production across the Labour and Supply Departments.[34] Labour politicians had previously proposed the establishment of a 'Ministry of Industry'; indeed, in 1930 Clement Attlee had argued that such a ministry should plan the rationalization of contracting sectors.[35] In 1939, the Royal Commission on the Distribution of the Industrial Population had recommended that a new 'Ministry of Industry' should be created to deal with the location and planning of industry and stimulation of economic development in regions of unemployment or expected unemployment. Wartime developments in political and social attitudes meant that both the Board of Education and the Ministry of Labour were presented with the prospect of becoming authoritative departments at the centre of government social and economic policy. Traditional, liberal ideas about education, the economy and the proper conduct and role of government, however, would not easily be jettisoned.

A Ministry of Education

War brought about an intensively planned economy in which efficiency and democracy were closely connected; reconstruction presented advanced thinkers with the opportunity to 'refashion the state machine in their own image'.[36] The intrusion of the state into areas that had previously been matters of private concern provided opportunities for the redrawing of former boundaries both in departmental and policy terms. The theme of centrally directed, post-War reconstruction gathered an intellectual momentum which envisaged leading roles both for the Board of Education and the Ministry of Labour. The conflict itself stimulated the demand for scientists and technologists, and the 1940s saw a convergence of thought between industrial trainers and educational progressives. Sir Fred Clarke's declaration that 'to separate culture and vocation in our thought, in our education and in our common life is not to solve a problem, it is to intensify a disease which, unchecked, may finish us' reflected the urgency and radical sentiment of much wartime debate.[37] Educational issues were widely discussed, and a reformed structure was seen as the best means of securing a fairer and less wasteful treatment of the majority of the population. This was in sharp contrast to the 1920s and 30s, when only a small minority was educated beyond 14 and only the children of the rich proceeded to higher education.[38]

Until relatively recently, this wartime mood of radical collectivism was seen by historians as a catalyst for far-reaching changes in social and welfare provision, exemplified in the Education Act of 1944. The alternative interpretation is that the War should not be seen essentially as a period of 'revolution' in social structures and attitudes, but as a continuity in old institutions and policies. Proposals for fundamental change were headed off by elites careful to preserve the content, if not the form, of traditional hierarchies.[39] According to this view, the 1944 Act was a continuation of policies put forward in the Hadow and Spens Reports. It represented a victory for the Board of Education's officials rather than any radical break with the past. If the historical process is seen as an interaction of interests and ideologies, however, the emerging social and economic agenda of the period may best be explained as a compromise between radical reformists on the one hand and conservatives on the other.

Schooling was seriously disrupted by the outbreak of the War and the Board of Education was thrown into confusion. Evacuation, with its exposure of the deplorable educational and physical standards of many children, brought renewed criticism upon the Board. As Peter Gosden has argued, in the early months of the War, the 'chillingly ingrained capacity of the Board to avoid fighting for its own – and therefore education's case – within the government had become chronic'.[40] The campaign for educational reform gathered pace.[41] The Board responded with strenuous efforts to seize the initiative, and to channel the growing pressures for reform into an acceptable legislative shape. In November 1940, some of the Board's top civil servants formed the Committee of Senior Officials on Post-War Educational Reconstruction, in order, as the Permanent Secretary, Maurice Holmes, explained, to 'lead rather than follow' the growing movement for change.[42] The Committee provided a means of securing a major change in the Board's traditionally advisory role, and of achieving a more active presence within Whitehall. Sir Robert Wood regretted the missed opportunities of the inter-War years. In particular, he cited the Board's loss of status during Lord Eustace Percy's period of office (1924–1929): 'I do not think that we have recovered from the damage of that period.'[43] In 1940, Wood wrote a paper which acknowledged the change in the balance of power between the Board and the LEAs since the 1902 Act. The local authorities had grown in confidence and independence while the Board had tended to react to events rather than anticipate them.[44] Memoranda produced by the Committee of Senior Officials provided the basis for the Board's *Education After the War* of 1941 (the 'Green Book') and for the White Paper, *Educational Reconstruction*, of 1943.

Documents such as these emphasized the need for central direction, and a concentration on national policy and national standards, in place of the disparate provision of the LEAs. The case for a stronger Education department was supported by virtually all concerned with post-War reconstruction. Under the terms of the 1944 Act, the President and Board of Education were replaced by a Minister and Ministry. The new Minister was given the duty:

> to promote the education of the people of England and Wales and the progressive development of institutions devoted to that purpose, and to secure the effective execution by local authorities, under his control and direction, of the national policy for providing a varied and comprehensive educational service in every area.

The Consultative Committee, suspended for the duration of the War, was replaced by two Central Advisory Councils for England and Wales, whose members and terms of office were to be decided by the Minister.[45] As the balance between the new Ministry and the LEAs was expected to change, an internal committee was set up to review departmental organization and staffing. The territorial organization, established in 1922 but suspended during the War, was re-introduced and nine divisions were set up. These would facilitate relationships with the LEAs, while policy issues would be decided in the branches which were reorganized into primary, secondary and further education. The technical branch was split between secondary (dealing with technical schools) and further education (dealing with young people's colleges). The increased authority of the new Ministry would soon raise questions about its relationships with other government departments, particularly the Employment department which was also growing in confidence.

A Ministry of Labour and National Service

The Military Training Act in May 1939 required young men on reaching the age of 20 to undergo six months' military training. In consequence, the Ministry of Labour was transformed into the Ministry of Labour and National Service. On the outbreak of the War, the continuing dominance of the old non-interventionist culture resulted in an economy drive in the department. Financial concerns increased, and the Ministry's circulars of the winter of 1939–1940 calling for reductions in staffing, stressed that 'the need for stringent economy should be borne in mind'.[46] Ernest Brown, appointed Minister of Labour in 1935 and who served until the advent of the Coalition government in May 1940, was 'an ex-regimental sergeant major with the loudest voice in Parliament'.[47] When, in late 1939 and early 1940, unemployment increased rapidly, Brown disowned responsibility, arguing that the reduction of unemployment was 'an industrial process' rather than a matter for his department. This ensured that the best use was made of available skills: 'so that every skilled man shall go to the job in which he is competent, and then the semi-skilled man shall follow him, and the unskilled will follow the semi-skilled'.[48] This process, he said, could take up to three years to complete. The idea of a hierarchical 'industrial process' rankled, and calls were made for all workers, not just the skilled, to be mobilized. Many people were afraid of what might happen over the next few months if Britain's workforce were not mobilized and if War production did not improve. Brown's response reinforced the general dissatisfaction with the complacency and *laissez-faire* attitudes of the Chamberlain government and a particular discontent with the Ministry of Labour and National Service.

War soon produced conditions under which state intervention and compulsion in matters of employment were raised to previously un-imagined levels. Emergency powers legislation of 1939 and 1940 enabled the Minister to control civilian employment and to establish a planned labour force, powers which the new Minister, Ernest Bevin, was to use to the full. The official historian of the Ministry during the War, H.M.D. Parker, concluded that 'The advent of Mr Bevin in May 1940 marked the beginning of the transformation of the Ministry of Labour and National Service into a major Department of State'.[49] The Factory Department of the Home Office was transferred to the Ministry and a Welfare Department, a Labour Supply Inspectorate and a Manpower Statistics Branch were established. Employment exchanges were given responsibility for a huge programme of registration and for the administrative work of mobilizing the population into the armed forces. Government Training Centres (GTCs) were expanded, and provided courses for 350,000 men and women during the War. In 1941, the Ministry was divided into two sectors. One controlled industrial relations, juvenile employment, un-employment insurance and other pre-war functions; the other assumed responsibility for manpower statistics, recruitment to the services and civilian War work, as well as for general training. In the following year, an Appointments Office was established with a Technical and Scientific Register, designed to ensure the efficient deployment of professional and scientific personnel. In 1943 a Nursing Appointments Office was set up to promote recruitment into nursing.

The employment exchanges: 'a living contact with the working people'

During the depression of the 1930s one senior official, Wilfred Eady, had written that the department had a 'special responsibility' to government because 'we alone of the Departments have a living contact' with the working population.[50] This contact was organized through the employment exchanges which were the core of the Ministry's distinctive role; they were also the objects of severe criticism both from public and press. Labour exchanges had been set up in 1909. Although renamed employment exchanges in 1916 the former name stuck in the popular mind, perhaps because of their association with the Ministry of Labour. Despite claims made at their inception by Churchill and others, the exchanges soon acquired a poor reputation as the place to sign on for dole payments rather than a place to find work. Their public image further deteriorated throughout the inter-War period, as they became the focus of a hatred fuelled by the government's parsimonious treatment of the unemployed. Rodney Lowe has argued that the exchanges constituted 'a success story', and that in assessing the Ministry's successes and failures, the historian should take particular account of the 'sheer executive efficiency' of the exchanges' work.[51] In 1939, however, when the Ministry also became responsible for national service, the dilapidated premises and understaffing of the exchanges were brought to the attention of a wider public. During 1939, despite the increased volume of work involved in registration for national service, financial constraints determined that money would only be made available for air raid defences and not to improve the general condition of the premises. According to numerous letters of complaint by exchange staff published in the Ministry of Labour Staff Association's *Civil Service Argus*, some offices lacked running water and proper sanitary facilities.[52] Difficulties faced by exchange staff, however, were routinely ignored. The press commonly portrayed them as 'snoops', while the *Daily Mirror* described them as 'swollen-headed tin gods'.[53]

A survey of London's exchanges in 1940 found 'a social tradition of hostility' towards them, based on their failure to fulfil the expected function of neutral contact between employer and employee, and their perceived prejudiced and bullying treatment of applicants.[54] Many people complained that they had been 'treated like dirt' and had been assumed to be loafers and malingerers. This was such a widely held feeling that people would easily accept hearsay evidence about poor treatment at the exchange even if their own experience had been unremarkable. Lowe argues that the 'historian should not be so gullible' and regards the criticism as exaggerated, based on unrealizable expectations. Nevertheless, it is necessary to ask why such an impression should persist under differing circumstances. Understaffing, the run-down nature of the buildings, their positioning out of sight in slum streets, and the lack of privacy within them encouraged complaints and a feeling of injustice and discrimination, arising out of different experiences but nevertheless shared by unemployed, waged and salaried workers alike. Bevin visited some of the exchanges at the end of 1941 and found them extremely depressing in their 'prison like appearance'.[55] As the *Manchester Guardian* maintained: 'What the Treasury deemed good enough for the working classes in 1911 or 1920 is not good enough today.'[56] Bevin's public defence of the staff, however, served only to encourage criticism, 'which continued to be bitter'. Much of this bitterness came from women, angry that their difficulties in moving from home to workplace were treated with disdain. Between the outbreak of the War and the end of 1942, 24 million people were registered with the exchanges, and women were interviewed at the rate of 50,000 per week.[57]

Calls for the separation of social security and employment work were to become crucial to the future of the department. Surprisingly, the situation intensified during the first year of the War as the contraction of the economy proceeded more rapidly than the redirection of labour into the forces and munitions work. Unemployment persisted, and the exchanges still had to provide a substantial number of benefit payments. In January 1940, *The Times* puzzled over 'obstinate' unemployment which 'baffles present analysis'.[58] Papers of the Manpower Survey, commissioned by the government in 1939–1940 in order to establish where labour shortages existed or where labour could be withdrawn for diversion to munitions work and the forces, provide useful information about conditions in London. Local investigators under the direction of G.D.H. Cole were engaged to gather information and to visit workplaces to talk to employers and unions. During the first 12 months of the War, the dislocation of the economy in London caused:

> a gradual running down of all motivating energy. Directors sit at desks clear of paper; the telephone rings seldom; they can see one almost in one's own time. They do not ask for help for each is engaged in a desperate competitive attempt to maintain as long as possible a facade of business activity. But their manner and their comments betray their total hollowness. There is no drive, no determination, no vision; no plans for change over to commodities for which there is current demand. This atmosphere permeates each firm, and the workers daily wait to be put off.[59]

Many people spent days going from place to place looking for work, bemused by the sight of wildly contradictory statements on newspaper placards, for example:

> 'BIG INCREASE IN WAR EFFORT CALL UP ACCELERATED'

at the same time as:

> 'ONE AND A QUARTER MILLION UNEMPLOYED INCREASE IN WOMEN'S UNEMPLOYMENT'[60]

Women and national service

Old prejudices died hard and many women over the age of 30 were turned away from munitions work because of their age. The launch of the Land Army was regarded by many as a fiasco when thousands enrolled, some giving up jobs to do so, only to find themselves still at home months later. This was not just a question of bottlenecks; no preparations seemed to have been made for the employment of females. Factories said they were short of labour, but the employment exchanges could not find vacancies for unemployed women. Failures such as these reinforced the groundswell of opinion in favour of the establishment of a true employment service, separate from the administration of social security. In 1942 Ministry staff were heartened by press reports that the Beveridge Committee was considering a proposal that a Ministry of Social Security would take over benefit work, while a separate Ministry of Industry would be responsible for employment, training, industrial relations and factory inspections.[61]

As benefit work continued to expand, alongside that of placement and registration, the basic dichotomy in the role of the department became ever more apparent. An inherent conflict in function existed. This can be illustrated by the situation regarding women's registration. In the spring of 1942 a report on women's treatment at the exchanges was commissioned from an external source.[62] Complaints from women in London had been common throughout 1941, as no distinction appears to have been made between those who were unemployed and those who were volunteering for work. The report argued that 'striking changes' were necessary to show that the Ministry meant what it said about the new place of the exchange, and of employment policy, in national life. Front line staffing needed to be strengthened and premises improved. Above all, training must be given to staff in 'selling' national service. This early 'corporate' approach was backed up by a suggestion that a colour should be identified with National Service, as red was with the Post Office, orange with United Dairies and green with Lloyds Bank. It was to be 'a shade approved by advertising experience to arouse most public attention' anticipating, perhaps, the development of job centres some 30 years later. Local department stores might be able to provide training in customer care for staff in the new colourful exchanges.

The report's recommendations confirmed that even the best exchanges had failed to win the confidence of women, while the worst 'still reek of unemployment and social defeat'. Women only ventured into exchanges when every other means of getting a job had been explored. The report suggested 'that the time is more than due to complete the change from unemployment to National Service of the most proud and vigorous kind'. This, however, would be difficult to achieve. At the outbreak of War it was hoped that the exchanges' identification with industrial depression and unemployment would disappear; when they refused women War work they 'suffered a cruel setback'.

A further complication in the transition to a concept of 'national service' arose from the potential conflict between the new attitude that 'the customer is always right' and the Ministry's powers of compulsion to direct women into specified areas of employment. This conflict was noted by the regional controllers, who were asked for comments on the report during May and June 1942. The need for a major relocation of the service was recognized, as the existing back street premises had originated at a time when it would have been 'deplorable to have the unemployed on parade in public'.[63] Yet the concept of selling national service was flawed; the Ministry could not 'complete the sale' unless direction was used, as they had no powers over employers. Therefore, 'the question is not so much one of confidence in the exchanges as of education in citizenship'. It was really a matter of:

> whether or not too much is expected of the [local office] organization
> in the direction of teaching people to be public spirited. The whole effect
> of manpower and womanpower policy is necessarily and inevitably to
> bring [local offices] in conflict with employers, workers and those who
> do not wish to work.[64]

It was not possible simply to break the association of exchanges with unemployment, indeed, there were still over 150,000 unemployed people, and seasonal increases were expected. Nor was it desirable, as the exchanges 'will no doubt have to deal with them again in the post-War period'. Therefore, the 'doctrine of direction' needed 'more elaboration', so that 'humanisation' and 'enlarged citizenship' would be accepted as justification for the government to do whatever was necessary to win the War.[65] This meant directing workers to where they were required, not selling them a service. The exchanges would need to make a 'living contact' with the working population in the context of Bevin's concern to make the idea of 'citizen' synonymous with 'labour'.[66]

Ernest Bevin

Ernest Bevin was Minister of Labour and National Service from 1940 until 1945 when he became Foreign Secretary. Born in 1881 into a poor family and orphaned at the age of seven, Bevin had worked as a van boy and driver in Bristol before becoming a Baptist lay preacher and a paid official of the dockers' union. In 1920, he acquired the title of the 'dockers' KC' for the skilful presentation of his union's claims at a wages tribunal. His position and reputation were consolidated as general secretary of the mighty National Transport and General Workers' Union, which he built up from some 32 separate unions.

Bevin's central concern, expressed at various conferences of regional controllers, was to avoid the problems of instability of the previous post-War period. The gap between management and workers must be bridged so that the Ministry could 'promote a new kind of industrial democracy at the end of the War'.[67] One method of achieving these goals was to decentralize the Ministry's functions: 'He likened the regions to dioceses; the exchange manager should be like a parish priest looking after the industrial welfare of the people and the Regional Controller like a bishop'.[68] Given Bevin's own career pattern, the backgrounds of some of the new regional industrial commissioners, appointed in 1941, were indicative of the way in which the new interventionist, decentralized 'clergy' were expected to work.[69] Some of these men were on good terms with the unions, nevertheless the emphasis was on people of high calibre in conventional Civil Service terms, and not on those who had direct experience of trade unionism. In 1940 Bevin, himself, had suggested that employment exchanges might benefit from the appointment of trade union clerks, but the regional controllers were of the unanimous and firm opinion that no improvement could be gained by their recruitment.[70] The regional industrial relations officers were also appointed from the ranks of first class officers. It was argued that they should be people who, by way of status and experience, were able to maintain contact with both unions and employers and be regarded as neutral. But, in a neat piece of Ministry logic, it was held that as bad management was at the bottom of most disputes, they would have to be people who knew how management worked, and therefore should be from that background.[71]

Bevin set out to transform the Ministry from an unpopular and lowly provider of unemployment relief into a modern 'Ministry of Employment'. Indeed, this was his preferred title, echoing the recommendation of the Haldane Committee. At the end of 1943, Bevin argued that after the War the Ministry would be 'in the forefront as one of the great economic departments of the state'.[72] The situation during the War prompted many comparisons with the social and economic changes which had arisen after the First World War. Mass observation and government reports showed that, until 1943–1944, many people thought that the War would end in unrest, unemployment and, on the European continent, even in revolution. Government schemes were needed to counter the anticipated instability of the post-War period. These included a strategy to combat any repetition of the press and business campaign which had ended with the 'Geddes axe' after the First World War. There should be no sharp return to the status quo ante. Economic controls should be retained and social reform instituted in order to create a smooth transition to peace. A policy of full employment suggested, at least to Bevin, that the Ministry's role had changed fundamentally. In a memo to the War Cabinet's Committee on the Machinery of Government, he argued that between the Wars the ministry had been given responsibility for unemployment, but few powers to increase the volume of employment.[73] The War had turned the Ministry of Labour and National Service into the predominant voice in the supply, distribution and use of labour, and had brought it into daily contact with employers and workers through the exchanges and regional offices. After the War, this organization should be adapted for the purpose of co-ordinating employment policy, the location of industry and long-term development. Information about future economic trends should be harnessed to equip workers with the skills required for new or expanding industries.[74] This approach would require a shift in focus – from the alleviation of unemployment to the initiation of measures designed to prevent it. Bevin's argument demonstrated the enduring nature of debates about the economic and social functions of the Employment department.

It also raised fundamental questions about the relationships between the Education and Employment departments.

Relations between the departments: the Youth Service and training policy

The Youth Service was established under the Board of Education in 1939, as youth issues, especially delinquency and juvenile employment, were given added urgency by the War. Voluntary youth organizations had existed for many years, but pressure arose to bring such organizations under state control, as had already occurred in many other European countries. In October 1939 the Board assumed responsibility for youth welfare from the National Fitness Council. A National Youth Committee was set up to oversee the welfare of those who had left full-time education and, in December 1941, the government decided to require all 16–19 year olds to register with local authorities and provide details of any youth organizations to which they belonged. The registration programme was carried out by the Ministry of Labour and National Service, which then passed the cards to the LEAs. In 1942, the National Youth Committee was replaced by the Youth Advisory Council, as the Board of Education sought to ensure that the expansion of youth services would continue after the War. In 1945, the Council was subsumed within the Central Advisory Council established by the Act of 1944. Thus, the Board of Education's sphere of responsibility was extended into areas which other departments, particularly the Ministry of Labour and National Service, saw as their domain. Once again, the nature of the relationship between the state and its youth became a matter of dispute across lines of departmental demarcation which had become blurred by a relaxation of Treasury control.

The imperatives of War not only overrode Treasury conservatism, but also ensured that the concerns of the Malcolm Committee about national industrial policy in relation to youth employment acquired 'additional force'.[75] Criticism, indeed, arose over the Ministry of Labour's perceived inactivity in the youth field. At the outbreak of War, its youth advisory work had been suspended as part of the economy drive, and the Board of

Education and LEAs had taken advantage of this suspension to expand their influence. In 1940, a prominent member of the Malcolm Committee, Sir Max Bonn, wrote to Sir Frank Tribe, a key Ministry of Labour and National Service official, to the effect that he was 'afraid of our giving back to the Board of Education much of the ground we had won after many struggles in the 1925–1930 period'.[76] The Ministry was expanding, but in its employment exchange and registration work, rather than in areas formerly disputed with the Board of Education. The Board had been in confusion as the peacetime conventions of compulsory schooling were disrupted, but it was attempting to find new avenues of advance in the youth field. The Ministry was growing; the Board was shrinking. The notion of a transformation of the Board of Education into an all-encompassing 'Ministry of Childhood and Youth', responsible for all areas of policy relating to children between the ages of two and 18, including youth training and employment, had been mooted in the Commons. In the event, this policy was not pursued as the difficulty of reaching an agreement with the Ministry of Health and the Home Office was thought to be too great.

Nevertheless, the deliberations of the various joint committees and informal groups of Board and Ministry officials (which met throughout the War to co-ordinate technical education and training policy) indicate that there was no sharp separation of educational and industrial spheres in the minds of the civil servants, rather an uncertainty over how they could best complement each other. During the War, the Board was drawn into employment issues through membership of interdepartmental committees with the Ministry of Labour and National Service. From 1940 onwards, policy on the use of technical colleges as training centres for the needs of the armed services, and their direct use as workshops producing radios and other technological items, was developed at the meetings of these committees.[77] Co-operation between the two departments grew, for example over the supply of equipment and the design of courses. Regular contact between HMIs and the Ministry's Regional Officers took place over the use of technical colleges. The policy areas of education and training were becoming blurred. On the one hand, officials were attempting to bring them into an efficient relationship and, on the other, to keep lines of departmental demarcation clear enough not to prejudice post-War developments, for example by maintaining a separation between the roles of technical colleges and the GTCs.[78]

One notable feature of the joint committees was the willingness of Board officials to challenge industrial interests over the use of education to improve national efficiency. For example, they proposed a modernization of the engineering industry's apprenticeship system involving a practical and theoretical technical college course for secondary schoolboys prior to entry to industry. The scheme was intended to produce in six months the same standard as that of two years of part-time study by ordinary apprentices.[79] When the Engineering Employers Federation (EEF) 'very definitely' opposed this, the officials considered working with other employers' associations. In the end, they reluctantly concluded that 'while the EEF would have to face the issue in connection with post-War training, the scheme would have to be abandoned for the present'.[80] Wider issues were raised by such proposals, for the Ministry of Labour's industrial relations department would have to be involved, while future relationships between the two departments would be dependent on overall reconstruction policies for the post-War era. Given these constraints, the relationship between education and industrial policy was gradually defined in terms of those elements which made for continuity between school and work. For example, the Board had been asked by the Institute of Industrial Psychology to make a grant to assist in training LEA staff in psychological testing for the 'selection of schoolchildren for secondary education and for choice of employment purposes'. The interdepartmental committee on training agreed that the two issues would have to be considered jointly as they were 'bound up' together.[81] The War was breaking down barriers between educational and economic decision-making and, in this sphere at least, the two departments were working together to create a new set of relationships.

Bevin, Butler and the Youth Employment Service

The War brought about increased intervention in the youth labour market. Such intervention required co-ordination between government departments and the development of an agreed set of policy objectives. As President of the Board of Education, Butler has been criticized for being more concerned about the religious controversies relating to the 1944 Act than with developing an education system that would contribute to national economic efficiency. Nevertheless, in late 1941 Butler met Bevin to discuss education reform, and the two men clearly shared key concerns over the relevance of youth employment and training policy to industrial efficiency. Bevin had obtained a copy of the 'Green Book', the draft plans for reform drawn up at the Board, and wanted to put forward his own views before the Board's proposals were too far advanced. The education system, he argued, was over-academic and should be made more practical, in opposition to wishes of 'doctrinaire administrators', by which he meant the LEAs.[82] Bevin thought that 'schoolmasters were a spoiled lot. They were the blue-eyed boys and girls of the family who had all the sacrifices made for them.'[83] Bevin, indeed, was so suspicious of LEA personnel that he blocked a proposal to make his own Parliamentary Secretary, George Tomlinson, Chairman of the National Advisory Council on Juvenile Employment because Tomlinson had been chairman of a local education committee. Bevin wanted more technical education at school, military service at the age of 20, residential state secondary schools using Ministry of Labour camps, and a reduction in the influence of parents and teachers in educational matters. He claimed that his proposals, including an immediate raising of the school-leaving age to 16, would improve 'the productive capacity of the nation'.[84]

Although he was dubious about some of the proposals, Butler's account of the meeting with Bevin makes it clear that he agreed with Bevin's opinion of the Fisher Act as being too academic and supported the principle of education for national efficiency. Sir Robert Wood argued that the day continuation schools, which Bevin disliked, should be seen as a means of solving the problem of creating a proper system of industrial training.[85] The Permanent Secretary, Maurice Holmes, maintained that technical education was essential, in association with industrial training, for the maintenance of the country's economic advance.[86] The widely publicized rise in juvenile delinquency and the employment of youths in unfamiliar, allegedly highly paid, occupations had provoked a rapid reorganization of youth services and employment regulations. In describing his concept of the role of the day continuation schools, Butler informed Bevin:

> I conceive of the system as providing for … just that body of adolescents whose work in and by itself cannot be wholly satisfying. Equally too, the system would facilitate, as you suggest, the provision of the technical education which, if we are to maintain our industrial skill and technical advance, must be associated with industrial training.

Ministers and officials of the two departments believed that a 'concordat' was needed to define the areas of industrial and educational supervision of school leavers.[87]

From 1943, the Ministry of Labour and National Service expanded its youth work in an attempt to regain lost ground. Officials from both departments, however, became increasingly preoccupied with the role of the LEAs. Burgess and Gosden have both described how in 1942 a small group of officials, including Tribe from the Ministry of Labour and Wallis and Wood from the Board of Education, began to meet to discuss post-War policy on technical education.[88] The group considered the general question of education in relation to industry but quickly saw that:

> There is a question of the direction and control of Technical Education: in particular whether this provision, so essential to the industrial life of the country, can be left simply to the initiative of local authorities whose interest and capacity may vary materially from area to area.[89]

In 1943 discussions on the future of the juvenile employment service took place, discussions which preceded the setting up of the Ince Committee in 1945 and which largely determined its conclusions. Bevin felt that the existing locally controlled situation was not conducive to national planning and efficiency in the context of full employment, and 'this raises big issues – particularly in the matter of how far the necessary national direction in the interests of employment policy can be effectively reconciled with the independence of local government'.[90] Nevertheless, the Ministry of Labour and National Service conceded that it would be impossible for the Ministry to attempt to control youth employment and 'oust' the LEAs in the interests of national efficiency.[91]

Officials at the Board told the Ministry of Labour and National Service that the inclusion of a clause in the Employment Bill (later to become the Employment and Training Act 1948) requiring LEAs to supply the Ministry with information necessary for vocational guidance purposes and the national planning of youth employment would be impossible. The two departments would have to work together to put pressure on 'slack or obstructive' LEAs.[92] Sir Godfrey Ince (Permanent Secretary at the Ministry of Labour and National Service, 1944–1956) then drew up a scheme which contained the outlines of a new youth employment service. This scheme saw the Education Act as helping the cause of national control of youth employment by abolishing the Part III authorities. It was essential that the LEAs 'should be required to conduct their administration in accordance with general rules and directions issued by this Ministry though this will be resisted by the authorities'.[93] A central executive body would be required. The scheme would later emerge, relatively unscathed, as the Ince Committee's recommendations. This Committee, made up of Ministry of Labour and National Service, Ministry of Education and LEA representatives, began meeting in 1945 in order to 'consider the measures necessary to establish a comprehensive Juvenile Employment Service'.[94]

The Ince Committee, itself, can be seen as a method of drawing the LEAs into the process of change planned by the Education and Employment departments. It began work where the Malcolm Committee had ended, and discussed the reorganization of the youth employment service with specific reference to the national economic interest and to national industrial efficiency.[95] At the first meeting of the Committee, the Ministry of Labour and National Service insisted that it accept the principle that more than a local knowledge of industry would be necessary in the economic conditions to come.[96] Sir Robert Wood was more disposed than Ince to give the central executive body supervisory, rather than advisory, powers over LEAs but, once again, the opposition this would provoke was reluctantly seen as insurmountable. In the meetings of the Committee both the Education and Employment departments attempted to manoeuvre and browbeat the LEAs into relinquishing local control. Differences existed between the two, but both were attempting to delineate areas of responsibility involving the educational and industrial supervision of youth, in order to bring them into relationship with each other. As one civil servant said, it was a hard task, but only impossible if, like the LEAs, you did not want to do it.[97]

Conclusion

During this period, both departments clearly showed that they could step outside of their former circumscribed roles. The Ministry of Labour demonstrated that it was not averse to operating an extensive training system – even if training within industry remained primarily a matter for the two sides of industry itself. The Board of Education proved itself to be sensitive to industrial imperatives – even if its officials continued to maintain a passive approval of divisions of social class and between the academic and technical within post-compulsory education and training. In contrast to today's common conception of a gulf between the senior officials of the two departments, only small differences in background and in strength of adherence to the general Whitehall political culture existed. Where the Board of Education boasted E.K. Chambers, the Ministry of Labour had Humbert Wolfe, both literary gentlemen. Where the Board was staffed by Oxford men, the Ministry added a leaven of London University graduates.[98] In the final analysis, both embraced the strictures of orthodox economic theory and the traditional view of the relations between education and industry. Vocational training would have no place in the expansion of secondary education. Turf wars over youth policy took place at various levels as the state shifted into a higher gear in social and economic policy. Nevertheless, a shared youth agenda developed in the negotiations and agreements conducted between Bevin and Butler, and in the extensive inter-departmental co-operation that took place over industrial- and college-based vocational training.

Paradoxically, by the end of this period the development of such relations had framed and tested their distinctive departmental cultures. These had emerged from their very different administrative experiences and methods of organization at the lower levels. The Ministry of Labour's army of clerks staffing the registration and unemployment programmes in the employ-ment exchanges entailed a very different style of administration and internal ethos from that of the Board of Education. The former was con-cerned with processes of change: enhancing the workings of the economy through the smooth training and supply of labour and the maintenance of voluntarism in industrial relations. The latter was concerned with processes of preservation: managing its relations with the LEAs so that a balance of interests was preserved and its ideal version of secondary education protected.[99] Chapter Five examines how, after the War, some of the dis-tinctiveness and increased status acquired by both departments gradually disappeared. During the long post-War boom, the Ministry of Labour and National Service would fail to secure a permanent role as an economic department of state, while the Ministry of Education would become increasingly isolated from the other business of government.

Notes

1. Weiler, 1993, 75.
2. De la Mothe, 1992, 40.
3. For Tawney see Wright, 1987.
4. Wiener, 1981, 194.
5. See, for example, Joseph and Sumption, 1979.
6. Tawney, 1931.
7. Quoted in Wright, 1987, 45.
8. Wright, 1979, 51.
9. Williams, 1961, 223.
10. Reeder, 1979, 127.
11. Savage, 1996, 75.
12. Savage, 1996, 42.
13. For a discussion of this theme see Harris, 1992.
14. Burgess, 1995, 42.
15. Board of Education, 1930. See Burgess, 1995, 42.

16. Burgess, 1995, 46. The first Advisory Council for Further Education was established in Yorkshire in 1928. This followed a report from Her Majesty's Inspectorate (HMI) and discussions with Percy, the President of the Board. No more advisory councils were set up until after the Second World War.

17. Burgess, 1995, 48.

18. Gosden, 1976, 7.

19. Lowe, 1986, 11, footnote.

20. Bullock, 1967, 119.

21. Savage, 1996, 157.

22. Quoted in Deakin, 1996, 49.

23. Sheldrake and Vickerstaff, 1987, 17.

24. Sheldrake and Vickerstaff, 1987, 17.

25. *Civil Service Argus*, July 1929, v, 7, issue 180. The *Argus* was the newsletter of the Ministry of Labour Staff Association which represented the clerical officers and some of the middle-ranking civil servants in the department. In 1973 the Staff Association merged with the TUC-affiliated union, the Civil and Public Services Association (CPSA). See also Lowe, 1986, 34.

26. *Civil Service Argus*, August 1929, v, 8, issue 181.

27. Savage, 1996, 137.

28. Quoted in Wright, 1987, 45.

29. Replies to Mass observation survey; MO File Report 1269, 'Opinion about Post-War Education', May 1942.

30. *Hansard,* H of C, 19 January 1944, 396, 215. Butler was introducing the second reading of the Education Bill.

31. Quoted in Addison, 1975, 172.

32. Hinton, 1994, 178.

33. *The Times*, 3 July 1940.

34. Gibbon, 1940, 12. See also Hinton, 1994, 41.

35. Lowe, 1986, 133.

36. Hennessy, 1989, 84.

37. Address to the Union of Lancashire and Cheshire Institutes (1945), quoted in Perkins, 1957, 4. Clarke was Director of the Institute of Education, University of London, 1936–1945.

38. Gordon, Aldrich and Dean, 1991, 35–36.

39. See, for example, Smith, 1986, 101.

40. Gosden, 1989, 188.

41. Gosden, 1989, 189.

42. Gosden, 1976, 23.

43. Gosden, 1989, 188.

44. Gosden, 1989, 188.
45. Gosden, 1989, 191.
46. PRO LAB 12/119; Staffing Basis Scheme. Circular 12/328(S), 24 November 1939.
47. Hennessy, 1989, 94.
48. *Hansard,* H of C, 16 April 1940, 359, 837.
49. Parker, 1957, 215.
50. Parker, 1957, 153.
51. Lowe, 1986, 145, 189.
52. Letters, *Civil Service Argus*, February 1939, xv, 2, issue 295.
53. Letters, *Civil Service Argus*, February 1939, xv, 2, issue 295.
54. Mass Observation File Report 433, 1940.
55. PRO LAB 12/294; Reports of Regional Controllers Conferences, September 1939–December 1941. Report of Conference, 10 October 1941.
56. PRO LAB 12/125; Employment Exchange service, organization of local offices. Cutting from the *Manchester Guardian*, 8 May 1944.
57. *Civil Service Argus*, December 1942, xviii, 12, issue 341.
58. *The Times*, 9 January 1940.
59. G.D.H. Cole papers, Nuffield College Library: Manpower survey, F2/56/3/8.
60. For the many problems faced by women in wartime see Burton, 1941.
61. *Civil Service Argus*, December 1942, xvii, 12, issue 341. Beveridge entered the Board of Trade in 1908 and was director of labour exchanges, 1909–1916.
62. PRO LAB 12/109; Procedures for dealing with women at Employment Exchanges. Report by Majorie Haywood, 7 April 1942.
63. PRO LAB 12/109; Procedures for dealing with women at Employment Exchanges. Letter, North Midlands RC to HQ, 11 May 1942.
64. PRO LAB 12/109; Procedures for dealing with women at Employment Exchanges. Letter, North Midlands RC to HQ, 11 May 1942.
65. PRO LAB 12/109; Procedures for dealing with women at Employment Exchanges. Letter, Edinburgh RC to HQ, 18 May 1942.
66. Weiler, 1993, 28.
67. PRO LAB 12/294; Reports of Regional Controllers Conferences, September 1939–December 1941. Report of conference, 10 October 1941.
68. PRO LAB 12/294; Reports of Regional Controllers Conferences, September 1939–December 1941. Report of conference, 10 October 1941.
69. PRO LAB 12/190; Regional Industrial Relations Officers; general questions, 1941.
70. PRO LAB 12/294; Reports of Regional Controllers Conferences, September 1939–December 1941. Report of conference, 14 August 1940.

71. PRO LAB 12/230; Regional Industrial Relations Officers; general questions, 1943.
72. *Civil Service Argus*, December 1943, xix, 12, issue 353.
73. PRO CAB 87/74; War cabinet: Machinery of Government. MG (43) 7, 22/6/43, 'Post war responsibility for employment policy. Memo by the Minister of Labour and National Service'.
74. Weiler, 1993, 138–139.
75. PRO ED 136/292; Education after the war: discussions and correspondence with the Ministry of Labour. Letter, Sir Max Bonn to Secretary, Ministry of Labour, 15 October 1941.
76. PRO LAB 19/45; Policy on Juveniles. Minute, Tribe to Blunden, 17 June 1941, reporting a previous communication.
77. PRO ED 136/669; Technical Education – Miscellaneous. Letter, M.G. Holmes to Principals of Technical Colleges, 30 December 1940.
78. PRO LAB 18/176; Joint committee with education departments on training. Minutes of meeting, 29 November 1943.
79. PRO LAB 18/173; Joint committee with education departments on training. Minutes of meeting, 26 June 1942.
80. PRO LAB 18/173; Joint committee with education departments on training. Minutes of meeting, 27 July 1942.
81. PRO LAB 18/174; Joint committee with education departments on training. Minutes of meeting, 3 May 1943.
82. PRO ED 136/292; Education after the war: discussions and correspondence with the Ministry of Labour. Minute to President, 9 September 1941.
83. From the diary of Chuter Ede, 19 November 1943; Jefferys, 1987, 153.
84. PRO ED 136/292; Education after the war: discussions and correspondence with the Ministry of Labour. 'Summary of Proposals for post-war development in education and juvenile employment. (n.d.)
85. PRO ED 136/292; Education after the war: discussions and correspondence with the Ministry of Labour. Note, Wood to President, 4 September 1941.
86. PRO ED 136/292; Education after the war: discussions and correspondence with the Ministry of Labour. 'Draft letter to Mr Bevin' (n.d., probably October 1941).
87. PRO ED 136/292; Education after the war: discussions and correspondence with the Ministry of Labour. 'Draft letter to Mr Bevin' (n.d., probably October 1941).
88. Burgess, 1993, 383; Gosden, 1976, 307.
89. PRO ED 136/669; Technical Education – Miscellaneous. Note, Wood to Butler, 24 February 1942.
90. PRO LAB 19/112; Letter, Bevin to Thomas Johnston, MP, 25 August 1944.
91. PRO LAB 19/112; Minute, DGMP to Bevin, 2 May 1944.

92. PRO LAB 19/112; Letter, Wallis to Taylor, 7 December 1943.
93. PRO LAB 19/112; Minute, DGMP to Bevin, 4 May 1944.
94. Heginbotham, 1951, 122.
95. *Report of the Committee on the Juvenile Employment Service* (1945) London: HMSO.
96. PRO LAB 19/142; Committee on the Juvenile Employment Service: papers, minutes and agendas. Minutes of meeting, 30 January 1945.
97. PRO LAB 19/142; Committee on the Juvenile Employment Service: papers, minutes and agendas. Minutes of meeting, 30 January 1945.
98. Savage, 1996, 62.
99. Savage, 1996, 62.

5 Science, Democracy and Modernization, 1944–1973

Introduction

Chapter Four examined the distinctive cultures and functions of the Board of Education and the Ministry of Labour which developed during the 1930s and 1940s. Both departments secured a significant role in national life, thereby gaining in confidence and status. The Ministry of Labour and National Service became the key department on the 'home front'. It rattled the framework of traditional economic and employment policy by introducing manpower budgeting and a planned approach to the skill requirements of industry. The Butler Act 1944 brought education towards the top of the political agenda by introducing free secondary education for all. Hopes were raised of a new relationship between education and employment, based on a democratic and efficient approach to harnessing the potential of young people. Yet, with hindsight, the post-War settlement has been seen as one that sealed the fate of millions of children within a system which relegated them to second-class, dead-end schooling and jobs. By the 1970s, the education system was being condemned in that 'it failed too many young people too much of the time'.[1] This chapter examines the nature of the post-War settlement and the extent to which hopes for radical change within education and employment policy were realized.

The post-War period was characterized by incessant discussion about modernization. During the late 1950s and early 1960s, the proposition that the British establishment was indifferent to the needs of industry and to the education and training of its workers became received wisdom.

Thomas Balogh's *The Apotheosis of the Dilettante*, as developed in a
Fabian pamphlet entitled *The Administrators*, condemned all civil servants,
and Treasury officials in particular. The non-specialized Civil Service
was seen as a legacy of Victorian Britain's *laissez-faire* political ethos
which required no commercial or practical expertise on the part of civil
servants as the state would not be involved in industrial issues.[2] As
Tomlinson argues, 'declinism', the notion that a serious economic decline
had started during the nineteenth century and had continued unchecked
ever since, became rooted in British political, academic and journalistic
circles.[3] Following in the footsteps of the Edwardian Fabians, the 1960s
'national efficiency' reformers focused on reform of the machinery of
government and of the education system as the best means of arresting
the country's relative decline. On this occasion, however, a strand of
right-wing vocationalism, represented by Correlli Barnett amongst others,
would also take up the cudgels, and 'culture' would become the key
explanation for perceived national inadequacy. Human capital theory would
provide these reformers with a crucial new argument and unite social
democratic and conservative vocationalists. Tension grew as the Education
and Employment departments were required to respond simultaneously
both to the national mood for democratic reform and to the perceived
needs of industry. The early 1970s and the onset of economic crisis would
place the Department of Education and Science (DES) and the Department
of Employment (DE) at the centre of major critiques of the prevailing
political culture.

'Learners not earners': the post-War settlement

In the period prior to the Second World War, a relatively fluid relationship between education and employment policy had emerged. This had
been reflected in a changing division of labour between the two departments. The War stimulated much agitation and reformist sentiment
around industrial and welfare issues, culminating in the 1942 Beveridge
Report, and in the Employment White Paper and Education Act, both of
1944. These measures served to crystallize the roles and responsibilities

of the Education and Employment departments. The demise of the Board of Education and its replacement by a modern ministry was heralded as the coming of age of an Education department that would now assume its rightful place amongst the other departments of state. Internal organization was simplified to produce one schools branch and one further education branch.

It has recently been argued that the Butler Act was in effect the Board's Act, a continuity of pre-War policy, albeit within a very different economic and political context. The effect of the measure has also been challenged. For example, Ian Lawrence has argued that full employment and the Beveridge plan had a 'more significant' impact on educational provision than the Act itself.[4] The political significance and symbolic message of the creation of the Ministry of Education, however, was considerable; it occupied a central place in the new Welfare State legislation. The status of the Education department was increased significantly, both in relation to other government departments, and to the Local Education Authorities (LEAs). Nevertheless, the system was still largely decentralized and no one player had overall control.[5] A process of 'elite accommodation' provided an appearance of calm and consensus.

> Many policy decisions in education were taken over lunch at the National Liberal Club by a troika consisting of Sir William Alexander, Secretary of the Association of Education Committees, Sir Ronald Gould, the General Secretary of the NUT and the Permanent Secretary at the Department of Education. If these three agreed on some item of educational policy, it would, more often than not, be implemented.[6]

The first post-War Education Minister, Ellen Wilkinson, had a well-established reputation within the labour movement and was the first state-educated head of the Education department. Implementation of the Act of 1944, however, was not always easy, and Wilkinson had to fight against those who argued that raising the school-leaving age was against the national interest. At a time of labour shortages, industry would be deprived of a whole cohort of trainees. The tide of public and political opinion, however, was on Wilkinson's side, and in 1947, the year of her death, the leaving age was raised to 15. Her successor, George Tomlinson, was also well qualified in labour terms, having begun work as a half-timer in a mill at the age of 12, served as Parliamentary Secretary to Bevin at the Ministry of Labour and National Service during the War, and as Minister of Works (1945–1947). Tomlinson, however, did not have a high political profile and neither he nor the Ministry of Education was particularly newsworthy during the remaining years of the Labour government.[7] As an ex-chairman of the Association of Education Committees, Tomlinson was popular with the LEAs, but made little public impact.

In 1945, Sir John Maud (later Lord Redcliffe-Maud) succeeded Sir Maurice Holmes who had been Permanent Secretary since 1937. Maud, who had been a fellow of University College, Oxford and Master of Birkbeck College, London, before wartime service in the Ministries of Food and Reconstruction and in the office of the Lord President of the Council, was 'undoubtedly the most influential educational figure of the immediate post-War period'.[8] His status and expertise counter-balanced the relative political weakness of the two ministers. In common with other senior civil servants, Maud, who had been educated at Eton and New College, supported a programme of educational expansion, with the provision of greater opportunities for all children of high ability, but he was also keen to preserve the hierarchical structure of the school system. Expansion dominated the agenda, fuelled by fears of a post-War baby boom. Wilkinson, Tomlinson and Maud all saw the provision of more school places as essential. In consequence, in spite of arguments that technical education, science and industrial training should be the key elements in post-War development, priority was given to the school-building programme. Government policy was gradually steered away from the more radical proposals made by Labour Party members towards those of which the Ministry approved. Financial difficulties provided a further reason for restraint, in educational policy as in other fields, and spending cuts were imposed from 1948.[9] The Ministry of Education consolidated and strengthened its position within Whitehall but, at least in the early part of this period, developed in a state of relative isolation from the priorities and problems of industry and economic performance.

In contrast, the outcome of the post-War settlement for the Employment department disappointed those who advocated a new role for the Ministry of Labour, one more in keeping with the hopes of its founders. At first, those hopes were kept alive by the Attlee government's commitment to economic planning and to the need to boost exports. Although principally remembered for its creation of the Welfare State, the Labour government of 1945–1951 was greatly concerned with industrial modernization, a concern stimulated by the levels of inefficiency revealed during the War.[10] During the War the locally managed and fragmentary nature of social and economic structures had been challenged by a 'producers' alliance' of civil servants, industrialists and trade unionists intent, albeit often for different reasons, on trying to construct national educational, industrial and welfare systems.[11] As in the Edwardian period, state intervention was seen by the Labour Party as the one method by which modernization could take place and the United Kingdom could maintain its place in the world. In pursuit of these aims, Sir Stafford Cripps, Chancellor of the Exchequer 1947–1950, whose name was associated with the post-War austerity programme, attempted to turn the Board of Trade into a Ministry of Industry. Several new bodies were also created, including the Production Efficiency Board.

The more radical aspects of such thinking, however, were never seriously considered. Despite Bevin's attempts to create a more active economic role for the Ministry of Labour, in June 1945 responsibility for economic policy relating to the distribution of industry and the Development Areas, transferred from the Treasury to the Ministry in the 1930s, was lost to the Board of Trade. The Employment and Training Act 1948 repealed the Labour Exchanges Act 1909, and defined the Ministry's functions on the basis of the 1944 Employment White Paper. This had envisaged the Ministry of Labour as supplying unemployment information and statistics in order to plan investment and labour policies. However, the 1948 Act did not include the placement of labour nor, as Beveridge had recommended, remedies against the 'misdirection of juveniles'. The role of the Ministry was restricted to the provision of training courses and assisting workers in finding suitable employment.[12]

Dislocation immediately after the War caused by the demobilization of large numbers of troops led to a considerable expansion of Government Training Centres (GTCs). From 1945 to 1946 the number of GTCs increased from 17 to 65, with 23,700 places available.[13] Interrupted Apprenticeship and Further Education and Training Schemes were established to help those whose education or training had been disrupted by military service. By 1947, however, demobilization and the redeployment of military and munitions personnel were largely completed. The anticipated high levels of unemployment did not occur. In consequence, interventionist employment policies were scaled down. Wartime controls over job advertising, engagements, and vacancies were progressively relaxed and the Control of Engagements Order 1945, which governed the process of demobilization, was revoked in 1950. Between 1946 and 1948, GTC places were reduced by 75 per cent and continued to fall until 1962. In the post-War period, the Ministry's influence in the labour market rapidly declined.

Contemporary and subsequent perceptions of a lack of efficiency within central government, particularly in respect of policy towards industry, did not change. Tomlinson, for example, has argued that the Labour government's attempts to raise productivity lacked co-ordination and focus.[14] Certainly, the defects in administration, which had been discussed widely during the War, were not directly addressed. In 1942, Harold Laski had argued that 'we are on the threshold of an age of profound institutional reconstruction'.[15] His demands for the recruitment of specialists, a Civil Service staff college and planning sections within government departments, however, would still be on the agenda when the Fulton Committee considered reform of the Civil Service in the mid-1960s. In wartime, the operation of strict definitions and boundaries in respect of departmental responsibilities had been seen as inimical to efficiency and innovation. Nevertheless the old ways continued, and indeed some boundaries became more entrenched under the Attlee government.

The divergence of the Education and Employment departments was signalled by the recommendations of the Percy Committee on Higher Technological Education. Its report of 1945 led to the formation of the

National Advisory Council on Education for Industry and Commerce (NACEIC) in 1948. The NACEIC contained representatives of the Regional Councils, Regional Academic Boards, the universities and colleges of further education, employers and trade unions, and the Ministry of Labour. Its role was to advise the Minister of Education on the policy necessary to develop education in relation to industry.[16] But in the course of the Percy Committee's deliberations a clear definition of young people as 'learners not earners', part of the radical democratic reformist wartime mood, gained undisputed ascendancy, and the Education and Employment departments were firmly separated. This new definition of their respective spheres of influence was based on a particular notion of skill requirements. Investment in technology at higher education level was seen as necessary, but the training of the lower skilled mass of the workforce could still be left to industry itself, supported by the voluntaristic policy of the Ministry of Labour. Thus, the relatively fluid relations between the Ministry of Labour and the Board of Education which characterized the inter-War years solidified into a new institutional settlement which saw little contact between the departments. Substantial changes in the organization of the Education and Employment departments and of their areas of responsibility did not occur. Instead, the 1940s bequeathed a legacy of unresolved debates over industrial and social issues and about the relationships between democracy, modernization and science. In the 1950s and 1960s these ideas came to be seen as key cultural elements in the fight to arrest the country's slide into relative decline.

'Declinism'

During the 1950s, the notion of economic growth as a key policy aim grew in importance. In the context of the Cold War, a considerable threat was seen in the Soviet Union's rapidly developing economy and technological prowess.[17] Sputnik and the atom bomb were the most visible features of this competition, but additional evidence also suggested that the economies of other western European countries were performing better than that of the United Kingdom. In 1962, the annual report of the

United Nations Economic Commission for Europe was highly critical of British economic performance, and gave rise to newspaper articles with such headlines as 'Britain bottom of the class'. The United Kingdom was the only western country whose gross national product was practically unchanged from the previous year, and also the one country where the employment situation had deteriorated seriously.[18] The notion that Britain was suffering from serious economic decline, 'declinism' as Tomlinson terms it, became a common element in political and academic discourse by the end of the 1950s.[19]

Declinism was popularized beyond the academic and political circles by books such as Landes' *The Unbound Prometheus*, and in the journalism of the day. As Arthur Koestler, then editor of the journal *Encounter*, put it: 'When the war was won, Britain's political and moral prestige in Europe was at an unprecedented height; in less than 20 years her leaders managed to bring it down to an equally unprecedented low.'[20] He blamed the 'leaders' for their fondness for the classics at the expense of economic efficiency: 'Don't let's listen to the [politician] who tells us to be Greeks to the Romans, to let the Germans sweat and bustle while we recite poetry to each other at the fountain on the *Agora*.' This bias was a 'functional' rather than a 'structural' disorder. Structural diseases had objective, material causes, but functional diseases had subjective, psychological ones. Koestler was arguing against Marxian theories of the determination of the 'superstructure' by the 'base', of culture by economics. 'Psychological factors and cultural attitudes are at the root of the economic evils.' The problem was the class system and the cult of the amateur; the country needed a meritocracy.

This interest in declinism as a cultural explanation both of the present and the past, was also a reaction against the *laissez-faire* traditions which re-emerged during the long period of Conservative government, 1951–1964.[21] Indeed, for a relatively brief period in the mid-1950s, modernization was even contemplated in terms of a reduction in the role of the state. Proposals were made by the Cabinet Secretary, the Treasury and the Conservative Research Department to introduce education vouchers and student loans, and to transfer responsibility for welfare provision to executive agencies.[22] These proposals never reached fruition, but the Education and Employment departments were both affected by the new political situation. As Minister of Education from 1951 to 1954 Florence Horsbrugh was not included in the Cabinet until 1953, a sign of a new low in the status of the Education department. She was also criticized by LEAs who saw her as losing the battle for resources. In November 1954 she was replaced by Sir David Eccles. According to one account: 'Eccles was the high priest of the remnants of the nineteenth-century romanticism, bringing to the Ministry the imagined values and style of the rural community he represented.'[23] Nevertheless, in spite of his dandified image and nickname of 'Smarty Boots', Eccles acquired a considerable reputation as a vigorous and imaginative minister. Civil servants were impressed by his ability to win more resources for the department, and technical training was expanded. His second term of office, which began in 1959 after two years as President of the Board of Trade, was less impressive. His successors were short-lived and came under strong pressure to bring educational expenditure under tighter control. During the 1950s, the Ministry gained responsibility for agricultural education and for a number of educational bodies previously controlled by the Charity Commissioners, but it also lost responsibility for the training of disabled adults and the financial control of education in prisons and borstals.

The balance of power between central and local government began to change. In 1958, the position of the Ministry with regard to the LEAs was weakened as a consequence of the abolition of the education grant as a percentage of total LEA expenditure, and its replacement by the general grant (later the 'rate support grant'). Control of capital spending also passed to the localities.[24] Under the previous grant system the Ministry of Education had been able to encourage national policies, by sanctioning certain developments rather than others.[25] The transfer of grant-making functions to the Housing, Local Government and Environment departments would further weaken Education. Between the Wars, the Treasury had put pressure on the Education department to end the system of a separate Education grant, while the Geddes Committee had tried to transfer control to the local authorities. The Board of Education had resisted these attempts, but, after the War, the Ministry agreed to the Treasury's plan for a block grant system, in return for approval of major capital investment in school buildings.[26] Such developments might reflect an increased investment in education, but they did not increase the status and power of the Education department directly.

The Ministry of Labour suffered more directly under Conservative governments. The Notification of Vacancies Order 1952 was designed to help employers in key sectors to obtain workers in the context of a shortage of labour. Four years later it was rescinded, on the grounds that however useful it might be, such a level of intervention could not be justified.[27] During the 1950s the administration of regional policy was further fragmented over several government departments, while the number of adult placings by the exchanges fell from 2,600,000 per year in the mid-1950s to some 1,500,000 in the mid-1960s.[28] Between 1951 and 1964, 100 smaller exchanges were closed and there were three successive cuts in staffing. By the latter date, staff numbers had fallen to a mere 20,000, less than half of the wartime figure.[29]

Staff complained that 'we are living through difficult times in the Ministry of Labour' and commented darkly on 'those who have begun to re-assess the position of the Department in the national economy'.[30] The General Secretary of the Ministry of Labour Staff Association noted the 'dismal mood' and the 'current of anger that anybody should be so short-sighted as to deal so harshly with a Department which had given and was giving such a valuable and much needed service to the working community'. Staff felt that 'the Department or at any rate those at the top somewhere care nothing about the employment service except to ensure that there are offices able to cope with unemployment should it arise because that could be a serious political matter'. Some Ministry of Labour officials concluded that they were heading for a closure of the Ministry of Labour and National Service or a merger with some other department.[31] During this period, the 'hyper-emollient' Minister of Labour, Sir Walter Monckton, and his sucessor Iain Macleod, were concerned to demonstrate that the Conservatives were not the party of the pre-War dole queue.[32] In May 1957, however, Alfred Robens, Shadow Minister of Labour, claimed that the Conservatives' changes to the employment service amounted to the 'de-Bevinising' of the Department, returning it to a benefit-paying service.[33] Showler has argued that it is 'paradoxical' that during the 1950s a shortage of skilled workers was accompanied by a reduction in state-provided training facilities, and 'their concentration on limited social objectives rather than also meeting a serious manpower problem'.[34] In 1959, a further symbolic change occurred. Following the statutory ending of conscription, the Ministry dropped the words 'National Service' from its title.

Criticism of what appeared to be Conservative complacency in the face of mounting evidence of decline appeared in leaders in *The Times*, and in Anthony Sampson's *An Anatomy of Britain*, first published in 1962. The problem was attributed to an outdated class system, represented by such politicians as Harold Macmillan and an administrative establishment of hidebound civil servants. The education system was designed for the classical liberal elite, not for the technological and economic needs of a society locked in fierce competition with other rapidly developing nations. Conversely, some on the right of the political spectrum argued that there was too much emphasis on social justice and fair play, and that the trade unions were the main factor in obstructing increased levels of productivity. In 1963, in a letter to the *Spectator*, Correlli Barnett gave a typically forthright statement of this conservative version of the declinist view. He argued that nineteenth-century humanism, liberalism and parliamentarianism were:

> luxuries possible only to a world empire with a huge navy, a vast bank account, and few rivals. What faces Britain today is the more basic matter of survival, and survival in terms of developments in technology (with all their colossal sociological consequences) that our political traditions simply do not compass. What Britain must think about again is power. With power you can be a crook or a policeman. Without it, you simply do not count. I believe that modern technology necessarily so changes the conditions of life that any conceptions of liberty and individual choice worked out in the past no longer apply. Liberty will exist less in

a political sense as in a private sense; the ability to do what you like with a private life made rich by modern production. Government is becoming – and should become deliberately more so, faster – a combination of GHQ and head office of a cartel; the Prime Minister a presidential dictator subject to quinquennial plebiscites. The country needs a grand strategy. This must depend on the realities of technology and of power. The party caricatures of free enterprise and nationalisation will not do. The prejudices of the electorate will not do either. We are faced with technical problems; not limitless free choice according to taste. I share ... fears of British 'small-f' fascism. Yet if we follow the Weimar Republic in failure to be effective over economic and technological questions; if the 'nice' people fail, the nasty ones could be let in.[35]

In the later 1950s and 1960s Barnett was one of the 'tough young realists' who operated outside of the prevailing post-War consensus, warning of the dangers of the growing welfare agenda and of the decline of Britain as a great power.[36]

In contrast, many of those holding traditionally liberal views argued that the protection of the weak and the preservation of the peculiar 'quality of English society' were worth the price of a degree of inefficiency.[37] Elsewhere on the left, critics such as Austen Albu, former Deputy Director of the British Institute of Management, Labour backbencher and campaigner for technical education, were talking in more technocratic terms of a 'taboo on expertise'. In the early 1960s, Albu made a clear, left-wing declinist statement – the causes of national decline and the failings of British industrial management were to be found in 'social and historical roots going back at least into the middle of the last century'.[38] These causes dovetailed with those suggested by Barnett, Koestler, Sampson and *The Times*: the amateur tradition of the Civil Service; the neglect of technical education; the desire of the sons and daughters of businessmen to become landowners or professionals and to adopt an aristocratic outlook; the unwillingness to provide high-quality education for the majority; the function of education as a system of social recognition; the separation of professional and general education; the confinement of the working class to vocational education at evening classes; the weakness of industrial training.

The bulge in the school-leaving population focused further attention upon such criticisms. The Crowther Report, *15 to 18,* published in 1959, reflected some of the prevalent unease when it emphasized the need for improved education in the 15–18 age range in order to develop the new skills required by new technologies. As a starting point, the Committee unanimously recommended that between 1966 and 1968 the school-leaving age should be raised to 16 and that by 1980 half of all young people should remain in full-time education until the age of 18. These proposals were not adopted by Sir David Eccles, and the Ministry's civil servants, defending themselves from the prevailing criticism, were scathing about the Committee in their private briefing papers for him. The brief from the further education branch declared that the Central Advisory Council (which had set up the Committee) had not faced the fact that education was 'a minor partner of industry'. The further education branch was clear that, in the British system, apprenticeship and industrial training were primarily a matter for industry, whereas members of the Council 'were attracted by continental systems of full-time apprenticeship training under educational control'.[39] The Council had not produced any 'substantial set of suggestions for strengthening the links between industry and the college'. In respect of the 'bulge', the Council had diagnosed a problem, but had not worked out a practicable solution:

> The fact is that the problem of the bulge cannot be solved by educational means … . The only real solution lies in increasing the number of apprenticeships, learnerships, etc, offered by industry … . Departmentally this is a matter for the Ministry of Labour. This is the most important immediate issue in the whole of further education.[40]

The Council's recommendations on further education were in the right direction, but 'above all they demand a more rapid advance in industrial support for certain aspects of technical education than is yet in sight'. The sandwich courses and other education-based remedies advocated by the Council would remain marginal. They ignored the basic structure of industrial training – the strict division between state and industry.

In the area of industrial training, the government commissioned the

Carr Report, published in 1958, which examined the state of training for young workers and included a comparative analysis of the British system with those of other countries.[41] No major departures from the traditional voluntaristic methods of organizing industrial training were proposed. The 'climate of opinion' in favour of supporting industrial training by a development of the general education system was endorsed. In a context of popular concern over the morals of youth, especially 'Teddy Boys', it emphasized the social aspects of education and training in building character. As Morgan has commented, 'industrial training had a direct character-building influence that was linked to traditional views of male work roles, the existing division of labour and the combating of idleness amongst young people', a function which industry was to provide.[42]

From the early 1960s the traditional division of labour between government departments in the area of industrial training and technical education became a focus of declinist criticism. In June 1960, Albu called for responsibility for training to be transferred from the Ministry of Labour to the Ministry of Education.

> At present we are falling down because that responsibility is split. It is not that I have anything against the Ministry of Labour, but because I do not think that a department that is concerned with employment conditions, as the Ministry of Labour is, is the right department to deal with training which has become more and more an educational process.[43]

In April 1963 the *Economist* joined in the criticism of the Ministry of Labour as being immersed in 'clientelism' in relation to the unions and the employers. It stated that: 'At the Ministry of Education there is a much tougher tradition ... that government should lay down standards below which teaching must not fall. There is also a willingness to realize that government should pay.' The magazine called for responsibility for industrial training to be transferred to Education from Labour and described the latter department as one of the 'superfluous organs of government'.[44] In response, the government argued that industrial training at the apprenticeship level was a matter of industrial relations, not education, and that Britain had a system that was second to none. A series of White Papers attempted to build on the existing division of responsibility, but these documents came under renewed criticism for not specifying the link between technical education and industry, except by assuming a simple beneficial parallel development of day-release schemes and technical education courses. The government pressed on and in March 1962 the Employment Service was cut back as part of the Conservative government's reductions in public spending. The separate Technical and Scientific Register was closed and the Nursing Appointments Service merged with the General Exchange Service. This negative approach by the Conservatives increased public fears about skill shortages in engineering and construction, and in April 1963 a major expansion of GTC places was announced from the 4,500 then available to 11–12,000 per year.[45]

Outside of the Education and Employment departments, however, the period between 1957 and 1964 was one of great political and administrative change: 'From Macmillan's appointment as PM in 1957 the implicit, and after 1962 the explicit, objective of government policy was modernization'.[46] After the Suez crisis and the abrupt resignation of Sir Anthony Eden as Prime Minister in January 1957, a major re-evaluation of the United Kingdom's role in the world occurred. Macmillan's modernization strategy was accompanied by radical reorganization of the Treasury in 1962, the sacking of one-third of the Cabinet (including Eccles) in the 'night of the long knives' in July 1962, and a simultaneous change in personnel in the top three jobs within the Civil Service in January 1963. At the same time, the Prime Minister, himself, presided over a progress-chasing 'Steering Committee on the Modernization of Great Britain'. Whitehall Ministries underwent a prolonged period of change. In 1953, the Ministry of Pensions had been merged with the Ministry of National Insurance; in 1955, the Ministry of Food was merged with the Ministry of Agriculture and Fisheries; and, in 1964, the formerly separate service Ministries were merged with the Ministry of Defence. From 1964, Labour governments under Harold Wilson would, initially at least, increase the momentum behind modernization. A more active approach was displayed towards economic and employment issues, and a willingness shown to reform Whitehall.

The 'Two Cultures' debate and the Fulton Committee

From the publication of Balogh's *The Apotheosis of the Dilettante* in 1959 to the appointment of the Fulton Committee in 1966, there was an intensification of the debate about the need to reform technical education, industrial training and the Civil Service.[47] Within these debates, Fabian modernizers held the 'middle ground'; the 'Civil Service was accused of being "amateur" when the need was for professionalism'.[48] Thomas Balogh, the leading Fabian modernizer, was Economic Adviser to the Cabinet in 1964–1967 and Consultant to the Prime Minister, Harold Wilson, in 1968.[49] As Fry argues in his study of the Fulton Committee's investigation into the structure of the Civil Service, 'like their counterparts in the first decade or so of the twentieth century', from the later 1950s the 'national efficiency reformers' of the period held that reform of the machinery of government and an improved educational system could arrest or reverse relative national decline. Solutions to the problem of decline were often based on an association of science with democracy, as against classical learning and privilege. As Wilson said: 'In a recent interview, I was asked what, above all, I associated with socialism in this modern age. I answered if there was one word I would use to identify modern socialism it was "science".'[50] In this, he was supported by C.P. Snow, the physicist, novelist and polemicist who, at Harold Wilson's invitation, became the 'second-in-command' at the Ministry of Technology, taking a life peerage. The focus of the national efficiency modernizers on subjective factors within the education system and Civil Service, and on the cultural aspects of Britain's decline, would provide a rallying point for critics from all parts of the political spectrum.

Snow's Rede lecture, 'The Two Cultures and the Scientific Revolution', delivered at Cambridge University in May 1959, initiated a long-running controversy. This not only involved the famous confrontations between Snow and F.R. Leavis during the course of the 1960s, but also spread into a wider world. The two cultures were those of the literary intellectuals on the one hand and the natural scientists on the other. Between them existed a great gulf, damaging both to the nation and to the world at large.[51] Thus, as Stefan Collini argued: 'One can trace a specifically British genealogy for the "two cultures" anxiety, arising out of a distinctive development of the social institutions within which education and research were carried on.'[52] These institutions, which developed from the nineteenth century, were construed within a hierarchy in which the classical education offered at Oxford and Cambridge took pride of place, while the applied sciences were relegated to the status of 'inferior activities in both the educational and industrial worlds'.[53]

> The traditional culture, which is, of course, mainly literary, is behaving like a state whose power is rapidly declining – standing on its precarious dignity, spending far too much energy on Alexandrian intricacies, occasionally letting fly in fits of aggressive pique quite beyond its means, too much on the defensive to show any generous imagination to the forces which must inevitably reshape it.[54]

Snow's arguments and hostility towards 'literary intellectuals' were clearly compatible with Wilson's campaign to promote Labour as the party of the scientific revolution, in contrast to the supposedly effete, aristocratic Conservatism of Macmillan.

The 'two cultures' debate belongs to a period of British political and cultural history characterized by Harold Wilson's famous speech about the 'white heat of the technological revolution' which 'was presented as a charter for "modernising" Britain'.[55] Science, democracy and modernity were closely linked in the writings of Snow, Wilson and others of the time. The basic theme of modernization encompassed both the wider culture in society at large and the more specific culture of government and administration. Snow, himself, was the personification of the scientist/administrator/modernizer. He envisaged an 'end of ideology' era in which politics would become less a matter of competing ideologies and more of pragmatic government. Snow believed that the two cultures thesis showed the need for an agenda of modernization that would overturn the traditional hierarchies of education and be translated into policy by 'a small group of politicians and their advisers'.[56]

The increased concern for science was reflected in a reformulation of the Education department. In April 1964, following the recommendations of the Trend Committee on Civil Science and the Robbins Committee on Higher Education, the Ministry of Education and the office of the Minister for Science were merged to form the Department of Education and Science. The DES took over responsibilities for civil science and higher education previously belonging to the Lord President. The various Privy Council committees for civil science were later abolished and a number of research councils were established under the Science and Technology Act 1965, which also abolished the Department of Scientific and Industrial Research. Two junior ministers headed the independent sections for science and education.

The Fulton Committee on the Reform of the Civil Service, which was seen by Balogh, Snow and other modernizers as a battle waged against those whom Wilson called the 'classics boys' in the Civil Service, took up the second theme of specialist and political ministerial advisers.[57] Sir Edward (later Lord) Boyle, the former Minister, and Norman (later Lord) Crowther-Hunt, Minister of State at the DES (1974–1976) were members of the Committee, as was Sir James Dunnett, the Permanent Secretary at the Ministry of Labour. Since 1964, some Labour ministers had been bringing politically sympathetic 'irregulars' into government.[58] The Labour Party's evidence to the Committee, based on the work of the Fabians, attempted to formalize this. Short-term political appointments to 'posts of confidence' located at strategic points in the departments were proposed, 'with the aim of ensuring the implementation of particular policies'.[59] Several contributors, including Anthony Crosland, the Secretary of State for Education, argued for a French-style ministerial *cabinet* which could improve the flow of information to Ministers and counterbalance the restrictions imposed by the pyramidical hierarchies of civil servants.[60] However, as Fry noted, Crosland also argued that:

> whatever the general merits of that kind of system, in his department a ministerial *cabinet* would have to be manned by educationists and the nature of educationists was such that they would create antagonisms and disarray in the department. He now got the advice he needed from various sources. His PPS was a former school teacher. He was in close

touch with the Chairman of the back bench education group, also a former teacher. Both had served in LEAs. He invited groups of helpful people to his house in an informal way. His Permanent Secretary quite welcomed all that.[61]

The Permanent Secretary, Sir Herbert Andrew, was less convinced by Crosland's approach, and was wary of Fulton proposals for more extra-Civil Service advice. In his evidence to the Committee, given in March 1966, Andrew said he was against the idea of research or planning units within departments. Six months later, Crosland told the Committee that he was going to establish a 'long-term planning branch' at the DES.[62] In 1967, the Planning Branch was set up, which involved economists and statisticians from outside the department, as well as civil servants. In 1970, Sir William Pile became Permanent Secretary and the Planning Branch was replaced by a Department Planning Organization (DPO) which utilized the Programme Analysis and Research (PAR) strategy. Some accounts, however, argue that the insular instincts of the DES prevailed and that Pile, who chaired the Policy Steering Group which played an important role in guiding the policy-making process, blocked the effective functioning of the DPO.[63] In addition to advocating more advice and policy input from outside Whitehall, the Fulton Committee also recommended a move towards regionalism and the devolution of functions. It proposed that education, together with other aspects of social and industrial planning and communications, should form part of the remit of Regional Economic Planning Councils, to be established by the newly created Department for Economic Affairs. Such proposals, with their implication of a reduction in central control, were not welcomed at the DES.

In 1964, the Education department not only absorbed the office of the Minister of Science, but also assumed responsibility for the University Grants Committee, which previously had come under Treasury control. The two cultures debate had clear implications for the expansion of higher education.[64] Snow welcomed the Robbins Report of 1963, and strongly supported the establishment of new universities. In government, he was closely involved in the establishment of the Colleges of Advanced Technology. The remit of the DES was extended to sport and the arts, with government sponsorship for the latter transferred from the Treasury in 1965, along with responsibility for the Arts Council and the national museums and galleries. Such expansion in terms of activities and expenditure led to increased concerns about accountability. Not surprisingly, the Treasury insisted that the DES define its objectives and priorities more clearly.[65]

On the employment side, the 1960s saw a shift of emphasis towards active employment functions. In the mid 1960s, the Organization for Economic Co-operation and Development (OECD) sponsored a series of conferences on the theme of the role of the state in relation to labour market policies, and on the expansion of 'human resources' as envisaged by the new theory of human capital. It was increasingly argued that expenditure should not be wasted on the provision of Industrial Training Boards; instead subsidies should be paid to individual workers for their training, and industry should look after its own specific needs. The National Plan, published in the United Kingdom in 1965, gave an impetus to the proposed changes and, in the following year, a review of the Employment Service was carried out by the Ministry of Labour, which concluded that the Employment Service should take on an active economic role. In addition, following criticism of the numbers and quality of apprenticeships, the GTCs extended their role to providing one-year, off-the-job apprenticeship training. In 1962 4,149 people were trained under government vocational training schemes. By 1971 this had increased to 18,402.[66] New developments included the provision of an Adult Occupational Guidance Service and a further attempt to re-locate exchanges out of the backstreets. A new area management structure was introduced, together with an expansion of staffing in local offices. Government training facilities and youth employment services were increased in 1968. Perceived imbalances between the distribution of skills and jobs prompted a strengthening of links between the employment services, industrial training and regional policy. In his analysis of these changes, Brian Showler points out that the Ministry might:

have shown a little more regard for the history of the service by acknowledging that what they were stating as a changed role was precisely the initial role laid down for the service in 1909 by Churchill ... . The nature of the 1966 statement is a measure of the failure of the Employment Service to fulfil its original employment function.[67]

Nevertheless, as Freedland has argued, during the early 1970s, the government began to find it necessary to redesign the Employment department and to 'recast its ethos', a process which centrally involved the setting up of the Manpower Services Commission (MSC).[68] This process had begun in 1968 when the short-lived Department of Employment and Productivity was created and the emphasis on the department's work shifted from the 'human touch' in industrial relations to economic theory: 'the arrival in St James's Square of the incomes policy experts ... was likened by an old hand at the Ministry of Labour to "theologians entering a corrupt monastery, bearing texts"'.[69]

Industrial training, youth employment and the relations between the departments

In 1958 the Carr Report, *Training for Skill*, drew a clear distinction between education and training, arguing that government should not become involved in the latter. The White Paper on Industrial Training in 1962, however, acknowledged that such training could not simply be left to industry, and led to the Industrial Training Act 1964. This gave the Minister of Labour powers to establish Industrial Training Boards (ITBs) for certain industries, and to impose a levy on employers to pay for them. The Industrial Training Act (ITA) generated fresh debate and new interdepartmental links over the relationship between training and economic prosperity. In 1963, the Newsom Report, *Half our Future*, had weighed in from the educational side, stating that: 'The need is not only for more skilled workers to fill existing jobs, but also for a generally better educated and intelligently adaptable labour force to meet new demands'.[70]

The Conservative government now accepted the argument that the nation was suffering from a shortage of skilled workers; economic growth would be impossible without improvements in industrial training. This shift in policy coincided with negotiations between the Education and Employment departments, the LEAs and various educational bodies, particularly over the composition and functions of the proposed ITBs. The Ministry of Education was concerned that the Boards were to be given the power to provide courses of further education. This raised issues of demarcation and, in order to preserve its control over further education, the Ministry of Education argued, albeit reluctantly, that 'a distinction between courses of training and courses of education must be accepted'. The Ministry of Education wanted this distinction put before the Parliamentary Counsel in drawing up the Bill. This apparent concern with departmental interests, however, was based on the Education department's relations with the LEAs rather than any intellectual or cultural differences with the Ministry of Labour. The latter accepted the Ministry of Education's view:

> that the problem is largely a political one. They want to see further education specifically mentioned in the Bill without at the same time laying the government open to the charge that it is proposing to devolve onto the Boards responsibilities which properly belong to local education authorities. This is a perfectly reasonable objective ... .[71]

The two ministries joined forces to prevent the LEAs claiming that the ITBs should fund the expansion of further education. The Education department did not want the Boards to dictate the pattern of further education, while the Employment department did not want the Boards levying powers to pay for LEA buildings, equipment, etc. They agreed that the Boards would only be responsible for fees for FE courses provided as part of training schemes. The departments were further united in opposing attempts by LEAs to secure an amendment to the Bill requiring the Minister of Labour to consult with the Minister of Education over the Boards' recommendations. This offended against the principle that government is 'one and indivisible'. Nevertheless, it was included in the Bill in respect of the appointment of members of the Boards, as a 'valuable gesture to educational feeling'.[72] The two groups of civil servants exchanged letters on the best way to approach the LEAs and other 'purists', for example by wording a letter on consultation with educational bodies to omit reference to technical education 'in case they [the words] were seized on by the purists to urge that considerations wider than those of technical education must be kept in view!'.[73] The Ministry of Labour's civil servants explained their view of the LEA representatives: 'If the educational members are to have the right to vote on the size of the levy then we shall not have achieved the purpose we intended to achieve, and will not have met the desires of the British Employers Confederation.'[74] There is no evidence that the Ministry of Education would have disagreed.

The Industrial Training Act was broadly welcomed by the political parties and its passage through Parliament was relatively smooth. The government clearly felt the need to create an impression of interdepartmental co-operation and the Minister of Education, Sir Edward Boyle, summed up the second reading of the Bill in the Commons. However, the lack of clarity over the role and financing of technical education within the Act meant that the issue of partnership between the Education and Employment departments again became a source of difficulty.[75] The Act soon came under fire. On the one hand, it was seen as a modernizing instrument and has been described as 'the end of voluntarism'.[76] However, it was also criticized on several grounds, notably for prescribing an essentially employer-led system based on individual industries, rather than on the training needs of the economy as a whole. The ITA represented the further development of government efforts to standardize training, not the end of voluntarism as a guiding principle. The previous departmental demarcation was left untouched; the institutional structure of industrial training was still separate from education. By the mid-1960s, export performance was worsening and further planning attempts were either aborted or became merely symbolic as domestic reform was sacrificed to the Treasury's prioritization of international economic liberalism.[77]

Tension between the two departments continued in the field of youth employment. The Employment and Training Act 1948 had embodied most of the Ince Report's recommendations concerning the youth employment service. It established the Central Youth Employment Executive, comprising officials from the Ministries of Labour and of Education, which made policy and controlled standards. A National Youth Employment Council representing employers, employees and LEAs was also formed. In 1964, in response to criticism over the service's effectiveness, the Permanent Secretary at the DES, Sir Herbert Andrew, suggested to his opposite number at the Ministry of Labour, Sir James Dunnett, that an interdepartmental committee be set up to deal with areas in which the responsibilities of the two ministries overlapped: careers guidance and the school curriculum. Youth employment services were 'patchy' and 'each of our Departments functions independently to a significant degree in our separate spheres'.[78] Civil servants at the Ministry of Labour saw this as part of a wider project which, on the one hand, involved a greater vocationalization of the secondary school curriculum and, on the other, the ambition of the DES finally to take over the youth employment service. They warned that:

> There are already signs that some Education Authorities who at present rely on our services may wish to take them over and, indeed, that a fresh attempt may be made by the Education Department to take the whole service over. [We need to] consider the present situation, possible developments and the state of our defences, assuming that we remain of the opinion that we should maintain the position in the field that we at present occupy.[79]

The Ministry of Labour considered that the expansion in education that had taken place since the War had not been matched by a similar development of its own remit. A gap in the provision of youth employment and careers services existed for those whose full-time education ended in between secondary modern school and university – in particular students at FE colleges. The growth of FE had clouded the distinction between the traditional types of education, and comprehensivization was further blurring them within the secondary sector. The Ministry of Labour should develop its careers service to match the situation. Its civil servants preferred a national system, with control both at the centre and in the localities. However, as during the Second World War, it was decided that the 'uproar' that would be caused by depriving LEAs of their local functions would be insupportable. A narrower focus on further education students would be the best approach.[80]

The Ministry also recognized the need to improve the professional quality of its youth employment officers (YEOs) in line with the higher standard of LEA staff. The number of YEOs was increased from 600 in 1956 to more than 1,550 in 1965. Advisory interviews took place for 90 per cent of those leaving school at the earliest age, placing 40 per cent in jobs.[81] However, a widespread view persisted that the Youth Employment Service (YES) was ineffective in developing children's knowledge of employment opportunities. This was attributed to a role confusion. Parents and children expected assistance in finding jobs but the YEOs concentrated on the educational guidance role.[82] Poor training and recruitment of officers was blamed by the Albermarle Report of 1960, but it also seemed to be the case that most YEOs saw themselves as providing professional careers guidance, not as enhancing contacts between the school population and the world of work. Concerns grew in the 1970s, as opportunities for youth employment declined. The 1970 OECD Report, *Manpower Policy in the United Kingdom,* recommended the integration of the YES into a vocational scheme for all ages. Education and vocational training, it argued, should be seen as a continuous process, a position given additional force by the expansion of educational provision post 18. This issue was considered by a working party of the National Youth Employment Council, established in 1969 to review the structure of the service. The majority of its members favoured making provision mandatory on the LEAs, but the minority argued for an Employment-department based service, as part of an overall national employment structure. The Conservative government accepted the majority recommendation. Under the Employment and Training Act 1973, responsibility for youth employment was transferred to the LEAs and was renamed the Careers Service. Officials at the Ministry of Labour were left to ponder on the course of events. As one member of staff put it: 'We allowed most of the youth employment work to be taken away from the Ministry of Labour and it has been regretted ever since.'[83] Following local government reorganization in April 1974, dual administration of the service was finally ended.

The early 1970s and the onset of crisis

Although by the end of the 1960s the DES had made few direct gains in status, increasing expenditure on education was propelling it towards the role of a major government department. The department had general responsibility for the University Grants Committee and civil science for the United Kingdom as a whole, as well as for education in England and Wales. Although in November 1970 the Welsh Office took control of primary and secondary education in the principality, in the following year responsibility for junior training centres and the education of mentally handicapped children was transferred to the DES from the Department of Health and Social Security. In 1938–1939 education accounted for nearly 8 per cent of tax and rate-borne public expenditure. By 1974–1975 it had risen to 12 per cent.[84] Nevertheless, as Sir William Pile acknowledged, 'a fair criticism of the post-War years, or at any rate of those who claim to have shaped them, is perhaps that they pre-occupied themselves too much with the shell of the system and not enough with the inner mystery of the process itself'.[85] By the early 1970s, these 'inner mysteries' were being explored, once again in the context of a debate about 'adjusting education to industry'.

Margaret Thatcher was Secretary of State at the DES between 1970 and 1974, a longer period of office than any of her predecessors in the previous decade. Thatcher is widely seen as having provided a challenge to the broad-brush approach to expenditure of her civil servants and their refusal to countenance new proposals. Pile's description of the response of DES officials is quoted in Hugo Young's book, *One of Us*: 'We followed our old traditional course of speaking up for what the department has always done or what we thought the department should do, as opposed to what ministers were going to tell us to do.'[86] Thatcher insisted that expenditure be better targeted and she brought a clear view of the purpose of the educational system: 'The earning capacity of the nation depends on the highest level of achievement in the professions, in science and technology, industry and commerce. This is the wealth of the nation, coming from those who have the most talent.'[87] This view, however, did not mean an emphasis on cost-cutting. Thatcher presided over the White Paper, *Education: A Framework for Expansion*, issued in 1972, which set out optimistic plans for increased expansion of nursery education, school building, teacher training and higher education.[88] However, the White Paper, although warmly welcomed in some quarters, also received criticism from the OECD for ignoring the new labour market situation and the needs of the 16–19 age group. Too much emphasis, it was argued, had been placed upon higher education and not enough on central direction of the actions of LEAs. The MSC, established by the Employment and Training Act 1973, was based upon the premise 'that if Britain wished to regain its status as an industrial power of the first rank, society at large had to rethink its attitude to wealth and its creation'.[89] This purpose, however, was rarely understood, especially as the MSC was soon forced to focus on measures to alleviate youth unemployment.[90] By 1973, and the onset of world recession, deflation had already set the tone for policy-making and little had been achieved by way of reconstructing national education and economic systems. As the MSC's sphere of operations expanded under a Labour government from 1974, it was clear that the configuration of employment and educational interests, decided at the end of the Second World War, had begun to break down.

Conclusion

This chapter has shown how, after the War, the nation's political process was dominated by a consensus based upon full employment and the Welfare State. For many years, demand for youth labour was relatively stable and the Education and Employment departments could agree on a strict definition of the division between education and training. Maintenance of this status quo was reinforced by the solid complex of interests operating within the apprenticeship system. In contrast to the years of economic crisis and War, the policies of the two departments were developed largely in isolation from each other as, in the post-War boom, young people were clearly categorized as 'learners not earners'. Nevertheless, tensions between the two, and between central and local government were contained within the post-War consensus.[91] From the late 1950s, fears about the relative decline of the United Kingdom stimulated widespread criticisms, including criticism of the complacency of Whitehall. Indeed, the culture of Whitehall became a serious political issue. In the 1970s and 1980s, these cultural concerns would come to focus directly upon the Education and Employment departments.

Many elements in the policies of the modernizers of the 1980s and 1990s can be identified as arising in this period, more broadly within the 'two cultures' debate and in particular in the recommendations of the Fulton Committee. The Committee proposed the establishment of planning units within ministries and of semi-autonomous boards, the latter development particularly supported by Sir William Armstrong, the joint Permanent Secretary to the Treasury.[92] These suggestions were resisted by the respective Permanent Secretaries at Education and Employment, Sir Herbert Andrew who gave evidence to the Committee and Sir James Dunnett who was a member. During the 1960s, such proposals were construed within a Fabian, left-wing, modernizing framework, aimed at reducing the inhibiting affect of cautious men like Dunnett. They were later to be identified with the privatization drive of the Conservative right. The use of specialist agencies and political advisers was a feature of the governments of the 1980s and 1990s, and continued under the Labour government of 1997, not least at the DfEE. A movement towards large departments also made it possible to include all ministerial heads of department within the Cabinet. This meant that many problems of co-ordination and status would now be tackled in a less public way – within, rather than between, departments.[93] For example, in 1968 the Foreign Office and Commonwealth Office were joined and the Ministry of Social Security (which had been the Ministry of Pensions and National Insurance) was merged with the Ministry of Health. In 1970 the new Conservative government of Edward Heath brought together the Ministry of Housing and Local Government, the Ministry of Transport and the Ministry of Public Building and Works to form the Department of the Environment. This type of solution to the tensions surrounding education and employment would appeal to the modernizers of the 1990s.

The modernizing policies of New Labour are based on the premise that the former divisions between left and right, and between unions and employers, have been rendered irrelevant by processes of globalization and economic change. These processes also present, it is claimed, an opportunity to end the long-standing civil war between the 'two cultures'. In the 1960s there was a convergence between the technocratic left and right as vocationalists from varying political backgrounds agreed on the causes of Britain's relative decline. Similarities are apparent between Snow's administrative ideas and Barnett's presidential dictatorship. Both argued for the irrelevance of older, liberal traditions. Snow was criticized for extending his claims about the work of a few Modernist writers to a critique of what he called 'the traditional culture'. Similar criticisms were made of the work of Barnett. In both cases, a particular view or aspect of culture was identified as a national one. Snow and Barnett tried to dispense with politics by identifying the fundamental problems as those whose solution lay in the ending of ideological and cultural alternatives, so that economic and technological change could remove the need for conflict between political aspirations, whether in terms of a left-wing meritocracy or a right-wing utilitarianism. Culture emerged as the key subject of debate and explanation of decline for many people, both on the left and right of the political spectrum. In the period prior to the merger of 1995 it was forged into a political weapon that would be used against both the Education and Employment departments, and with potentially damaging effects. As Collini has argued:

> Laments about archaic, gentlemanly cultural values obstructing 'modern-isation' in Britain are themselves part of a long and still vigorous British tradition, and the danger, as the years since Snow's death chillingly demonstrate, is that they mainly succeed in giving ideological comfort to the most reductive kind of commercial philistinism.[94]

Chapter Six provides further commentary on these issues, and particularly upon the nature and extent of historical continuity between the 'national efficiency' modernizers of the 1960s and those of the 1980s and 1990s.

Notes

1. Barber, 1994, 354.
2. Newton and Porter, 1988.
3. Tomlinson, 1998.
4. Lawrence, 1992, 7.
5. Ranson, 1980.
6. Bogdanor, 1979, 161.
7. Kogan, 1978, 29.
8. Lawrence, 1992, 13. Maud was strongly supported by Herbert Morrison, the only member of the War Cabinet to oppose the upgrading of the Board of Education to a Ministry.
9. Gordon, Aldrich and Dean, 1991, 64.
10. Tomlinson, 1994, 166.
11. Hinton, 1994.
12. Showler, 1976, 25.
13. Showler, 1976, 24.
14. Tomlinson, 1994, 166, 183.
15. Laski, 1942, 6.
16. The NACEIC was wound up in 1977 and its functions were passed to the Business and Technician Education Council.
17. Tomlinson, 1998, 4.
18. *The Guardian*, 9 April 1962.
19. Tomlinson, 1998.
20. Koestler, 1963, 6.
21. Newton and Porter, 1988, 129.
22. Lowe, 1997, 604.
23. Lawrence, 1992, 26.
24. Ranson, 1980, 85.
25. Gosden, 1966, 198.
26. Gosden, 1966, 194.
27. Showler, 1976, 25.
28. Showler, 1976, 26.
29. *Civil Service Argus,* September 1964, xl, 9, issue 600.
30. *Civil Service Argus,* January 1957, xxiii, 1, issue 510.
31. *Civil Service Argus,* January 1957, xxiii, 1, issue 510.
32. Hennessy, 1989, 453.
33. Extract from *Hansard,* reproduced in *Civil Service Argus*, June 1957, xxiii, 6, issue 515.
34. Showler, 1976, 83.

35. Barnett, 1963, 292.
36. Fairlie, 1963, 11.
37. Fairlie, 1963, 12.
38. Albu, 1963, 45.
39. PRO ED 136/729; Central Advisory Council, 15 to 18 (Crowther Report) Briefs. 'FE Branch Brief' (n.d.).
40. PRO ED 136/729; Central Advisory Council, 15 to 18 (Crowther Report) Briefs. 'FE Branch Brief' (n.d.).
41. National Joint Sub-committee Report (Carr Report), 1958.
42. Morgan, 1994, 46.
43. Quoted in Morgan, 1994, 49.
44. Quoted in Morgan, 1994, 75.
45. PRO LAB 18/940; Interdepartmental committee on training for skill. Paper, 'Training in Government Training Centres', November 1964.
46. Lowe, 1997, 601.
47. Fry, 1993, 5.
48. Fry, 1993, 9–10.
49. Fry, 1993, 5.
50. Harold Wilson, speech at Daresbury, Cheshire, 17 June 1967, quoted in Foot, 1968, 331.
51. Snow, 1959.
52. Collini, 1993, xi.
53. Collini, 1993, xiii.
54. Collini, 1993, xxv–xxvi.
55. Collini, 1993, xli.
56. Collini, 1993, lxx.
57. Fry, 1993, 243.
58. Fry, 1993, 109.
59. Labour Party, 1967, 23.
60. Fry, 1993, 108.
61. Fry, 1993, 108.
62. Fry, 1993, 119.
63. Lawrence, 1992, 87.
64. Collini, 1993, xl.
65. Gordon, Aldrich and Dean, 1991, 83.
66. Showler, 1976, 84.
67. Showler, 1976, 27.
68. Freedland, 1992, 277.
69. Jenkins, 1970, 8, quoted in Freedland, 1992, 279.

70. Quoted in Gordon, Aldrich and Dean, 1991, 78.
71. PRO LAB 18/834; Consultation with Ministry of Education and Scottish Education Department about proposals in White Paper published in December 1962. Minute, Clucas to Lokyer, 8 May 1963.
72. PRO LAB 18/834; Consultation with Ministry of Education and Scottish Education Department about proposals in White Paper published in December 1962. Letter, Mitchell, Scottish Education Department (SED), to Clucas, Ministry of Labour, 30 August 1963. Letter, Clucas to Mitchell, 4 September 1963.
73. PRO LAB 18/834; Consultation with Ministry of Education and Scottish Education Department about proposals in White Paper published in December 1962. Letter, Donnelly, SED, to Stewart, Ministry of Labour, 30 December 1963.
74. PRO LAB 18/834; Consultation with Ministry of Education and Scottish Education Department about proposals in White Paper published in December 1962. Minute, Clucas to Stewart, 16 October 1963.
75. Morgan, 1994, 80, 91.
76. Morgan, 1994, 63.
77. Newton and Porter, 1988, 147.
78. PRO LAB 19/779; Suggestion by the DES for an interdepartmental working party to review questions of careers guidance and school curriculum. Letter, Sir Herbert Andrew to Sir James Dunnett, 31 July 1964.
79. PRO LAB 19/779; Suggestion by the DES for an interdepartmental working party to review questions of careers guidance and school curriculum. Minute to Pickford, 1 October 1964.
80. PRO LAB 19/779; Suggestion by the DES for an interdepartmental working party to review questions of careers guidance and school curriculum. Memo, 'The Youth Employment Service after 1970', n.d., probably October 1964.
81. Royal Commission on Trade Unions and Employers' Associations, 1965, 127.
82. Showler, 1976, 65.
83. Letter from M. Green, *Civil Service Argus,* 1964, xl, 3, issue 594.
84. Pile, 1979, 229.
85. Pile, 1979, 233.
86. Young, 1989, 72.
87. Gordon, Aldrich and Dean, 1991, 86.
88. Gordon, Aldrich and Dean, 1991, 92.
89. Ainley and Corney, 1990, 2.
90. Ainley and Corney, 1990, 36.
91. Mason, 1988.
92. Fry, 1993, 102–106.
93. Stacey, 1975, 83–86.
94. Collini, 1993, xlii.

6 From Vocationalism to the Enterprise Culture, 1973–1995

Introduction

From 1973, the development of the Education and Employment departments occurred within a new context. Policies of government spending as a means of stimulating the economy were abandoned. A dramatic rise in oil prices altered the United Kingdom's position within the international trade system and heralded a period of prolonged inflation. This was an era of rapid and fundamental change in post-War social, economic and education policy, which included the 'revolution' of the Thatcher governments which presided over extensive privatization programmes and the decline of manufacturing industry. More specifically, the 1970s and 1980s saw the raising of the school-leaving age to 16, the 1982 Employment and Training Act, the creation (and abolition) of the Manpower Services Commission (MSC), and the 1988 Education Reform Act.

The ascendancy of 'new right' ideology left a lasting impression on Conservative and Labour Party policy alike. This ideology emphasized the creation of conditions for growth, abhorred state intervention in the economy, and undermined old ideas of how education could contribute to economic growth or social justice. At the same time, the traditional methods of decision-making in education moved from consensus to contention.[1] The recession and accompanying growth in unemployment re-focused attention on the disillusionment with the educational system which had developed in the 1960s. The relationship between education and economic performance became a matter for urgent investigation.

At this point in the history of the Education and Employment departments, the issue of departmental cultures arose, for the first time, in the sense in which it is used today. In the preceding period, the Civil Service in general had become the target of critics who focused on the subjective causes of national economic decline. The crisis of the mid-1970s saw a change in emphasis to questions of competitiveness and an enterprise culture. Correlli Barnett's work, together with that of Martin Wiener, was taken up by elements of the Conservative Party and used to underpin the agenda of the 'Thatcher revolution'. As an explanation for Britain's relative decline, 'cultural bias' displaced any rivals which pointed to change within economic policy or interference by the state in industry and trade. The cultural critique centred on the Education and Employment departments which now found themselves singled out within Whitehall. Merger followed, and the neo-liberal economic trend which concentrated on supply-side education and training measures in tackling competitiveness and unemployment gained institutional form.

The Department of Education and Science (DES) and the Department of Employment (DE) under scrutiny

A report of the Organization of Economic Co-operation and Development (OECD), *Education Development Strategy: England and Wales*, published in 1975, prompted a new period of examination of the workings of the DES and of the nature of policy-making in the department.[2] As indicated in Chapter Five, the DES was in advance of most of the rest of Whitehall in modernizing its internal procedures. The Planning Department had been set up in 1967 and the DES was one of the earliest to use the Programme Analysis and Research (PAR) system to review its programmes. Nevertheless, the OECD report argued that planning within the department was deficient and that the DES needed to develop new institutional and administrative methods which would allow it to respond and contribute to changes in society rather than continue with outmoded decision-making processes. The DES's 1972 White Paper, *Education: A Framework for Expansion*, was overtaken by economic events, and criticized for ignoring the new labour market situation and the needs of the 16–19 age group. The OECD alleged that too much emphasis had been placed upon higher education and not enough on central direction of Local Education Authority (LEA) actions. The report focused on the inadequate relations between the DES and other bodies with educational interests, particularly the Department of Employment, arguing that its secretive culture had inhibited policy-making.

Prompted by these criticisms, in 1976 the House of Commons Expenditure Committee, chaired by Janet Fookes, carried out an extensive study of the organization and policy-making process in the DES. In its evidence to the Committee, the DES defended itself against the OECD by claiming that educational planning involved a large degree of uncertainty as it was based on long-term projections of demographic change. The several 'time lags, resistance and frictions' within the system meant that major changes of direction and pace could be achieved only slowly:

> It has to be recognized that educational planning by central government is necessarily concerned more with quantity of input than with quality of output – in part because educational content is the preserve of the local authority and the individual institution, and in part because there is no satisfactory way of measuring the quality of output in its totality.[3]

The officials believed that the long-term nature of policy-making made it essentially an a-political matter. This view reflected the overall conception of education and training prevalent during the post-War period. Expansion of the system was thought to lead directly to greater economic efficiency and, at the same time, greater social equality. In the mid-1970s this assumption of a simple congruence between education and training for employment came under intense scrutiny, as youth unemployment rose sharply and economic crisis created unease in political circles. The DES's civil servants became the main object of this scrutiny.

For decades a process of slow, demographically determined, politically low-profile educational planning had been generally accepted. By the mid-1970s the world had changed, and such a style of policy-making came to be seen as a self-serving bureaucratic project which denied ministers their rightful authority over education policy. At the Fookes

Committee hearings, the impression of a culture of secrecy and complacency in the Education department was quickly established. The OECD
had warned against a 'permanent officialdom' which 'becomes a power
in its own right'. Professor A.H. Halsey was one of several witnesses
attending the Committee who put forward similar views, arguing that
since the days of Morant, 'policy-making has historically been more the
function of the DES civil servants than of their Parliamentary masters'.[4]
Professor John Vaizey argued that 'a departmental view' had dictated
practice not only before the War but also during the 1950s and 1960s.[5]
These authoritative opinions established a link between the culture of the
DES's civil servants and subsequent changes in policy which sought to
redistribute responsibilities and authority within the education system.
For example, Halsey argued that too much power lay with civil servants
and LEAs and not enough with ministers, schools and parents – a recur-
rent theme from this period onwards. He advocated an increase in the
number of parent governors at the expense of LEA education committee
members, and advised that there was a:

> case ... for much more direct allocation of resources to the governing
> bodies of schools ... I would prefer to see a strengthening of central
> responsibility for the collection and provision of information and an
> increase in the autonomy of the schools at the expense of the LEA
> intermediary ... .We must realize that the costs of ... mistakes are not
> borne by the local education authority or by their staffs, they are borne
> by the children in the schools. There comes a point when the Secretary
> of State must say centrally 'I can do better than that and I am going to
> do it.'[6]

Halsey, the OECD and other critics established the view that the accretion
of power by DES civil servants and their culture of self-protection had
rendered the department incapable of contributing to the regeneration of
the British economy. By the end of the Fookes Committee's deliberations, it was widely believed that such a contribution was essential.

Relationships between the Education and Employment departments
formed a central element of this new agenda. The OECD report had argued

that 'The role of the educational system is not reviewed or related to the functions of different departments concerned with educational matters such as, *inter alia*, the Department of Employment.'[7] For Vaizey, this was the 'crunch question'.[8]

> What links ought to exist between the DES and other departments? It is quite clear that historically education has regarded itself as apart, or separate from the rest of Whitehall. This has good historic reasons. But it is lamentably true now that the DES does not play an active part in the formulation of economic policy for example. Thus in the recent discussions of a new national plan, the sections on manpower are unbelievably weak … . All this, to my mind, points to the radical proposal that the DES in its present form should be dissolved.[9]

Vaizey painted a picture of a swollen, complacent Education department. He emphasized that in the post-War period the growth of the DES, both 'numerically and politically', had made it a 'powerful Department of State' which was now a substantial obstacle to the regeneration of the British economy.[10]

The Education department had indeed grown. By 1950, it had more than 3,000 staff and by 1970 more than 4,000. Vaizey, however, was arguing for more than a simple reduction in size or influence. Vaizey's 'radical proposal' was based on a new approach to the relationship between education and employment, one grounded in a supply-side approach to skills and the creation of economic well-being. The Employment department also came in for criticism and was censured by the OECD for not 'fulfilling its role as an agent of economic policy'.[11]

Perceived imbalances in the economy between the distribution of skills and jobs prompted government to make links between the employment services, industrial training and regional policy. The Heath government (1970–1974) was keen to implement the recommendations of the Fulton Committee on the Civil Service. These had placed considerable emphasis on establishing separate units within departments as independently managed agencies. In 1972, the Department of Employment issued a discussion document, *Training for the Future*, and, after consultations with employers and trade unions, agreed to set up a National Training Agency hived off from the DE. The MSC, the Health and Safety Commission and the Advisory, Conciliation and Arbitration Service (ACAS) were constituted under the Employment and Training Act 1973, the Health and Safety at Work Act 1974 and the Employment Protection Act 1975, respectively. King has argued that the decision to set up the MSC was motivated by short-term considerations of placating the unions as part of an attempt to reach agreement over pay in 1972–1973.[12] Certainly, a corporatist rationale lay behind the MSC, and its membership contained equal representation of employers and unions. Nevertheless, the MSC laid the foundations for future training policies and can be seen as a catalyst for policy and administrative developments. It got the job done 'above the niceties of public accountability and control'.[13] Some discussion took place over whether it should be located in the DES, but Margaret Thatcher, as Education Secretary, lost that particular turf war.[14]

Initially, the MSC was divided into two bodies, each with its own organizational structure: the Employment Services Agency and the Training Services Agency. Ainley and Corney have argued that the 1973 Act gave the Secretary of State for Employment unprecedented powers of direct intervention into the education system, powers which would be matched by those of the Education Secretary only after the 1988 Act.[15] Nevertheless, the establishment of the MSC was not particularly contentious at the time, for there was a broad consensus about the desirability of a national training organization. LEAs, the teaching and lecturing unions, employers and trade unions gave support.

In its early days, the MSC came to represent a new vision of society and the economy. Its leading personnel, Sir John Cassels (Director, 1975–1981) and his successor, Sir Geoffrey Holland, emphasized the importance of vocational education and training in economic regeneration. They argued that Britain needed a new social ethic, or culture, which corresponded to its political aspirations for economic modernization.[16] Holland was a leading figure in developing MSC policy and a long-term advocate of the abolition of the academic/vocational divide within a new, modernized system of education and training. The aim was to construct a modern and effective training culture, but after 1974 the MSC's main role was to manage the unemployment crisis for both Labour and Conservative governments. The return of mass unemployment 'blurred' the debate about the role of training in economic performance. Training programmes became associated with unemployment, rather than with the skill requirements of industry. The development of training policy is considered in the Chapter Seven. At this point, it is sufficient to note that the MSC was consistent in its attempts to abolish the dichotomy between education and training. Its 'great rival' in such projects was the DES.[17] After 1973, the MSC expanded its training activity at a rapid pace, so that the Training Opportunities Scheme (TOPS), for example, doubled in scale between 1974 and 1976 at a time when the DES was under severe pressure to cut costs. The DE staff numbers rose from 35,000 in 1974 to nearly 60,000 by 1987.

The Fookes Report of 1976 advised that:

> although it was not said in so many words, relations between the two departments probably had been under considerable strain during the past two years … . The DES and the Department of Employment are, in a sense, competing for resources and liable to be judged, one against the other, by results … . The TSA [Training Services Agency] has moved at a tempo which the DES could not (and, indeed, should not try to) emulate. Equally clearly it has trodden on some corns in the education service. We are not unduly worried about these early tensions. We are satisfied that the machinery for co-operation between the two departments at national level is adequate and that both services mean to make it work. We welcome the initiative and enthusiasm displayed by the TSA. It is clear, however, that tensions will occur at local level if national policies to improve the quality of education and training are implemented, not on the basis of an equal partnership, but by the agency of one Department of State having extra resources with which to dictate developments.[18]

The following period was to be marked by a level of interdepartmental wrangling not seen since the 1920s. In May 1975, the TSA's *Vocational Preparation for Young People* sent 'shock waves' through the DES.[19]

It proposed a vocational preparation scheme financed by government and industry and led to the Unified Vocational Preparation scheme. By the end of 1975, there was a feeling of 'war' between the two departments.[20] At this stage, the DES was coming under a dual pressure: to respond to the new requirements of industry as well as to address inequalities within the educational system. The configuration of employment and educational interests, as constructed at the end of the Second World War, began to break down. The shift to a supply-side approach to problems of economic growth and unemployment, and the politicization of education policy-making, meant that the DES was a prime target for those who wished to advance their interests within a new settlement.

The 'Great Debate' and changes at the DES

The Fookes Committee had established the agenda within Westminster and Whitehall for the political consideration of the roles of the Education and Employment departments. James Callaghan's famous Ruskin College speech in 1976 opened up these issues to wider public discussion via the 'Great Debate'. It also marked the beginning of a period of change in Whitehall personnel. Gerald Fowler, Minister of State at the DES was removed by Callaghan after only nine months in the job and replaced by Gordon Oakes, who was in favour of close links between industry and the polytechnics.[21] Sir William Pile was replaced by Sir James Hamilton as Permanent Secretary. This was a matter of some controversy, allegedly involving Downing Street intervention, and it soon became clear that Hamilton was ready to respond to criticisms of the DES in a novel way. A DES briefing paper which accompanied the Great Debate:

> identified teachers as convenient scapegoats, rather than conceding that concern at the state of education reflected rather upon the department nominally responsible for state education. Rather than courting consensus the DES appeared willing to countenance contention.[22]

This approach also involved a willingness to centralize power and to disturb the traditional relationships with LEAs. According to Fletcher, rather than strengthening its hand within the partnership with LEAs and teachers, the DES, aided by HMI, made use of the Great Debate as a 'window of opportunity' to try to escape from its traditional approach and to 'advance and implement contentious policies'.[23]

The Callaghan speech brought an end to the post-War period of educational expansion. It also officially laid the blame for the lack of trained workers imbued with the necessary skills and attitudes at the door of the education system.[24] Education, and the Education department, were now identified as a cause of the crisis, as manifested in the rise of youth unemployment, rather than as a potential remedy. The Ruskin speech meant that education could no longer be left to the educators. Industry had to be involved; a renewed emphasis on training for the young unemployed was required. Although the 1976 debate was framed in Education department terms, the MSC was widely believed to be the government's desired instrument of change. In his evidence to the Fookes Committee, Lord Alexander of Potterhill, General Secretary to the Association of Education Committees, advised that the MSC was 'making a take-over bid for a substantial part of the educational system'.[25] The advantage of the MSC's semi-autonomous status was that it did not have to go through a lengthy consultation process before making changes. According to the Chief Executive of the Training Agency, this difference in method produced a different culture at the MSC. At the DES, the consultation process meant that it had to 'think about these things more profoundly'.[26] The Work Experience Programme was introduced in 1976, and in 1978 the Youth Opportunities Programme (YOP) was established, not by the DES which had attempted but failed to maintain Education's hegemony over youth issues, but by the DE.

The Treasury saw the problem much as it had done since the mid-1920s: 'the economic climate and imperatives are clear; the task is to adjust education to them'.[27] The DES was not opposed to the Treasury view. As Stewart Ranson wrote in 1983:

> The driving force for change, however, has not been an external source
> of influence but the DES itself. The policy of reconstructing the education

service has been led by the Department who have championed the
initiative of strengthening the ties between school and work, between
education and training in order to improve the vocational preparation of
the 14–19 age group.[28]

Many officials in the DES recognized the need for reform of post-
compulsory education and training which focused on the transition from
school to work.[29] Differences of opinion within the department were
inevitable, however, as the DES was being pulled in two different directions
at once. Her Majesty's Inspectorate (HMI) and others were criticizing the
department for failing the majority of young people who did not go into
higher education. Employers were complaining about the lack of attention
to the needs of industry. As Mason has argued: 'The former utilized a
"social" argument, i.e. giving priority to the needs of the less able
academically in the form of practical courses and the latter claimed that
school leavers lacked the basic skills to benefit from technical education.'[30]
Divisions between the schools and further education branches were apparent over control of the curriculum, but a consensus grew around the need
for the vocationalization of 16–19 education, and a convergence of departmental views and objectives gathered pace. Temporary agreement was
reached that the curriculum should have a vocational focus and that priority
should be accorded to the needs of employers.[31] Both branches of the
DES accepted that the curriculum should be vocationalized and that the
recession would lead to a rationalization of educational provision. These
developments would steer students into particular vocational routes
according to ability, aptitude, attainment and maturity, 'bearing in mind
the need to promote even-handedness of treatment and parity of esteem
within 16–19 education'.[32] The internal consensus at the DES was
achieved on the basis of an 'overt stratification' of young people in order
to meet the needs of industry.[33]

Conservative governments

Following the election of Margaret Thatcher's first Conservative government in 1979, there was a firm drive towards centralism in education.

Moves to weaken the LEAs were apparent under the first two Secretaries of State, Mark Carlisle (1979–1981) and Sir Keith Joseph (1981–1986), for example by increasing parental rights and representation on governing bodies. They came to a head with Kenneth Baker's Education Reform Act 1988. Joseph, who was Secretary of State for Industry (1979–1981), was the longest serving Education minister since George Tomlinson and the embodiment of the first Conservative administration's emphasis on cutting central government spending. He closed the Schools Council in 1982, and his period of office is remembered by many as one of acrimonious relations with teachers.[34] Joseph represented the formative years of Thatcherite education policy within the context of high unemployment and the continued existence of the MSC as a tripartite body. In 1983, Joseph was joined by a new Permanent Secretary, Sir David Hancock, an ex-Treasury man who reinforced the impression of a right-wing, cost-cutting agenda.[35] The Conservative government made further use of the MSC to intervene in the preserve of the DES, thus bypassing the traditional forms of control of vocational education and training. During the early 1980s the move towards vocationalism was to gather pace as unemployment precipitated political stresses and sharp changes in policy.

Measures to decrease the power of LEAs proved successful. Rate-capping placed them under severe financial pressure and the DES increasingly used specific grants to fund many aspects of the curriculum.[36] Extra funding for LEAs came from the MSC, but further altered the nature of the central/local relationship. For example, the MSC's Technical and Vocational Education Initiative (TVEI) was seen as breaking the mould of previous policy-making in education. The Department of Employment's *A New Training Initiative*, issued in 1981, stated that pupils and teachers needed to gain a closer understanding of economic and industrial aspects of society.[37] It also recommended the adoption of 'a position where all young people under the age of 18 have the opportunity either of continuing in full-time education or of entering a period of planned work experience combined with work-related training and education'.[38] This aim – and its underlying assumption that working life would begin at 18, rather than 16 – echoed the thinking of *A Time for Youth*, published in

1978 by the Conservative Study Group and discussed in Chapter Two of this book.

A Time for Youth had argued for the transference of responsibility for training from the Employment department to the Education department and for the creation of a new Department of Education and Training. Few regarded this as a feasible option in 1981, but the MSC was seen as a vehicle for more closely integrating the school curriculum, post-compulsory education and entry into the labour market. In November 1982, Margaret Thatcher announced the TVEI as an MSC initiative without the usual formal consultation with Education department interests. Norman Tebbit declared that the initiative, which commenced in the autumn of 1983, heralded 'the rebirth of technical education',[39] an interpretation that also appealed to Sir Keith Joseph. Joseph broke with 'departmentalism' and supported the MSC's inroads into education via the TVEI, despite the implication of inadequacy on the part of the DES. At the 1984 Conservative Party Conference, Joseph announced: 'David Young and the education service together are making sure that a technical ingredient is returned to more and more curricula in more and more of the country; they are just beginning.'[40] The Conservatives were 'impatient of the effort to change education from within, [and] used the MSC to subject education to changes from without'.[41] The TVEI allowed the MSC to be involved in the curriculum and to bypass established methods of funding school education. In addition, Non-Advanced Further Education (NAFE) funds were allocated to the MSC to re-imburse further education colleges directly, rather than from LEAs. Harland argues that the MSC's use of categorical funding marked a departure from previous practice that was subsequently imitated by the DES. Power could be exercised through the authority conferred by the use of resources, thus establishing a principal–licensed agent relationship, rather than through the former partnership model.[42]

Relationships between the LEAs and the MSC became increasingly strained as TVEI 'tested territorial and professional boundaries'.[43] A British Educational Management and Administration Society conference took place under the title 'Education Fights Back',[44] while other organizations, including HMI, were openly sceptical about the contribution of TVEI to the secondary curriculum. A resolution by the National Association of Teachers in Further and Higher Education (NATFHE) condemned what it saw as a government attempt to 'transform education into training and transform the bulk of the 14–18 age group into a pool of ill-educated labour'.[45] The apparent weakness of the DES in the face of the MSC spurred some educational organizations to couch their 'fight back' in the form of calls for a new Department of Education and Training. For example, the National Association of Head Teachers (NAHT) believed that the continued separation of education and training 'may mean that the Department of Employment and the MSC together control the future shape of the education service and of the main lines of curriculum development'.[46] The notion that a new Department of Education and Training would serve to protect the interests of educational organizations was based on the assumption that the DES was attempting to defend itself from the new vocationalist approach. In reality, *A New Training Initiative*, as well as the launch of the TVEI, had the backing both of Sir Keith Joseph and of Norman Tebbit, the Employment Secretary. Joseph had not taken part in the initial discussions on the scheme but, rather than demonstrate any antipathy towards the Employment department, he quickly gave it general support, by arguing that it would help to re-invigorate education for the 'bottom 40 per cent' in schools.[47] Thus, at a ministerial level the Education and Employment departments were operating with a shared understanding about a redefinition of the relationships between education and employment and between central and local government.

In 1985, Chris Patten, then an Education minister, argued that the DES had been involved in government decisions on vocational education and training since 1979. This 'convergence of interest' in education and training, as Mason has described it, was spelt out by Patten as entailing a government strategy which was now being expressed through *both* the DES and the MSC. The two organizations had a differential ability to intervene. The DES was an 'orchestrator' of the partnership between central and local government. The MSC was a 'direct drive programme deliverer' in a recognized, although sometimes abrasive, relationship with the LEAs. These were two arms of a single education and training strategy and the government's primary concern was the content of the various programmes 'not where the education bits came from'.[48] Notwithstanding the note of administrative diplomacy in these pronouncements, they indicate that hopes, or fears, of the creation of a Department of Education and Training were missing the point. The two elements of policy were already becoming merged. Despite their different traditions and experiences, both departments were focusing on changing central–local government partnerships and forming closer relations with employers and industry.[49]

Such convergence was based upon a strict supply-side approach to the problem of unemployment by way of an injection of free-market economics into suspicious, Keynesian Whitehall offices. This has been portrayed as the transformation of the Education department into a copy of the interventionist, hands-on Employment department. During the 1970s, however, the Employment department itself underwent a transformation based upon neo-liberal principles, and in the 1980s both departments were objects of the Conservatives' drive for an enterprise culture. The series of Green Papers emanating from the Employment department in the 1980s showed a marked change from the traditional style of consultation documents which set out the options in a detached manner. These Papers were, in Freedland's judgement, 'texts or tracts single-mindedly reflecting ministerial ideologies in which the discourse of collective *laissez-faire* has little enough place'.[50] In 1986, the Employment department, then under Lord Young, issued a White Paper entitled *Building Businesses ... not Barriers*, which announced a fundamental redefinition of its goals. The previous principles of voluntarism and collective self-government in industry and training policy were replaced by a new aim which was to:

> Encourage the development of an enterprise economy. The way to reduce unemployment is through more businesses, more self-employment and greater wealth creation, all leading to more jobs. The key aspects of the Department's work are to
> 1. Promote enterprise and job creation in growth areas such as small firms, self-employment and tourism.

2. Help businesses to grow and jobs multiply by cutting 'red tape' … .
3. Improve training arrangements.
4. Help the young and those out of work for some time to find work.[51]

The change from a labour ministry to the 'Department for Enterprise and Efficiency', and from 'the public guardian of collective *laissez-faire* to being the focus of governmental promotion of free enterprise in a deregulated and individualized labour market', involved an ever-shrinking field of direct operation. This was particularly so in the area of training, which from 1990 was semi-privatized under the Training and Enterprise Councils (TECs).[52]

The convergence of interest of the two departments involved a powerful top-down, ministerial-level, ideological intervention, which cut across the professional concerns and agreed 'spheres of influence' of civil servants. One senior civil servant complained that the 1984 initiative, *Training for Jobs*, was 'sprung on us by ministers, as we didn't want to implement it'.[53] Pressure from ministers for corporate responsibility gave rise to factions within the DES and the MSC, so that there were 'stronger affinities across the boundary than within each organization'.[54] Once again, as in the 1920s, a strong political lead was directed at establishing new norms or, as in the 1980s a new culture, within which the main educational and training interests would have to operate. This new culture was based on neo-liberal, supply-side economics and vocationalism for the mass of young people. In general, it aimed at a unification of education and training, but the fulfilment of this aim would require the development of a new overarching political philosophy – the enterprise culture.

The enterprise culture

The theory of 'cultural bias' as an explanation for the economic problems of society brought further pressure for change in the internal culture of the DES. In 1978, in the wake of the 'Great Debate', Correlli Barnett wrote an article entitled 'Obsolescence and Dr Arnold' in which he argued that the British problem, the 'English disease', dated back a century and more. Although the first industrial nation of modern times, the British had never developed a 'genius for technology' and were unable to respond to the industrialization of other countries. From the mid-nineteenth century onwards, 'The bias of English middle- and upper-class culture has remained anti-pathetic towards industry and industrial progress ever since; a major influence in our decay.'[55] A 'crucial element of the English disease' was the 'special character of the British urban working class as a culture apart, an alienated group often embittered and hostile'.[56] Barnett's article identified the impact of the rise in unemployment during the 1970s as the main source of popular dissatisfaction with the education and employment systems, and as the stimulus to reform. He defined the culture of British people as 'the patterns of thought and behaviour, of feeling, the ideals and expectations, the belief in their "rights" to this and that, which took shape in the era of their wealth, success and security'.[57] The implication was that the population needed to accept a reduction in rights in the interest of improved employment prospects. Barnett drew the conclusion (echoing Koestler and others in the 1960s) that the crisis facing Britain was not simply a material one with an economic diagnosis and prescription, but a matter of change in 'our very national character and outlook'. This was not an issue for great debates, but rather of strong leadership, an alternative to the weakness of past government and its concessions to malcontents and interest groups. Barnett's 1978 article contained the seeds of Thatcherism's later approach to 'making Britain great again'. Its attack on liberal education as unsuited to the mass of the population sowed the seeds of the successful disarming of the left's traditional hostility to vocationalism. The inner city riots of the summer of 1981 formed the context of a renewed general concern with unemployment and youth training schemes.

Barnett's work contributed to the idea and ideal of an enterprise culture. This was developed at the Centre for Policy Studies (CPS) and other think tanks, and in the work of Lord Young.[58] According to Sir Keith Joseph, since 1945 all governments had pursued anti-free market policies. The resultant 'semi-socialism' was the cause of Britain's relative decline. In 1978 he argued that the English disease stemmed from the two World

Wars and the 'mood they produced': a desire for an expansion of government.[59] For Joseph, as for Barnett, the greatest damage had occurred during and after the Second World War. This had produced a mood of 'naive utopianism' and a 'debilitating compassion'. The illusion of an expanded, compassionate government had taken the form of encouraging demand (such as full employment policies and industrial subsidies) while discouraging supply (anti-enterprise attitudes, vindictive taxation and restrictive practices). For example, Joseph argued for the ending of university grants as a means of inculcating respect for industry among students.

Members of the radical right saw themselves as fighting for a 'new conservatism' against socialism and Butskellism (a convergence of policy identified with the Conservative R.A. Butler and the Labour Hugh Gaitskell) which was associated for them with the denigration of business. Thatcherism proclaimed that Victorian-style industrialism would encourage self-improvement among the workers, a genuine radicalism, and a respect for the market. The Centre for Policy Studies (CPS), which was intended to 'think the unthinkable',[60] focused on existing barriers to the development of an enterprise culture, in particular the British class system, the trade unions and state intervention. In contrast to the original idea of unshackling self-interest, from the mid-1980s there was a stress on the morality of the market. The CPS made the link between education and this moral approach to the successful working of the economy a central part of their argument: 'The stress is on motivation, creative ambition, religious factors and striving for excellence – factors to be instilled through education. Enterprise is thus considered to be teachable.' [61] A consensus grew among the think tanks that barriers to the enterprise culture were not of an economic nature and, therefore, could not be removed by changes to economic policy. The 'vested interests created by the particular British historico-cultural and psychological realities' would block the workings of the free market unless there was a concerted effort to educate new generations in enterprise.[62]

Lord Young has been described as the architect of the enterprise culture, although its roots may be found in a strand of intellectual activity that stretched back to the late 1950s and challenges to the post-War consensus.[63] Young argued that 'the welfare state stifles enterprise by generating dependency' and that 'in the past, there was an unfortunate and unnecessary bias against enterprise in British culture ... . We must strive to bring schools, universities, and other educational institutions to a closer understanding of the needs and hopes of the enterprises in which their pupils and students will one day work.'[64] In a lecture delivered in 1985 he addressed the seeming paradox of a government committed to the free market interfering in such areas as education. In terms almost identical to those of Barnett and Wiener, he argued that the nation's political culture had thwarted the development of the original Victorian entrepreneurial spirit. The educational system and the trade unions had managed to corrupt the natural propensity for enterprise within human personality. The solution was the promulgation of a community of interests: one nation and one set of cultural values.[65] Thus, the fully developed notion of enterprise culture, which began life as a description of the withdrawal of government from the workings of the economy, revolved around the question of education and the inculcation of the values and attitudes appropriate to a free market. It was no coincidence that Lord Young was a leading advocate of a merged department of education and training.

In the 1980s the works of Barnett and Wiener's account, *English Culture and the Decline of the Industrial Spirit, 1850–1980* (1981), gained powerful influence in political and academic circles, in policy reports, and in the media.[66] Barnett and Wiener gave the prevailing general criticism of the Civil Service and the education system a hard right-wing edge by counterposing economic and social policy. They argued that the dominant political culture was incompatible with wealth creation. For too long social improvement had been promoted at the expense of economic efficiency. In the mid-1980s, employers' organizations launched campaigns to improve the status of industrial activities. Some of these were more successful than others. For example, the question of why there was no 'Engineers' Corner', alongside Poets' Corner, in Westminster Abbey, led to red faces, when it was pointed out that there was! Radio and television were castigated by the Aims of Industry organization for anti-industrial stereotypes in pop songs, *Women's Hour*, the *Nine o'clock News* and in other broadcasts.[67] The intelligentsia had been hijacked by Marx, and the disease of the spirit had infected Oxbridge, the newspapers, the Treasury and the BBC.[68] The chief message of this campaigning was the notion that two different cultures existed, those of industry and of education, cultures which must be brought together.[69] The campaign culminated in 1986 in the Confederation of British Industry (CBI)'s Industry Year which, for the CBI, was a declaration that poor economic performance was in part attributable to the anti-industry culture fostered, if not caused by, the educational system.

Numerous persuasive critiques of the Barnett–Wiener hypothesis appeared. Economists argued for the primacy of economic, over social and cultural, explanations of economic decline. Historians suggested that only by a highly selective use of sources was it possible to maintain that an exceptionally anti-industrial culture had existed in Britain since the nineteenth century.[70] British high culture was the least hostile to industry and enterprise of European countries, and all Western intellectual culture can be seen as containing anti-industrial elements. Several important industrial and technical initiatives had occurred in the second half of the nineteenth century, for example the foundation of civic universities and polytechnics. British economic decline, which was relative rather than absolute, was a natural consequence of the growth of more populous states such as Germany and the United States of America. Even in the twentieth century, the problem was a relative one: for most of this period, the rate of growth of the British economy was reasonably good. Critics of the education system and of civil servants, moreover, should take account of other priorities, for example the existence of a British Empire which necessitated the production of an imperial administrative elite.

However, despite such academic scrutiny of the Barnett–Wiener thesis and a recognition that the state of the economy was the product of many factors, cultural defects became widely accepted as the major explanation for Britain's decline. The extent of the economic crisis and the apparent permanence of unemployment, especially among the young, created a need for a powerful new political philosophy. Declinism simplified the understanding of economic growth and provided a mono-causal explanation and panacea for poor past performance. Education and training were the main culprits and the past was re-interpreted in terms of their deficiencies.

In the 1980s, as Wiener's volume acquired cult status, contributions to the debate were supplied both from the left and right of the political spectrum. For example, Perry Anderson, a well-known Marxist writer on the decline of Britain who, like Wiener, interpreted the contemporary situation in terms of a 'crisis of capitalism', provided a favourable review of *English Culture and the Decline of the Industrial Spirit, 1850–1980*. Wiener's attack on the role of liberal policy-makers and educationists was taken by neo-liberals as evidence of the ineffectiveness of welfarism, and by the left as proof of the irrelevance of the English pastoral tradition and old class distinctions. Barnett and Wiener shared with more progressive critics of the system a view of British institutions as insufficiently modernized. The transition to modernity in the United Kingdom had been incomplete and old elites and institutions continued to dominate policy-making. Both sets of critics accepted the existence of a sharp separation between a City of London/finance/commerce group of business interests and a Northern/manufacturing group. British social and economic policy was seen as being driven by the former, via the power of the Treasury within Whitehall. The policy implications of such analysis included the need to assert much greater central control over the old financially based elites and parochial local interests. A further attack on liberal education and on divisions between the academic and the vocational was required. Unemployment became the central issue, both for Conservative vocationalists and for progressive educational reformers. Convergence between the two sides was based on the lowest common denominator between the two positions – hostility towards liberal education and the old academic traditions of the DES.

The promotion of an enterprise culture commanded wide support. In a speech in 1982, Sir James Hamilton (Permanent Secretary at the Education department, 1976–1983) claimed that he detected a 'growing consensus' that the secondary curriculum should be reformed in order to become more practical and a better preparation for working life. This consensus included teachers, LEAs, employers and policy-makers, who were coming together under banners such as 'skills for working life' and 'education for capability'.[71] The dominance of the new vocationalism continued throughout the 1980s. Schools formed new business links, embraced initiatives developed by the Schools Council Industry Project (SCIP) and became more adept at securing sponsorship and work experience placements for their pupils. Another important development was the establishment between 1988 and 1993 of 15 flagship secondary schools or City Technology Colleges (CTCs), bearing the names of such firms as ADT, Dixons and Harris (Carpets). Levels of private sector funding for CTCs, however, were much lower than expected.[72]

The introduction of an enterprise culture into schools and colleges did not meet with universal approval. For example, it was condemned by those who interpreted it as a new means of social discipline, an adaptation of the ideology of self-improvement and self-discipline to the new technological conditions of production and consumption.[73] According to Cohen, vocationalism was 'a pretext for dismantling the whole cultural apparatus of working-class apprenticeship' and for ensuring that 'knowledge is radically disconnected from the power of social combination'.[74] Although such critiques from the left, including those of the Centre for Contemporary Cultural Studies, gained considerable prominence in academic debates, they had 'almost no impact on the formulation of alternative education policy'.[75]

From vocationalism to traditionalism

In 1984, the White Paper, *Training for Jobs*, called for an integrated approach across government departments, with the MSC exerting more control over spending on vocational education and training. The Chairman of the MSC suggested that the LEAs were the authors of their own downfall, having failed to 'encourage the introduction of industry and the world of business into the school system'.[76] Despite this willingness to reject the traditional division of departmental labour, however, and despite the concept of a training policy that would utilize the co-ordinated services of the Education and Employment departments, the government's focus shifted to introducing the market into education. Morgan has argued: 'As a consequence, the links between the MSC and the DES were not developed as they might have been in a closer tying together of training and education in a nationally co-ordinated strategy under a unified government department.'[77] In the mid-1980s, this shift in thinking about the relationship between education and the economy was seen by several writers in terms of Raymond Williams's description of a changing balance between various class fragments or interest groups.[78] These were classified as old humanists, industrial trainers and public educators. Bowe and Whitty, for example, saw the struggle over exams at 16 plus as one of the on-going series of compromises between these groups.[79] The universities, some Conservatives, and the General Certificate of Education (GCE) boards were the old humanists; employers and the corporatist elements among both Conservatives and Labour were the industrial trainers; the Certificate of Secondary Education (CSE) boards, teachers, LEAs and traditional elements of the labour movement were the public educators. In contrast to the early 1980s, which had been characterized by the dominance of the new vocationalism, the growing influence of the old humanists became apparent prior to reform of the GCSE system in 1986, the year in which Kenneth Baker succeeded Joseph as Secretary of State. The academic model of education once again prevailed, to the consternation of the industrial lobby. With the return of a third Conservative government in 1987, the emphasis changed from vocationalism to an endorsement and strengthening of traditional systems of curriculum and examination.

The Education Reform Act 1988, with its commitment to the National Curriculum and national testing, represented the renewed dominance of the old humanists and of a traditional academic culture. The Act transformed and enlarged the powers and functions of the DES, and of its civil servants. In contrast, the powers of the LEAs were severely curtailed. Indeed, the largest of them, the Inner London Education Authority (ILEA), was simply abolished. Polytechnics and larger colleges were removed from LEA control and even schools were allowed to opt out and assume grant-maintained status. The 1988 Act brought about some of the changes anticipated by Halsey in 1976. For example, LEAs no longer had a majority on governing bodies and parents had the right to see all curriculum documents. Parents even began to take part in discussions over school budgets. The Act was seen as a fundamental reform in favour of the consumers of education as against the providers, and as a central part of the Thatcherite attack on the Welfare State. In consequence, the DES was placed in the unfamiliar position of being at the leading edge of government policy: 'In the late 1980s the DES found itself a place in the Whitehall sun for the first time in 20 years but at the cost of abandoning its quietist mixed tradition of high spending and great self-restraint. From now on DES money was to talk.'[80] The unification of education and training no longer appeared to be a major policy objective. Under Baker's direction, the DES travelled along the alternative road of a national curriculum, national testing and the reform of school management.[81]

The Conservative manifesto for the 1987 election portrayed the MSC as working on a single policy area, that of training. Its days as a strategic force in the labour market linking up with the Education department in a new approach to the 16–19 group were clearly numbered. In 1988, an employment training programme was introduced with the aim of redirecting training to the specific needs of the labour market. Critics such as King, however, have suggested that it was an extension of the dominant new right approach which was aimed at returning training to its voluntaristic roots, undermining the unions and linking unemployment benefits to participation in training schemes similar to the US workfare projects.[82] Under the terms of the Employment Act 1988, the MSC was renamed the Training Commission (TC). The Training Agency and the Employment Service, which had been divisions both of the Department of Employment and of the MSC, were set up as executive agencies. From this date, the Department of Employment was also known as the Employment Department. From 1988, the Conservatives made a major change in the administration of training programmes by devolving them to TECs. Each TEC was chaired by a local business person who communicated directly with the Employment Secretary. The Trades Union Congress (TUC) voted to boycott the Employment Training (ET) programme and the government, deciding that the Training Commission could no longer be relied on to support its initiatives, abolished it.[83] The life of the TC was effectively 10 days.[84] The functions of the TC were returned to the Training Agency. In October 1990, it was announced that the Training Agency was to be broken into three directorates as part of the government's overall strategy of giving responsibility for training to local industry and to the TECs.

Conclusion

The recession of the 1970s signalled a tightening of educational expenditure and a more vocationally centred approach to educational provision for the 16–19 year old group. By the middle of the decade concerns about a gap between the traditional organization and administration of education and the urgent problems brought about by economic crisis and the rise in youth unemployment had escalated. In consequence, attention was focused once more upon the culture of the DES and of its civil servants. Former critiques of the educational system were revived and used to condemn the DES's relationships with other organizations and departments, and its perceived lack of openness in terms of policy-making. The DES tried to arrest the decline in its influence and reassert control by carrying out various centralizing measures.[85] Nevertheless, control was diffused across Whitehall, as in this period the Employment department and the MSC were involved increasingly in areas of traditional educational concern. Outside intervention was needed in order to tune education policy to employment policy, or to 'adjust education to industry' as the process had been known during previous periods of economic crisis. The Education Reform Act 1988, however, transformed the situation. The new vocationalism, which implied a unification of education and training, was replaced by an emphasis on the market and traditional Conservative educational values. The 1988 Act 'placed the DES ... in the van of the movement to by-pass local government wherever possible and, in crude Whitehall terms, activity plus high and sustained ministerial attention = high relative status'.[86]

The dynamic and confident style of Kenneth Baker and the substantial nature of the 1988 Act brought the DES centre stage: 'the impressions conveyed were of authority, and of control'.[87] The National Curriculum, however, was not easily implemented. It was widely regarded as being overloaded, and the DES came under renewed pressure. In 1992, when responsibility for the research councils was transferred to the Office of Science and Technology and the department changed its name to the Department for Education (DfE), the department's senior officials once again attempted to 'mark out its legitimate territory, much as an animal marks out its patch by the pungency of its scent'.[88] In 1993, the teaching unions regained some authority by successfully boycotting the testing regime, and John Patten (Secretary of State, 1992–1994) became the object of universal opprobrium. By 1995, the DfE appeared to have retreated on several fronts, with the original confidence of its central control over the system considerably shaken. Gillian Shephard took a more conciliatory approach and was rewarded by John Major with the new DfEE.

The Employment department began the period as a secure feature of the post-War corporatist state, then battled its way through a period of mass unemployment when it attempted to forge a new training role for itself, and finally fell victim to the old arguments about its abolition. In 1995 its functions were dispersed across Whitehall, much as Churchill had advocated in the early years of its existence. The wheel had turned full circle. The abolition of the Employment department was accompanied, as was its creation, by uncertainty about the best way to co-ordinate departments concerned with industry, labour and training.

During the 1980s and 1990s a process of convergence of views and objectives took place within the Education and Employment departments at ministerial level. This convergence revolved around the proposition that education should be brought into a closer relationship with industry and employment. Whilst retaining different traditions of relating to their respective client groups, pressure from the top was towards a new, shared policy goal and internal departmental culture. This convergence took place primarily in the area of 16–19 policy, or post-compulsory education and training (what used to be called the 'youth question'). It involved a process of negotiation within a structural context of a more or less powerful local control of educational and employment matters. As central power increased in the 1980s and the departments' objectives further converged, tensions re-emerged and, lacking avenues of expression at the central government level after the formation of the DfEE, were pushed down the system to the local level. Many conflicting interests now operate in the education and training fields – further education colleges, trade unions, employers and TECs. Chapter Seven looks at the operation of these interests and the development of tensions between them in the key policy areas of training and 16–19 education.

Notes

1. Fletcher, 1995.
2. OECD, 1975.
3. Tenth Report from the Expenditure Committee, Session 1975–76, HC 621. *Policy-making in the Department of Education and Science.* London: HMSO. Minutes of evidence, memo by the DES, para. 26.
4. Quoted in Gordon, Aldrich and Dean, 1991, 96. Tenth Report from the Expenditure Committee, Session 1975–76, HC 621. *Policy-making in the Department of Education and Science.* London: HMSO. Memo by Dr A.H. Halsey, 191, para. 3.
5. Tenth Report from the Expenditure Committee, Session 1975–76, HC 621. *Policy-making in the Department of Education and Science.* London: HMSO. Memo by Professor John Vaizey.
6. Tenth Report from the Expenditure Committee, Session 1975–76, HC 621. *Policy-making in the Department of Education and Science.* London: HMSO. Memo by Dr A.H. Halsey, 193, para. 10, and minutes of evidence, 9 February 1976, q. 720.
7. OECD, 1975, 35.
8. Tenth Report from the Expenditure Committee, Session 1975–76, HC 621. *Policy-making in the Department of Education and Science.* London: HMSO. Memo by Professor John Vaizey.
9. Tenth Report from the Expenditure Committee, Session 1975–76, HC 621. *Policy-making in the Department of Education and Science.* London: HMSO. Memo by Professor John Vaizey.

10. Tenth Report from the Expenditure Committee, Session 1975–76, HC 621. *Policy-making in the Department of Education and Science*. London: HMSO. Memo by Professor John Vaizey.
11. Mason, 1988, 11.
12. King, 1993, 219.
13. Ainley and Corney, 1990, 46.
14. Low, 1988, 215.
15. Ainley and Corney, 1990, 19.
16. Ainley and Corney, 1990, 1–2.
17. Ainley and Corney, 1990, 1–2.
18. Tenth Report from the Expenditure Committee, Session 1975–76, HC 621. *Policy-making in the Department of Education and Science*. London: HMSO, para. 70.
19. Ainley and Corney, 1990, 38.
20. Ainley and Corney, 1990, 38.
21. Lawrence, 1992, 72.
22. Fletcher, 1995, 139.
23. Fletcher, 1995, 142.
24. Ainley, 1988, 81.
25. Tenth Report from the Expenditure Committee, Session 1975–76, HC 621. *Policy-making in the Department of Education and Science*. London: HMSO. Minutes of Evidence, 5 April 1976, q. 1326.
26. Tenth Report from the Expenditure Committee, Session 1975–76, HC 621. *Policy-making in the Department of Education and Science*. London: HMSO. Minutes of Evidence, 5 April 1976, q. 1310.
27. Treasury official quoted in Ranson, 1983, 11.
28. Ranson, 1983, 12.
29. Sheldrake and Vickerstaff, 1987, 31.
30. Mason, 1988, 12.
31. Ranson, 1983.
32. Mason, 1988, 13.
33. Ranson, 1983.
34. Lawrence, 1992, 98–99. Apart from Sir David Eccles who served twice, 1954–1957 and 1959–1962.
35. Lawrence, 1992, 105.
36. Fletcher, 1995, 140.
37. Ainley and Corney, 1990, 58–63.
38. Quoted in Deakin, 1996, 85.
39. Quoted in Moon and Richardson, 1984, 24.
40. Quoted in Knight, 1990, 174.

41. Ainley, 1988, 65. As, at this time, education funds from central government were absorbed into local budgets, the payment of TVEI money in this way was a means of ensuring that it was spent as intended.
42. Harland, 1987, 40.
43. Mason, 1988, 24.
44. Mason, 1988, 24.
45. Deakin, 1996, 90.
46. House of Commons Education, Science and Arts Committee, Session 1982–83, HC 133-1. *Education and Training, 14–19 year olds: the new TVEI.* London: HMSO. Memo submitted by the NAHT, 'NAHT Response to the Government's Technical Education Initiative for the 14–18 age group'.
47. McCulloch, 1986, 44.
48. Speech at FEU/FESC conference, Bristol, 8 December 1985. Quoted in Mason, 1988, 32.
49. Mason, 1988, 3, 33.
50. Freedland, 1992, 283.
51. Quoted in Freedland, 1992, 286.
52. Freedland, 1992, 289, 294.
53. Mason, 1988, 27.
54. Parkes, 1985, 167.
55. Barnett, 1978, 32.
56. Barnett, 1978, 33.
57. Barnett, 1978, 34.
58. Morris, 1991, 22, 28–32.
59. Joseph, 1978, 100.
60. Morris, 1991, 22.
61. Morris, 1991, 24.
62. Morris, 1991, 29.
63. Young, 1992, 29, 34.
64. Young, 1992, 30.
65. Young, 1992, 30.
66. Raven, 1989, 188–189.
67. Raven, 1989, 194.
68. Raven, 1989, 201.
69. Marsden, 1989.
70. See, for example, the contributions to Collins and Robbins, 1990.
71. Hamilton, 1982, 9.
72. Chitty, 1992, 65–66.
73. Cohen, 1984, 114.

74. Cohen, 1984, 115.
75. Jones, 1995, 235.
76. Quoted in Mason, 1988, 25.
77. Morgan, 1994, 218.
78. Williams, 1961.
79. Bowe and Whitty, 1989, 403.
80. Hennessy, 1989, 429.
81. Morgan, 1994, 236.
82. King, 1993, 215.
83. Morgan, 1994, 236.
84. Ainley and Corney, 1990, 6.
85. Ranson, 1983, 12.
86. Hennessy, 1989, 428.
87. Fletcher, 1995, 142.
88. Fletcher, 1995, 145.

7 Towards Lifelong Learning

Introduction

During the week that followed the announcement of the merger between the Education and Employment departments, Michael Bichard, at that time uncertain of his own future, appeared before the House of Commons Employment Select Committee. The 'meat of the merger', he told the Committee, was to be found in the 'middle ground' of policy, adult and youth training, and further and higher education. Success in these areas would be crucial because 'that is where the opportunities are and that is where some of the problems could be if we do not get it right'.[1] As earlier chapters of this book have indicated, post-compulsory education and training had not only been an arena for overlap and potential conflict between the departments, but also the terrain on which relationships between the departments had developed. The merger of Education and Employment in 1995 generated great expectations about the creation of a coherent post-compulsory education and training system for England and Wales.

This chapter examines the significance of vocational education and training initiatives during the 1980s and early 1990s and the still more recent pursuit of lifelong learning. Some broader perspectives are highlighted, for example in relation to employment and unemployment trends, to educational, technological and occupational changes and to new conceptions of the Welfare State.

The battle against unemployment

Unemployment worsened significantly as a result of the economic recession of the late 1970s. Five per cent of the British workforce was unemployed in 1979, rising to 9.4 per cent in 1981 and 10.6 per cent in 1983. Youth unemployment rates were higher still: 8.9 per cent of 16–19 year olds were unemployed in 1979, 22.7 per cent in 1981 and 25.1 per cent in 1983.[2] This situation led to a fundamental change of direction for the Manpower Services Commission (MSC). It was 'pressed into service to provide emergency unemployment schemes and soon lost sight of its original goal of creating comprehensive and high-quality skills training for the long-term needs of the national economy'.[3]

A range of MSC initiatives, including the Youth Opportunities Programme (YOP) 1978–1983 and the Youth Training Scheme (YTS) 1983–1990 were introduced, designed to 'soak up the growing pool of unemployed youth'.[4] Although the YTS was to be extended from a one-year to a two-year programme, it was widely seen as a cheaper and poorer quality replacement for apprenticeship training, offering neither certainty of employment nor certification for trainees.[5] By 1987, 60 per cent of all 16 and 17 year olds were 'on a YTS' and it has been suggested that the scheme had become almost a rite of passage, rather as National Service had been for the previous generation.[6]

The YTS was 'cobbled together at breakneck speed without many of the preconditions for high-quality training'.[7] Pressure to meet numerical targets meant that little regard could be given to the quality of placements. All too frequently, this resulted in low-level work, inadequate training and little or no education. Some employers saw YTS basically as a source of cheap labour. The trainees, themselves, according to one survey, judged schemes primarily according to the prospects of being 'kept on'.[8] Many YTS trainees failed to gain a qualification of any kind,[9] while others found that, having obtained a basic-level award, employers prevented them from pursuing further study.[10] Although some individuals benefited from their YTS placements, the programme 'never managed to throw off the reputation for low-quality training which had dogged all previous MSC training schemes'.[11] The MSC and Department of Education and Science (DES) were seen as developing 'new palliatives to manage the dispersal and decline' of Britain's shrinking industrial base, rather than contributing towards its regeneration.[12] Although Youth Training, the successor to YTS from 1990, was administered at a more local level and placed under the control of Training and Enterprise Councils (TECs), it attracted similar criticisms. The 1993 National Commission on Education reported that, six months after completing Youth Training programmes 'one-third of young people had neither a job nor a full or part qualification'.[13] It should be noted, however, that the British response to the crisis of youth unemployment was not unique. Several other countries introduced similar programmes, memorably described by one commentator as 'no more than "parking places" for the young'.[14]

In spite of such criticisms, in May 1997 when Tony Blair's Labour government came to office, UK claimant unemployment figures stood at 1.635 million, their lowest since the start of the decade.[15] Youth unemployment was less than the European average. In opposition, Labour had pledged to improve the employment prospects of a range of groups and to replace Youth Training. Within weeks of coming to office a New Deal Task Force had been established. Under the leadership of Sir Peter Davis, the Chief Executive of Prudential Insurance, the Task Force membership included enterprising role models for young people, such as Shami Ahmed, the founder and Managing Director of Joe Bloggs Jeans Ltd, a self-starter turned international businessman. The New Deal for Young People, which commenced in January 1998 in 12 'Pathfinder' areas and nationally three months later, targeted those aged between 18 and 24 who had been claiming Jobseeker's Allowance for at least six months. Those joining the New Deal first entered a 'Gateway' to assistance from the Employment Service, the DfEE's specialist employment agency. Here they were offered help to improve their employability and to find unsubsidized employment. Four options were available to those who emerged from the Gateway without work: first, a private sector job subsidized for six months by the government; second, work with a voluntary sector employer with a weekly wage in excess of the rate for welfare benefits; third, work for the government's Environment Task Force; or, fourth, full-time study on an approved course.

The scope of the New Deal was soon broadened to include the long-term unemployed aged 25 or over, lone parents, those receiving incapacity and disability benefits and partners of unemployed people. Gordon Brown, the Chancellor of the Exchequer, and David Blunkett, the Secretary of State for Education and Employment, carefully presented the New Deal not as 'another government scheme',[16] but as a social justice measure to empower those sections of society that have traditionally been excluded from work.[17] The principles of welfare-to-work, however, should also be located within Labour's concerns to eradicate benefit fraud and the culture of dependency. There was an urgent need for 'third way' solutions that would meet the costs of Britain's aging population and its increasingly expensive Welfare State. In May 1999 in a speech to DEMOS, the left-of-centre think tank, David Blunkett explained that:

> In our drive to modernize the Welfare State we face those on one side of the political spectrum, advocating rampant individualism, and on the other, well-meaning people calling for dependence based on debilitating welfarism. ... The welfare system should provide work for those who can, and security for those who cannot.[18]

The favourable economic conditions that have coincided with the launch of the New Deal make it difficult to assess its true impact and success. Employment Minister, Andrew Smith angrily dismissed an early critique of the hidden costs of the initiative by the Centre for Policy Studies, as 'a shoddy and shabby affair'. Smith countered that 'those who used to believe in supply-side reform have suddenly got cold feet at the first whiff of success'.[19] The Institute of Directors offered a more favourable assessment, although these findings drew upon a survey of just 207 out of its 47,000 members. Surprisingly, this research also revealed an ignorance of basic information about the New Deal among employers, information that could readily have been obtained from the local job centre.[20] In its first year almost 70,000 participants on the New Deal for Young People had found 'sustained' work, mostly in unsubsidized jobs. The total number of unemployed claimants aged 18–24 stood at its lowest level since 1974.[21] The UK's employment rate, meanwhile, was the highest among the larger European Union countries and second only to Denmark.[22]

Qualifications and targets

For much of the 1980s, the Thatcher governments' vocational education and training policy focused upon reducing youth unemployment. Towards the end of the decade, however, there was shift of emphasis. First, there was a drive to improve both the system of accreditation and the numbers gaining qualifications. Second, responsibility for vocational education and training reform was handed over to employers and the market. From the 1980s, as preparations were made for the operation of a single European market, a number of international surveys of vocational education and training reinforced concerns that the British workforce was poorly prepared. For example, in 1991 it was reported that only 42 per cent of British workers possessed qualifications relevant to their employment.[23]

During the last 20 years, both Conservative and Labour governments have pledged to maintain GCE A-levels as a 'gold standard' of post-16 academic excellence. The suggestion of the Higginson Committee in 1987 that sixth-form students should study a broader range of subjects, in line with the practice of a number of other countries, was summarily dismissed by the then Secretary of State for Education, Kenneth Baker. Over the following decade, the proportion of young people passing A-levels and proceeding to university rose steadily. In 1989, only one in six went on to higher education; by 1994, it was one in three.[24] Few, however, ventured to suggest that this rise was a consequence of higher standards of pupil attainment. Instead, critics – including many powerful voices from the worlds of business and commerce – suggested that the tendency of many syllabuses to introduce more coursework at the expense of written examinations and modular approaches were the root causes of grade inflation. Significantly, during his brief 11-month tenure as Permanent Secretary at the DfE, Sir Geoffrey Holland appointed the industrialist Sir Ron (later Lord) Dearing to the post of chief executive of the Schools

Curriculum and Assessment Authority (SCAA) rather than David Pascall, the outgoing chairman of the National Curriculum Council. Over the next four years, Dearing was to earn a reputation as the 'educational Red Adair',[25] heading inquiries into the National Curriculum, post-16 education and training and higher education, prior to taking up a part-time post as Chairman of the University for Industry. Government efforts to involve business people in the evolution and execution of education policy could not allay fears that steady improvements in GCSE and A-level pass rates disguised a relaxation in examination standards. For example, in 1998 the Institute of Management indicated that 60 per cent of its members did not regard their employees' GCSE grades as a reliable indicator of knowledge, while 80 per cent thought that they were a poor predictor of an individual's competence in the workplace.[26]

In the mid-1980s, Margaret Thatcher's Conservative government deliberately sought to avoid similar doubts being raised about the rigour of vocational education and training awards. In 1986 a new quango, the National Council for Vocational Qualifications (NCVQ), was established to regulate the awarding bodies and their qualifications. Increased responsibility was also devolved to employers, for example, to design competence-based training programmes. This 'new' approach was reminiscent of the standards-based training associated with various Industrial Training Boards during the 1960s and 1970s but, according to critics of the NCVQ, the work of these bodies was deliberately not acknowledged, nor were these earlier initiatives developed.[27]

Under the auspices of the NCVQ, new types of vocational qualifications were developed to complement those of longstanding bodies such as the City and Guilds of London Institute and the Royal Society of Arts.[28] National Vocational Qualifications (NVQs) were introduced at five levels leading to 'craft', 'technician', 'sub-degree', 'degree' and 'post-graduate' awards. NVQs were presented as a means of accrediting capability in the workplace from basic foundation competencies to professional and managerial skills. In 1995, Gillian Shephard, as Secretary of State for Education and Employment, commended the new qualifications for providing both motivation for students and measurable benefits for employers.

Some employers were quick to praise NVQs. A spokesman for the Chemical, Pharmaceutical and Allied Industries awarding body, for example, suggested that NVQs led to improved efficiency, a reduction in waste of expensive raw materials, less downtime, lower risk of accidents, less absenteeism and increased motivation.[29] The first awards were made in 1988 and, by 1999, more than two million NVQs had been awarded.[30]

On the other hand, the numbers of workers holding and currently working for NVQ qualifications have been disputed.[31] On the very day of Labour's general election victory the *Independent* reported that one-third of NVQs had never been completed by a single trainee and that a further 50 out of the 878 existing NVQs had been achieved by just one person. It continued:

> Among the nation's least popular NVQs are level two qualifications in pest control, maintaining fire-extinguishing equipment, spectator control and funeral service, none of which has yet been awarded. Certificates in amusements, carton manufacture and steel hot rolling have also yet to be gained.[32]

The credibility of NVQs has also been undermined by reservations, including those set out in the 1996 report by Sir Gordon Beaumont, about the excessive number of awarding bodies, the rigour and jargon-ridden nature of assessment procedures and the reductionist nature of competence testing.[33] In 1993, the National Commission noted with curiosity that the structure of NVQs:

> places emphasis on jobs as they are currently organized, with no regard to how they might develop in the future. It also emphasizes practical capability at the expense of the understanding of underlying principles and knowledge, so that, for example, while a bricklayer must be able to calculate how many bricks he [sic] requires for a length of wall, he is not expected to have a mathematical grounding which can be built on later.[34]

Others have questioned whether the competence model pays sufficient attention to the social skills that the successful bricklayer, plumber or electrician, among others, must practise when dealing with customers.[35]

To date, the vast bulk of NVQ awards have been at the lower levels and in such occupational areas as hairdressing, childcare, retailing and the armed forces. As Professor Alison Wolf has argued, it cannot simply be assumed that the NVQ initiative can transform the nature of the UK economy and vocational training.[36]

Interestingly, the most successful dimension of the 1990s drive to improve the quality of workplace training marked a return to the past. The Modern Apprenticeships scheme for 16–24 year olds became available nationally from September 1995. By January 1999, 225,000 young people had completed Modern Apprenticeships at NVQ levels three or above. A further 126,000 were in the process of training, working in some 80 different industrial sectors. In 1998, a parallel scheme, National Traineeships, replaced Youth Training with the intention of offering vocational qualifications to NVQ level two.[37] According to David Blunkett 'The idea of revitalising the oldest tradition in training has caught the public imagination.'[38] Plans for an accelerated version of the Modern Apprenticeships scheme, however, were quietly withdrawn as a result of poor enrolments.

In 1992, a further NCVQ initiative was launched when some schools and colleges began to offer post-16 General National Vocational Qualification (GNVQ) programmes at foundation, intermediate and advanced levels in such areas as health and social care, business studies and leisure and tourism. These were intended to be the vocational equivalents of GCSE and A-levels, although the difficulties of making such comparisons are legion.[39] Within a relatively short period of time, it became apparent that GNVQs were playing an important part in improving full-time post-compulsory education participation rates. By 1995, 68 per cent of the British 16–18 cohort were in full-time education or training, some 20 per cent higher than five years earlier.[40] Officially, GNVQs have been hailed as a success both by the previous Conservative and current Labour governments. 'Part One' GNVQs for 14–16 year olds were subsequently introduced on a pilot basis as alternatives to GCSEs. There have also been criticisms. Reports by Dr John Capey and Sir Ron Dearing questioned the complex and expensive assessment arrangements for GNVQs.[41] Others have voiced doubts about the acceptability of the qualifications to employers and higher education institutions. According to DfEE statistics, 82,000 GNVQ students gained a full award in 1996,[42] of whom 20,000 applied for a higher education place. An encouraging 92 per cent of the higher education applicants received offers, yet only 61 per cent finally took up a place.[43] It has also been suggested that these qualifications are more likely to have a currency in the 'new' rather than the 'old' universities.[44]

Improved access to higher education since the early 1980s has not boosted the employment opportunities of all graduates. In 1995, it was reported that Barclays de Zoete Wedd, one of the leading merchant banks, was so doubtful about the quality of emerging university graduates that it had decided to target just five universities – Cambridge, Durham, Edinburgh, Oxford and Trinity College, Dublin – during the recruitment 'milk round'.[45] A graduate recruiter for Mobil Oil commented: 'We target the older, long-established universities where access is difficult. If everybody can get a degree, then some degrees are more valuable than others. A degree is no longer a guarantee of success in the workplace.'[46]

Although graduate employment rates were relatively high throughout the 1980s and 1990s, increasing numbers have proceeded from university into low-paid clerical work. In 1995, Alan Smithers, then a professor of education at Manchester University, reported that 'Jobs done 10 years ago by 16-year-old school-leavers were five years ago being done by those with A-levels. Now it's graduates. It's an inevitable effect of mass higher education.'[47]

Some powerful voices from the business world have been sceptical about the rigour and relevance of both academic and vocational qualifications. Nevertheless, the drive to raise the average level of individuals' qualifications has been strongly supported by many employers. Indeed, in 1991 the Confederation of British Industry (CBI) initiated a policy of setting national targets for foundation and lifelong learning as a strategy for encouraging Britain's global competitiveness. The targets were subsequently adopted, revised upwards and added to by the National Advisory Council for Education and Training Targets (NACETT), established in 1993. The targets now cover everyone involved in education, training or work from the age of 11. It is envisaged that by the year 2002 more learners of all ages will achieve vocational and academic qualifications, adults will receive greater access to training and more employers will encourage workplace learning. The challenges are considerable. Although the percentage of pupils gaining five or more GCSE passes at A*–C in recent years has improved, the proportion of pupils – mostly boys – leaving school with no qualifications has stubbornly remained at around 8 per cent. In November 1998, 75,000 young people were reported to be out of education, training or work, while a further 85,000 young people aged 16–17 were working in unskilled jobs without training or qualifications.[48] Some 52 per cent of people without qualifications were recently reported to be in employment. By contrast, 78 per cent of those with A-levels or equivalent were in employment, earning on average 25 per cent more than unqualified workers.[49] The most important targets, however, are those relating to performance in basic literacy and numeracy. In March 1999, a report by Sir Claus Moser indicated that seven million British adults encountered difficulties in these areas. The report suggested that one in five adults was unable to locate the page reference for plumbers in a *Yellow Pages* directory and one in four unable to calculate the change due from £2 when buying goods worth £1.35.[50]

TECs and the delivery of workforce skills

In December 1988, five months after the enactment of the most centralizing measure in the history of English education, Margaret Thatcher's Conservative government indicated that, henceforth, more control and responsibility for training would be exercised at a local level. The White Paper, *Employment in the 1990s,* was written, significantly, by civil servants in the Employment department, rather than by MSC personnel who by then were tainted by their closeness to the trade unions and by their preoccupations with short-term solutions to unemployment rather than with long-term economic success.[51] The White Paper announced the establishment of TECs in England and Wales and Local Enterprise Companies (LECs) in Scotland. According to Green, this development was consistent with the Conservative government's drive to reduce the influence of trade unions and to return to a 'demand-led, employer-controlled training system'.[52] As Evans has argued, however, another key element of government thinking was 'the repeated failure of British employers to commit themselves adequately to training'.[53] Rather than providing training themselves, TECs were to 'form contracts for its provision with private employers, public and voluntary bodies and private sector training agencies'.[54] The TEC initiative showed some similarity with Enterprise Zones and urban development corporations, both of which had sought to work with local authorities, employers and the voluntary sector during the early and mid-1980s.[55] It shifted control from the centre to the localities but, at the same time, ushered in a training market entirely under the government's direct management. The Training Agency (TA), as the MSC had become, was left with a diminished and contradictory role. TECs were to operate on market principles, but were ultimately answerable to the TA.[56] Government control was also exercised via a National Training Task Force (NTTF) which vetted applications to run local TECs. The shift towards decentralized training, therefore, was only partial.

In 1991, the formation of the first TECs and of a semi-privatized training service reduced the role of the Department of Employment (DE), causing some to speculate whether it had outlived its usefulness.[57] In early 1990 it was reported that the Prime Minister, Margaret Thatcher, wanted to abolish the DE, transferring its training functions to the DES.[58] The Society of Education Officers and the Association of County Councils shared this view, although for different reasons.[59] In July 1991 a leaked confidential memorandum suggested that tensions between DE civil servants and the TECs were increasing, a perception that had been apparent a month before in the evidence of two local TEC Chairs to the House of Commons Employment Committee.[60] Views about the TECs varied. John Major believed that they would stimulate enterprise and effect a closer association between training and economic development. Some saw them as essentially providing training for the unemployed, while others hoped that they would be the agents for a transfer from 'welfare' to 'workfare' and for the reform of social security policy.[61] Debates also focused on questions of accountability and whether the TECs should be exempt from Civil Service interference.[62] From the outset, therefore, the TECs suffered from an identity crisis, heightened by individual TEC managers' prioritization of a range of different objectives.[63]

After 1993, relations deteriorated between the TECs and further education colleges.[64] The incorporation of the colleges saw them engaged in power struggles with LEAs and TECs for control of sixth-form facilities, courses and funding. In April 1995 the controversial work-related further education programme was abolished; control of the funding was returned from the TECs to the colleges. The TECs, however, were authorized to approve colleges' strategic plans and controlled the £20 million 'competitiveness fund' earmarked to help colleges meet specific local labour market needs.[65] The absence of reciprocal arrangements contributed to the colleges' sense of injustice.[66] The head of the DfEE's further education branch recognized the 'potential tension' in these arrangements, but hoped for a 'fruitful synergy' between the Further Education Funding Council (FEFC) and the TECs.[67] Such hopes were in vain. Tension erupted into major hostilities as the TECs accused the colleges of 'buying' students to boost enrolment on franchised courses. In return, colleges complained that TECs, themselves, were seeking to provide training which should have been purchased from the colleges.[68]

The TECs hoped that the merger between the Education and Employment departments would resolve these potential conflicts. The division of junior ministerial responsibilities within the new department, however, seemed to accentuate them. Post-compulsory education and training was split between Eric Forth, who was placed in charge of higher education and the old Employment department briefs, Lord Henley, responsible for vocational qualifications, and James Paice, whose remit included further education and the TECs. Sir Geoffrey Holland, by this time installed as Vice-Chancellor of the University of Exeter, was scathing about the structure: 'There is no point in bringing the two departments together if you are not going to integrate them and that integration of programme, policy and organization needs to be reflected at ministerial level, when so far it has not.'[69]

Much international interest was aroused by the creation of the TECs. By 1994, however, the Organization for Economic Co-operation and Development (OECD) had reached the conclusion that they had 'fallen short of initial expectations'.[70] The growth of work-based training left some TECs resentful about 'churning out numbers on government programmes',[71] rather than matching skills training to employers' needs. The move to a system of payment-by-results funding was also to prove damaging. It has been suggested that this led to some TECs focusing on cheap, low-level NVQ training, reflected in a 1996 *Observer* headline 'TECs create a nation of service workers'.[72] The reputation of the TECs was further damaged by examples of financial mismanagement, as evidenced by the dramatic collapse of the South Thames TEC in December 1994 and various instances of fraud.[73] In April 1999, David Blunkett commented that the large severance payment awarded to the outgoing Chief Executive of a poor-performing TEC could have funded the training of some 200 unemployed persons.[74] These unfortunate episodes, together with the recent exposure of financial mismanagement within the FE sector, have raised questions about whether the move to a devolved system of training is actually more efficient than a centralized approach.

In advance of the 1997 general election, the Labour leadership let it be known that TECs were only guaranteed to survive the first two years of a Labour government. This inaugurated a period of intense lobbying by the TECs to secure a future.[75] In November 1996, Chris Humphries, then Chief Executive of the TEC National Council, argued that:

> TECs are not about running government training programmes. They are about addressing the fact that, in a modern economy, it is skills that make economic regeneration possible. By putting skills at the core of regeneration it is possible to merge economic success with social objectives leading to job creation, social cohesion and a reduction in disadvantage.[76]

In the event, the TECs survived the two-year amnesty, but their future remained under review. Friction resurfaced between the TECs and the Employment Service, following the announcement of the government's plans for the New Deal for the young unemployed.[77] An early Labour initiative sought to introduce greater accountability in the wake of a civil servant's admission that the TECs 'spend more than £1.5 billion a year but it is very hard to tell how well they are doing'.[78] Labour's first Minister for Lifelong Learning, Dr Kim Howells, introduced a system of performance tables similar to school league tables so that comparisons could be made between TECs, colleges and training companies.[79] Unsurprisingly, early indications were that the performance of individual TECs was variable.[80]

The creation of National Training Organizations (NTOs) in May 1998 and Regional Development Agencies (RDAs), in April 1999 placed a further question mark against the TECs' *raison d'être*. At the launch of the first 55 NTOs, David Blunkett commented that:

> For far too long industry has complained that education is not preparing young people properly for the world of work. We are addressing this through our drive to raise standards in schools and our commitment to creating a learning society. NTOs are ideally placed to contribute to both initiatives, since part of their brief involves telling schools, colleges and universities what skills are required by industry.[81]

In May 1999 David Blunkett announced that NTOs would play a more central role in relation to Modern Apprenticeships training, workforce development and NVQ training.[82] RDAs are now responsible for advising the government on appropriate regional strategies to determine skill requirements, thereby creating the possibility of a new turf war, this time between the DfEE and the Department of the Environment, Transport and the Regions (DETR). In 1998, the House of Commons Education and Employment Committee recommended that TECs should come under the control of RDAs.[83] Reports in the press, however, suggested that behind the scenes the DfEE was resisting such an outcome. If ministers agreed the transfer of funding arrangements from the DfEE to the RDAs (and hence to the DETR) 'that would be an abdication of their responsibilities to Parliament for promoting national training policies and ensuring important national objectives'.[84] Notwithstanding the creation of NTOs and RDAs some commentators have favoured the retention of TECs, though only as skills agencies responsible for the training of unemployed adults and to oversee the Modern Apprenticeships scheme. A classic Old Labour–New Labour dilemma may be detected in current disputes, with TECs occupying the battleground both between public and private and between central and local. An *Observer* editorial of March 1999 was uncompromising in its declaration that TECs were 'One of the most disastrous legacies of the Conservative years'. It continued:

> A handful have been innovative and progressive; the majority have not. A patchy, unpredictable system has developed, haunted by short-term budget crises and poor standards. Unrepresentative cliques have dominated policy in some areas; forward planning has been lamentable.[85]

At the end of May 1999, the *Financial Times* reported that issues of post-16 funding and delivery mechanisms for work-based training were to be considered by a Cabinet Committee. TECs, it speculated, would probably be abolished on the grounds that they had failed to solve skills shortages not only in such areas as management, information technology, customer care and technical skills, but also in low-paid and relatively unskilled work. This scenario, the report noted, would represent a victory for DfEE officials seeking to restore centralized control over training by 'emasculating' the TECs.[86]

Training, equal opportunities and economic efficiency

One of the more positive outcomes of the 'new vocationalism' of the 1980s was its commitment to work towards equal opportunities. The consensus that developed around such notions as 'employability' and 'upskilling' looked beyond traditional forms of schooling that had historically failed girls and women, reinforced institutional racism and marginalized the disabled. Formal commitments to equal opportunities were pledged by the MSC, the Careers Service and the Education and Employment departments.[87] For the MSC, as Evans has noted, the 'motive was clearly economic rather than social as the main intention was to exploit the full range of adult skills in the wider population'.[88] The MSC reasoned that economic recovery would best be served by opening up opportunities to previously excluded groups.[89] Such thinking lay behind the publication of *No Barriers Here*, which argued that although talent was equally distributed between the sexes, women were under-represented in higher management positions. Firms, therefore, should be proactive in encouraging change in the way women's jobs were conceived. Similarly, in 1986 the DE declared that:

> We must achieve a coherent vocational education and training system which serves the interest of all – wherever they live, irrespective of income, sex or race. ... But standards need to be defined and achievement of them recognised in a way which is widely understood. That is the role of the vocational qualifications system.[90]

These statements were widely welcomed. For example, in 1990, Gaby Weiner noted that improved training opportunities for women now determined 'that feminists have been provided with a foothold in the new system, which they never had in the old'.[91]

Women's participation on government training courses, however, remained low, despite the public position of the MSC and of the government. For example, in 1984 only three per cent of trainees on government skill centre training for the unemployed were women.[92] In the same year, Sir Keith Joseph argued that the problem was 'the attitude of parents and of girls themselves'. Young women, he suggested, were choosing not to take up places on MSC programmes and, in particular, were avoiding science and engineering courses.[93] Other explanations, however, were afforded. According to Caroline Benn, entry to a number of the better quality YTS schemes was controlled by criteria that favoured white middle-class males. Of the YTS, she has argued that:

> Despite much MSC jargon, there was little real skills training, much narrow male and female work patterning, racial inequality, health and safety failures, lack of accountability and impoverished educational input. ... Over-weighted with working class and ethnic minority youth, trainees suffered a shocking lack of rights, and no redress when employers failed to deliver on their side of the training bargain, a frequent occurrence.[94]

During the 1990s developments in training policy were characterized by equality of opportunity, rather than equality of outcome. The dominant view within the TECs and in government was that equality is a matter of providing equal life chances by preventing discrimination through legislation, that is by removing barriers to the free working of the market. In 1991, TEC directors presented their views on equal opportunities in oral evidence to the Employment Committee. Asked if he needed any additional resources to help women back into work, the Chair of the Hertfordshire TEC said 'no more so than for the overall population'.[95] The Chair of the Devon and Cornwall TEC added that 'if in Devon and Cornwall we were seen as treating women differently from men we would be greatly criticized because they consider themselves very much as equals and that is how we treat them'. He denied that there were any barriers to women gaining access to courses and jobs provided through his TEC, adding 'No. It is interesting in the West Country that we are see-ing the incidence of women increasing generally within the workforce.'[96] The TEC chairs saw their job as upgrading skills generally as part of an enterprise brief, not just as training the unemployed or otherwise dealing with the social side of the training question. Asked if he saw his role as challenging stereotypes, the Chair of the South East Cheshire TEC replied:

> No, not put that way, I do not think it is. I talked about getting the skill level of the whole workforce higher and that applies right across the board, whatever the ethnic origins, sex or whatever. It is an overall problem and I do not think we can differentiate or try to change that stereotyping.[97]

During the 1980s and 1990s, the position of girls and women greatly improved within the education system. The introduction of a National Curriculum and stronger coursework components into GCSE and A-level courses were adduced as explanations for the superior performance of girls in public examinations. In December 1995, Gillian Shephard indi-cated to the Employment Select Committee that her greatest anxieties revolved around boys' failures:

> Not that we are not delighted the girls are doing well, but we do not want disaffected boys turning into disaffected and difficult-to-employ young men. This is a bonus, you could say, that we have from the merged department, in that we can watch both developments, do something about them at school and college level, so that the problem does not feed through into the workplace.[98]

Boys' difficulties have also been attributed to such problems as the lack of male role models in primary education and often in the home, and being less skilled than girls in exercising communication skills at school.[99] The 1990s have also seen women comprise the majority of students both in further and higher education. Statistics for work-based training and from the labour market, however, showed less evidence of change. At a conference of the Girls' Schools Association in 1994, Shephard, then Secretary of State for Education, was generally positive that the nation was becoming more accommodating towards women's careers aspirations and domestic circumstances. She noted with approval an improvement in the employment rate for women graduates, but also recognized that further progress was needed. At that time, according to the Secretary of State, women comprised only 2 per cent of the membership of large company boards, 3 per cent of surgeons, 8 per cent of architects and 6 per cent of MPs.[100] At the lower levels of vocational training, too, there continue to be grounds for concern about equality, not only for women but also for ethnic minority groups and the disabled. Historically, 'women's work' has been generally defined as unskilled, regardless of the nature or complexity of the task.[101] Working-class girls, in particular, are offered few incentives or opportunities to train for high status, new technology areas.[102] A 1996 report by Unwin and Wellington found that nine out of 10 of the first 700 Modern Apprentices were white males. Trainees with disabilities were under-represented and recruitment was weighted towards those of above average ability, many of whom already possessed a vocational qualification.[103] More recent data for the Modern Apprenticeships scheme confirm that female participation differs widely between sectors, with very low proportions, for example, in construction and electrical installation engineering and very high proportions in the hairdressing and childcare sectors. Perhaps surprisingly, however, a majority of those working towards National Traineeships were female. These data also indicate that ethnic minority participation varies from 7 per cent in childcare to just 1 per cent in construction and plumbing. Disabled persons' participation ranges from 1 to 5 per cent across the sectors.[104]

In terms of equal opportunities, the New Deal is the most transparent of all the government programmes intended to combat unemployment since 1981. Detailed statistics are published each month. Prior to May 1999, 73 per cent of the 140,200 New Deal for Young People participants were male, 29 per cent of all participants were black and 13 per cent had a disability. The comparable statistics for the New Deal for those aged 25 and over were 84 per cent, 16 per cent and 19 per cent.[105] More data are needed, of course, to judge the effectiveness of the New Deal in challenging endemic discrimination. Individuals from ethnic minorities, including graduates, have consistently experienced difficulties in finding work that fully utilizes their skills and talents. In 1997 the ethnic minority unemployment rate was reported to be twice that for the white population. This question continues to present a major challenge, especially as over the next few years the ethnic minority section of the labour market is set to grow from the current 6 per cent to 10 per cent.[106] One recent newspaper report indicated that ethnic minority representatives have been largely excluded from some New Deal partnerships and that inequalities in the unsubsidized labour market continued disproportionately to exclude black jobseekers.[107]

Labour and lifelong learning

While British employment rates have fluctuated since the 1980s, there has been a consistent decline in job security. In 1995, a survey by Austin Knight, the private sector employment agency, revealed that fear of redundancy drove two-thirds of white-collar employees to work for 40 hours or more each week and one-quarter for 50 hours or more.[108] As Chris Humphries, Chief Executive of the TEC National Council and subsequently Director-General of the British Chambers of Commerce, has commented, the disappearance of job security marks the return to a more orthodox labour market:

> A job for life was only ever available to a privileged minority, and has in fact been a construct of the 20th century. It only existed for a limited period, but it has been a paradigm by which individual security has been judged and that is causing insecurity to enter the expectations of most of today's and tomorrow's workforce.[109]

The importance of 'lifetime learning', a term that had featured prominently in the 1993 National Commission report, underpinned the first objectives produced by the Department for Education and Employment in 1995.[110] At a political level, however, the Conservative government capitalized very little on the theme of lifetime or lifelong learning. This could not be said of the Labour Party. Many of its policy statements and publications envisaged a society in which continuous learning would be the norm. Early in 1996, however, Labour abandoned its longstanding commitment to impose a compulsory training levy on employers. The party was concerned not to alienate the CBI, already anxious about the possible consequences of the EU Social Chapter and the national minimum wage. *Learn As You Earn: Labour's Plans for a Skills Revolution* outlined a new partnership of individuals, enterprises and government to create a learning society.[111] Individual Learning Accounts, Investors in People status for employers and a University for Industry were key elements in this new scenario. In a major speech on education delivered at the University of Birmingham shortly before the 1997 general election Tony Blair recalled:

> When I was growing up, most people thought that you could go to school until the age of 16 or 18 and guarantee yourself a decent standard of living, a secure job, a chance to bring up your family well, and have something to retire on. But the old rules have changed. The new economy demands new skills and more education. We cannot survive on the belief that education ends at 16 or 18. That is why we will promote the idea of lifelong learning.[112]

Labour's election victory led to the appointment of Dr Kim Howells as the first Parliamentary Under Secretary for Lifelong Learning. The DfEE also re-organized its management structure, with the experienced Nick Stuart becoming Director-General of the Employment, Lifelong Learning and International Directorate. In January 1998, however, government critics suggested that the lifelong learning policy was in disarray, following a late decision to abandon a widely trailed White Paper on the subject. It was reported that Downing Street had taken the decision not to proceed because the Prime Minister balked at the costs involved in substantially increasing FE student numbers, as recommended seven months earlier by a committee chaired by Baroness Helena Kennedy.[113] Insiders also suggested that the aborted White Paper contained 'too much about trying to change the culture of training in Britain and not enough about standards and exams'.[114] National and local conferences having already been organized to coincide with its intended publication, in February a consultative Green Paper, *The Learning Age*, was published in its place.[115] Despite this unpromising background, the Green Paper attracted some 3,000 responses, most of them favourable. Labour seemed divided between a view of post-16 education and training as investment and a source of economic regeneration or as a drain on public spending. The former position was associated with David Blunkett and the DfEE; the latter with Gordon Brown and the Treasury.

The policy of lifelong learning has been presented within the context of the Prime Minister's aspirations for 'joined up' government. In a 1998 interview posted on the DfEE's lifelong learning website Nick Stuart candidly acknowledged the incoherence of post-16 education and training reforms over many years:

> Taking an historical perspective ... there was not really a concept of lifelong learning 10 years ago, even really five years ago. There was nothing at central government level that pulled together Further Education, Higher Education, Local Authority Adult Education, Community Learning, Advice and Guidance for Adults, Careers Education, help for the unemployed, Investors in People and workforce development more generally.[116]

Two central elements in the current drive for lifelong learning are the University for Industry (UfI) and Individual Learning Accounts (ILAs). The UfI has two principal aims: to stimulate demand for lifelong learning among businesses and individuals and to promote improved access to and availability of training and education through information and communication technology (ICT). Using a range of open and distance learning techniques, and with funding from the European Social Fund, private and public sectors, the UfI aims to stimulate demand for one million courses and learning packages a year by the year 2004. David Blunkett has predicted that the UfI will be a major force in 'improving business competitiveness and enhancing individuals' employability'.[117] The UfI is a university for the twenty-first century. Learning is expected to take place not only in schools and colleges, but also via the Internet and interactive digital television in libraries, the home, the workplace and even in shopping centres. ILAs are successors to the National Record of Achievement, free profiles introduced in 1991 to help 16 year olds to document their learning successes. The government has pledged to put £150 into each of the first million ILAs. From September 2000, discounts of up to 80 per cent will be offered on the costs of certain training courses, including some supplied by the UfI.

The success of the lifelong learning policy rests to a large extent upon whether the various agencies involved in its delivery – broadcasters, colleges, employers, government, LEAs and universities, among others – can interact and combine without creating the kinds of rivalries that have undermined previous training initiatives. Underpinning the current drive is a belief that ICT developments will fundamentally change the nature of learning, of business transactions and of national competitiveness in the early part of the twenty-first century. Immediate objectives include the linking of all schools to the Internet and the National Grid for Learning, the 'upskilling' of teachers and librarians in the use of ICT, more partnerships with digital broadcasters and a national network of ICT centres.

Education, employment and business

In 1995, the merger between the Education and Employment departments presaged closer relationships between schools, colleges and universities and employers. Gillian Shephard, herself a former careers adviser, required secondary schools to provide a programme of careers education and guidance for all students in years nine to 11 (ages 14–16). An action plan for the training of school advisers was also introduced, following criticisms from such bodies as the National Association of Careers and Guidance Teachers. In 1997 a spokesperson for this organization commented: 'In some cases, there are teachers who have been trained and in some cases, it is just a job which was, say, given to the Latin teacher after Latin became defunct, or to an ageing PE teacher.'[118]

The Technology Colleges programme, launched in September 1993, was subsequently extended to cover all specialist schools. Under Conservative and Labour governments this programme has sought to increase private sector involvement in the management of schools, notwithstanding the limited success of the CTCs. Among the current sponsors of specialist schools – of which there were 330 in October 1998, rising to 400 in September 1999 – are HSBC Bank, British Aerospace and Manchester United Football Club. A target of 500 such schools has been set for the year 2002.[119] The tendency for schools to develop business links, however, has not been confined to those with specialist status. It was recently estimated that almost half of English and Welsh primary schools and over 90 per cent of secondary schools have established links with the private sector.[120] As well as offering sponsorship and work experience it is not uncommon for companies to be working with schools in the areas of financial, ICT and management training and the mentoring of – usually disaffected – pupils.

During the 1980s and early 1990s there were frequent suggestions from those on the 'new right' that businesses could play a major role in the drive to improve educational standards. Since 1997, a new Labour government has also looked to the private sector to provide radical solutions to educational problems that the public sector has failed to solve.

Education Action Zones are one high-profile initiative to encourage business investment and involvement in the running of education services. The government hopes that leading businesses will work with poor-performing and/or disadvantaged schools and LEAs to raise standards. A second manifestation occurred early in 1999 when a business offshoot of Kingshurst City Technology College in Solihull called '3Es' – named after Tony Blair's election priorities of 'education, education, education' – was awarded a contract to revive a flagging school in Guildford.[121] The third, and most radical, development in this area may see failing LEAs swept away to be replaced by private sector contractors.

Over the past 20 years, links between higher education institutions and business have also been strengthened. Companies have sponsored research, equipment, campus buildings and professorial chairs. The expansion of undergraduate degree programmes in such areas as business and media studies has seen more students undertake a period of work experience, a practice previously more common with scientific and engineering courses. Students following courses in the arts and humanities, however, were unlikely to have contact with the worlds of business and industry before making applications for employment. This may soon change. In April 1999 the government signalled its expectations that universities should play a more central role in working with local businesses and stimulating regional competitiveness. In the future, a minimum period of work experience may become a requirement for all students in higher education.

Conclusion

Since 1979, successive governments have introduced a variety of schemes designed to prepare young unemployed persons for employment and to help those made redundant to learn new skills with a view to re-entering the labour market. For much of this period, resources were directed towards reducing levels of youth unemployment, while providing job-related training of variable quality.

During the 1990s, as unemployment decreased, more emphasis was placed upon educational standards, the acquisition of vocational qualifications and the provision of equal opportunities. All were seen as valuable in their own right, but also as essential to the improvement of national economic efficiency and competitiveness. At the same time, the receding possibility of a job for life and the developing concept of life-long learning reduced some of the old distinctions and contests between education and training. Lifelong learning implied not only a firm grasp of basic literacy and numeracy but also a concern with core transferable skills, for example problem-solving, communication, teamwork, Information and Communication Technology (ICT).

Another significant theme of the 1980s and 1990s was the promotion of closer co-operation between the worlds of education and business. The creation of the Department for Education and Employment seemed to confirm this policy, and it continued unabated following the Conservative defeat of May 1997. Indeed, since that date, a Labour government has not only encouraged closer links between the worlds of education and work, but also indicated that failures in public sector provision of education, whether at institutional, area or local authority level, may lead to the adoption of private sector solutions.

Where does the merged department fit in this scenario? In 1991, the Chair of the NCVQ, Sir Bryan Nicholson, suggested that 'what you have at the moment is a system in which a balance of interests often compete together but generally collaborate together' and where strongly differing viewpoints arose over an issue 'it is very useful to have two departments because you can appeal to one against the other'.[122] After the merger, LEAs, colleges, TECs, teacher unions and other educational bodies could no longer appeal to one department against another to settle disputes. Failure on their part to co-operate in support of government policy might well lead to further centralization of power or increasing recourse to private initiatives.

Notes

1. House of Commons Employment Committee. Session 1994–95, HC 458-ii. *The Work of the Employment Department*. London: HMSO. Minutes of Evidence, 11 July 1995, q. 242.

2. See Deakin, 1996, 82–83.
3. Green, 1995, 98.
4. Blackman and Evans, 1994, 2.
5. Green, 1995, 99.
6. Ploszajska, 1994, 49.
7. Green, 1995, 99.
8. Hurrelman and Roberts, 1991, 242.
9. Green, 1995; Ploszajska, 1994, 49.
10. Blackman and Evans, 1994, 14.
11. Green, 1995, 99.
12. Mason, 1988, 38.
13. National Commission on Education, 1995, 5.
14. Papadopoulos, 1994, 151
15. *DfEE News* 140/97, 11 June 1997.
16. *DfEE News* 133/97, 5 June 1997.
17. See, for example, *Financial Times*, 3 July 1997.
18. *DfEE News* 227/99, 19 May 1999.
19. *DfEE News* 550/98, 25 November 1998.
20. *DfEE News* 217/99, 17 May 1999.
21. *DfEE News* 238/99, 27 May 1999.
22. *DfEE News* 177/99, 21 April 1999.
23. *The Times*, 10 January 1991.
24. *DfE News* 213/94, 30 August 1994.
25. *Sunday Times*, 25 February 1996. Red Adair was a well-known international firefighter.
26. *Daily Telegraph*, 27 August 1998.
27. Blackman and Evans, 1994, 6–7.
28. Montgomery, 1965.
29. *Sunday Times*, 21 April 1996.
30. QCA website at http://www.org.uk/qlnvq22.htm.
31. See, for example, Robinson, 1996.
32. *Independent*, 1 May 1997.
33. See, for example, Beaumont 1995.
34. National Commission, 1993, 280.
35. See, for example, Hodkinson, 1997, 19.
36. Wolf, 1997.
37. *DfEE News* 17/99, 14 January 1999.
38. Quoted in *DfEE News* 574/98, 11 December 1998.
39. Wolf, 1997.

40. *The Times*, 10 April 1995.
41. Capey, 1995; Dearing, 1996.
42. *DfEE News* 270/96, 27 August 1996.
43. *DfEE News* 165/97, 27 June 1997.
44. Anderson and Haywood, 1996.
45. *Sunday Times*, 3 September 1995.
46. Quoted in *Sunday Telegraph*, 3 September 1995.
47. Quoted in *Sunday Times*, 28 May 1998.
48. *DfEE News* 506/98, 3 November 1998.
49. *DfEE News* 115/99, 11 March 1999.
50. Moser, 1999.
51. Evans, 1992, 131.
52. Green, 1995, 99.
53. Evans, 1992, 130.
54. Ploszajska, 1994, 53.
55. Mason, 1988, 31; Evans, 1992, 152.
56. Evans, 1992, 482.
57. See Evans, 1992, 152.
58. *Independent*, 5 January 1990.
59. House of Commons Education, Science and Arts Committee. Session 1990–91, HC 529. Sixth Report. *Education and Training for the 21st Century*. London: HMSO. Memos.
60. Evans, 1992, 185; House of Commons Employment Committee. Session 1990–91, HC 285-I. London: HMSO. Minutes of Evidence, 26 June 1991.
61. For example, King, 1995, 191; Jones, 1996, 145.
62. Bennett, Wicks and McCoshan, 1994, 123.
63. See Tonge, 1993, 21.
64. *TES*, 3 February 1995.
65. *TES*, 23 June 1995.
66. *TES*, 6 June 1997.
67. House of Commons Education Committee, Session 1994–95, HC 649. *Education and Training of 14–19 year olds*. London: HMSO. Minutes of Evidence, 12 July 1995, q. 4.
68. *TES*, 4 August 1995.
69. *Guardian*, 12 July 1995.
70. *Financial Times*, 6 July 1994.
71. *Financial Times,* 4 November 1997.
72. Jones, 1997; *Observer*, 16 June 1996.
73. *Financial Times*, 4 November 1997,

74. *DfEE News* 194/99, 29 April 1999.
75. *TES*, 20 June 1997.
76. Quoted in *Financial Times*, 22 November 1996.
77. *Financial Times*, 4 November 1997.
78. *Financial Times*, 26 August 1997.
79. *TES*, 31 October 1997.
80. *DfEE News* 457/98, 6 October 1998.
81. Quoted in *DfEE News* 235/98, 12 May 1998.
82. *DfEE News* 240/99, 28 May 1999.
83. House of Commons Education and Employment Committee. Session 1997–98, HC 265. Fourth Report, *The Relationship between TECs and the Proposed Regional Development Agencies*. London: The Stationery Office. 25 February 1998.
84. *Observer*, 7 September 1997.
85. *Observer*, 7 March 1999.
86. *Financial Times*, 31 May 1999.
87. Coles and Maynard, 1990, 298.
88. Evans, 1992, 85.
89. Mason, 1988, 23.
90. Department of Employment, 1986, 3, 16.
91. Weiner, 1990, 29.
92. Briar, 1997, 133.
93. Briar, 1997, 134.
94. Benn, 1992, 156.
95. House of Commons Employment Committee. Session 1990–91. HC 285-I. Fifth Report, *TECs and vocational training*. London: HMSO. Minutes of Evidence, 17 April 1991, q. 109.
96. House of Commons Employment Committee. Session 1990–91. HC 285-I. Fifth Report, *TECs and vocational training*. London: HMSO. Minutes of Evidence, 17 April 1991, qs 110-111.
97. House of Commons Employment Committee. Session 1990–91. HC 285-I. Fifth Report, *TECs and vocational training*. London: HMSO. Minutes of Evidence, 17 April 1991, q. 163.
98. House of Commons Employment Committee. Session 1995–96, HC 125. Scrutiny session. London: HMSO. Minutes of Evidence, 19 December 1995, q. 12.
99. *The Times*, 26 April 1997.
100. *DFEE News* 279/94, 9 November 1994.
101. Taylor and Henry, 1994, 108.

102. Brine, 1992, 156.

103. Reported in *TES*, 15 March 1996.

104. *DfEE News* 135/99, 26 March 1999.

105. *DfEE Statistical First Release* SFR 18/1999, 29 July 1999.

106. *DfEE News* 15/97, 28 January 1997.

107. *Guardian*, 22 May 1999.

108. *Independent*, 26 October 1995.

109. Speech at a 1998 DfEE conference 'The Learning Age: Towards a Europe of Knowledge' at http://www.lifelonglearning.co.uk/conference/sp09-ch.htm.

110. *DfEE News* 210/95, 27 September 1995.

111. Labour Party, 1996.

112. Transcript of speech delivered at the Barber Institute, University of Birmingham, 14 April 1997.

113. Kennedy, 1997.

114. *TES*, 13 February 1998.

115. DfEE 1999, *The Learning Age: A Renaissance for Britain* (Green Paper), Cmnd 3790.

116. At http://www.lifelonglearning.co.uk/iln6000/iln7001a.htm.

117. Quoted in *DfEE News* 242/99, 28 May 1999.

118. Quoted in the *Evening Standard*, 23 May 1997.

119. *DfEE News* 496/98, 29 October 1998.

120. *Sunday Times*, 28 February 1999.

121. *TES*, 12 February 1999.

122. House of Commons Education, Science and Arts Committee. Session 1990–91, HC 529. Sixth Report. *Education and Training for the 21st Century*. London: HMSO. Minutes of Evidence, 26 June 1991.

8 Conclusions

Introduction

The first purpose of this study – to provide an historical account and explanation of the relationship between education and employment in the United Kingdom in the twentieth century in its own terms – has now been achieved. Following a general introduction and an examination of the creation of the DfEE in 1995, the next four chapters traced the relationships between the Education and Employment departments from 1900 until 1995. These relationships were considered with three cultural frames in mind – broad intellectual and ideological contexts, complemented by specific political and administrative arrangements. The penultimate chapter explored those issues which have been identified as constituting the 'meat of the merger', and noted the emergence of the concept of lifelong learning.

This concluding chapter focuses upon a second purpose, indicated in the subtitle of the book, of placing the DfEE within that historical account and explanation. Historical perspectives are applied here to contemporary concerns. The discussion is organized under four subheadings: the creation of the DfEE; the status of the new department; current issues; and lifelong learning.

The creation of the DfEE

The creation of the DfEE in 1995 came as a considerable surprise to many. In terms of the historical and cultural perspectives employed in this book, however, it is perfectly explicable. Ideological conflicts on the international and national stages had been replaced by the triumphs of capitalism and competitiveness. In consequence, industrial strife and issues of unemployment had a lower profile within the United Kingdom than at any previous era in the twentieth century. This was reflected at the party political level in that New Labour was adopting much of the previous Thatcherite agenda. At the same time, the internecine strife that characterized Conservative Party politics in the spring and summer of 1995 provided both an opportunity and a justification for rewarding some politicians as opposed to others. The merger also made good administrative sense. Indeed, five of the six main reasons noted in 1984 by Pollitt for establishing new ministerial departments can be identified in the creation of the DfEE: to mark a change in policy or to give extra weight to an existing policy; to give a favourable public impression of dynamic reform; to adapt to major changes in the environment beyond Westminster and Whitehall; to promote better co-ordination, technical efficiency and administrative savings; and to enable the Prime Minister better to utilise the talents of his senior colleagues.[1] The sixth of Pollitt's reasons was to provide for the administration of a new government function. This was not applicable in 1995. Indeed, quite the opposite. The merger reflected the dispersal and relative demise of functions previously exercised by a single ministry.

The creation of the DfEE may also be located within a series of longer historical contexts. The first of these, which pre-dates the twentieth century and, therefore, the period subjected to detailed examination in this book, is the intimate connection between education and employment that has existed across the ages. In primitive societies, as in this country in previous centuries, almost everybody worked from a very early age. Education, therefore, frequently occurred within a vocational context. In common with employment, it might take place over a lifetime. It was for this reason that some medieval classrooms included people of all ages. These links between education and employment were weakened when compulsory age-specific schooling, introduced by central government in the late nineteenth century, was extended and reinforced in the twentieth. This ensured a fundamental divide between education and employment, a divide buttressed by legislation. In 1972 the school-leaving age was raised to 16. Since that date, a range of strategies has been employed to remove even more young people from the labour market. These strategies have included a massive expansion of higher education for some, and 'vocational' initiatives for the remainder.

A second historical perspective arises from the evidence and analysis contained in Chapters Three to Six. Although these reveal substantial changes over time, for example war and peace, boom and slump, they also demonstrate a number of continuities. There has been a recurring debate about the extent to which the modernization of education and employment and of the relationships between them have been impeded by governmental structures and traditional political and administrative elites. This and other debates about the problems of 'adjusting education to industry' have occurred within a range of fundamental contexts and contests, for example those of central and local, public and private.

Before 1995, twentieth-century relationships between the Education and Employment departments were construed within this framework. The artificial, age-related gap between education and employment defeated attempts, both by politicians and by civil servants, to bridge the divide. The problem was exacerbated by the fact that extended schooling, which essentially had been a means of preparing for a particular range of occupations, had become the norm for all. In the 1970s and 1980s, following the Ruskin College speech and the increasing influence of the 'vocationalist modernizers' of the Conservative Party, it appeared that the Employment department and agencies such as the Manpower Services Commission (MSC) had begun to reverse the passage of recent history. They appropriated to themselves substantial sections of the traditional agenda of the Education department.

The vocational initiatives of the 1970s and 1980s have been examined in the two preceding chapters. The logical administrative reform to accompany and co-ordinate such initiatives seemed to be the creation of a Department of Education and Training. This would provide a structure to bridge the perceived longstanding academic–vocational divide. Another key factor was the desire to bring to an end the turf wars, 'unnecessary and costly duplication and ... competition for ideas and resources that had become unproductive'.[2] The addition of Employment in 1995 was justified not only by general concerns that the worlds of education and of work were too far apart, but also by a belief that the provision of a skilled workforce was essential to future economic success.

Prior to 1988, a merged Department of Education and Employment might well have signalled the victory of the vocational modernizers. The Education Act 1988, however, signified a reassertion of the authority of the Education department. The National Curriculum marked a return to a traditional academic curriculum based upon subjects, while the national system of annual assessment was of a type unseen since the days of the infamous Revised Code of 1862.[3] Since 1995, and particularly since 1997, the DfEE has concentrated on schools and standards. David Blunkett has pledged that unless 80 per cent of 11 year olds reach the approved level in English and 75 per cent in mathematics by the year 2002, he will resign. This pledge has nothing to do with 16–19 year-olds, post-compulsory education or vocational training – the areas identified by Michael Bichard as constituting the 'meat of the merger'.

Status

The second conclusion concerns the status of the new department. Has the creation of the DfEE raised the status of Education and Employment within the national culture, and of its ministers and civil servants within the corridors of Westminster and Whitehall?

For much of the twentieth century, the Education and Employment departments were of low status. Employment was at its most prominent in times of national emergency, such as war – indeed the original Ministry of Labour was a wartime creation in 1916 – and in times of recession and unemployment. Conversely, the Education department was at its weakest in such times. From 1979 the determination of Conservative governments to create a free-market, enterprise culture seemed to threaten the status of both departments once more. The Education Reform Act

1988, however, was but the most prominent of several measures designed to increase the powers of the Education department and to reduce those of LEAs and teachers. In contrast, prior to the merger, the Employment department, although naturally more proactive than the Education department in promoting training within industry, as well as good labour relations and economic enterprise, had become marginalized under the Conservatives. For David Blunkett there was an acceptance that 'It was just a fact and a reality that life has changed and so having a department to try and reflect a bygone era did not carry a lot of weight in my view.'[4]

The capacity of ministers has also been important. For much of the twentieth century, both departments suffered under weak ministers. Nevertheless, the Employment department flourished under the leadership of Ernest Bevin in the 1940s, while in the 1980s and 1990s the Education department achieved a high profile with Secretaries of State such as Kenneth Baker and Kenneth Clarke at the helm. Proactive and powerful ministers might produce a great deal of extra work for civil servants. For example, Sir Tim Lankester noted that Conservative reforms at Education involved 'a lot of planning and a large programme of implementation – whether one is talking about the succession of complex education bills, the National Curriculum, the new inspection arrangements in schools, national testing, incorporating the old polytechnics and further education colleges, etc.'[5] The DfEE has boasted able and highly committed ministers in Gillian Shephard and David Blunkett, and a powerful administrative head in Sir Michael Bichard. There can be little doubt that since 1995, and particularly since 1997 and the election slogan of 'Education, education, education', the DfEE has enjoyed a relatively high profile. David Blunkett, as Secretary of State, is very close to, if not an actual member of, the inner circle of key ministers.

In the second half of the twentieth century, some departments, such as the Foreign Office, have seen a relative decline in their power. In contrast, the DfEE has gained a more important place on the political agenda. Billions of pounds have been won for such initiatives as the National Childcare Strategy and the New Deal. For most of the twentieth century, the Education department suffered from being a small entity which consumed a considerable amount of money over which it could exercise little direct control. In April 1998, in assessing his first year in office in an interview with the authors of this book, David Blunkett argued:

> I am not sure that without an amalgamated department I would have been as successful. For two reasons. One, there is an emphasis from us on recognizing the employability and skills agenda for the future rather than short termism in terms of getting people off the dole queue and just boosting the employment figures. Secondly, because a big department with an economic and an education brief actually does have some clout and Balkanized departments don't. Neither the DES nor latterly the Department of Employment had much clout separately. This department does have clout.[6]

Similarly, Sir Michael Bichard, a Permanent Secretary whose own social and educational background does not fit the traditional Whitehall stereotype, told the authors that 'the Department has got an economic arm which actually means that the new department has got a place at Cabinet Committee which Education never had access to. There is no department in Whitehall that is taken seriously unless it has got an economic dimension to it.'[7]

The limitations of the power of the DfEE, however, were apparent in the demise of the *Lifelong Learning* White Paper referred to in Chapter Seven. Downing Street and Treasury priorities triumphed over new thinking about the role of training and of enhanced skills in increasing productivity. There can be little doubt that Gordon Brown's influence as Chancellor of the Exchequer and a key architect of New Labour extends across the whole range of domestic policy. In May 1999, it was Brown who announced a pilot scheme to pay children aged between 16 and 18 of poorer parents some £40 per week to remain at school or college. Later the same month in a speech at the Institute for Fiscal Studies, he stated that 'a Labour Treasury would need to be not just a Ministry of Finance but also a ministry working with other departments to deliver long-term economic and social renewal'. As Peter Riddell has commented: 'In his

Budget speeches Mr Brown has at times seemed to treat the Social Security, Education and Employment and Trade and Industry Secretaries as divisional managers in his Whitehall-led empire. Every decision leads back to the Treasury.'[8]

What of the future? In spite of its many achievements, the application of long historical and broad comparative perspectives raises doubts not only about the efficacy of the DfEE, but also about its continuing existence. As demonstrated in Figure 2, significant changes have occurred in respect of the names and functions of the Education and Employment departments throughout the twentieth century. The processes which produced such changes are set to continue, notwithstanding the creation of the merged department in 1995. Indeed, given that, as indicated in Figure 1, other countries have not produced a similar merger of these two departments, pressures for change may increase rather than diminish. It is important to recognize that prior to the election of 1997 other options were considered. One was to give the DfEE two ministers of Cabinet rank; another was to demerge the department on the grounds that 'the Labour Party opposed it initially and have got a strong natural link to an Employment department'.[9] As Shadow Secretary of State for Education, David Blunkett's preference was for a Department of Education and Training. Although willing, in government, to accept either an Education or an Employment portfolio he concurred with the *fait accompli* of a merged department on the grounds that 'once you had taken the training and skills agenda out of the old Employment Department you did not leave them with a lot'.[10] Nevertheless, further changes, for example the creation of a Department of Trade, Industry and Employment, may yet pave the way for a Department of Education and Training.

Current issues

Current issues facing the merged department are identified here under three broad headings: the nature of education, training and employment; the relationship between education and employment; and cultural problems within and outside the DfEE.

Current priorities for the DfEE, as for many government departments, are demonstrated in the setting and achievement of targets. This is a process in which both ministers and civil servants are to be held accountable. The most highly publicized of these targets concern the achievements of school pupils in English and mathematics at age 11. Dramatic progress towards these targets occurred in the summer of 1999. Some 70 per cent of children tested at key stage two reached level four in English and 69 per cent reached level four in mathematics. These represented increases of five and 10 per cent respectively over the previous year. Similar progress was noted in the field of employment. Between May and July 1999, the numbers of those in employment rose by 54,000 to a record 27.41 million. In August, the number of people claiming unemployment benefit dropped to a 19-year low.

Improvements in test scores are worthy goals, but as Howard Gardiner and Charles Handy, among others, have argued, there are many categories of intelligence and ability and to concentrate on one very limited range of attainments is to run the risk of neglecting so many others. Similar cautionary points may be made about training and employment. As the historical perspectives provided in this book have shown, training has encompassed at least three elements: education, employment and welfare. Much of the training provided under the aegis of the MSC served to remove young people from the job market, rather than to prepare them for it. Indeed, the rise of 54,000 in numbers of the employed between May and July 1999 masked a decline of 24,000 in the number of 16 to 24 year olds in work. Training has been, and remains, a highly contested area, as the recent history of the Training and Enterprise Councils (TECs) has clearly demonstrated. The idea of human capital is widely accepted and Richard Layard, Director of the Centre for Economic Performance at the London School of Economics, is but one commentator who has drawn attention to the decline in the demand for unskilled labour in the United Kingdom and the consequent need for a skilled workforce and a reduction in the supply of unskilled people. The reduction in some types of unskilled or semi-skilled work, however, may be complemented by the mushrooming of others, for example in the service sector. In the second quarter of 1999, manufacturing shed 26,000 jobs, whereas the service industry added 129,000.[11]

Changes in the pattern of work are extremely difficult to interpret and to predict with certainty. Forecasts about further increases in homeworking and in the percentage of women workers have recently been modified. One clear feature, however, has been an increase in some types of paid employment for women. In 1994, Gillian Shephard told the Girls' Schools Association that although women still only represented 2 per cent of the members of the boards of large companies, 3 per cent of surgeons, 6 per cent of MPs and 8 per cent of architects, times were changing.

> Three out of the ten leading companies studied now take in more women graduates than men. ICL heads the field with women occupying as much as 65 per cent of their graduate intake. At Abbey National, half of their 600 branch managers are now women, compared with only a dozen 10 years ago. Twenty years ago, only one in ten newly qualified accountants was a woman; now it's nearly half.[12]

Uncertainties concerning the natures of education, training and employment are reflected in the second issue to be considered here: the uncertainty about the relationship between them. Understandably, leading figures at the DfEE are committed to the doctrine that investment in education and training is the best means of promoting national economic success and of minimizing levels of unemployment. Thus, in March 1999, in a speech in Dusseldorf, David Blunkett declared that 'Investment in human capital – in people and in their skills and knowledge – will be as important as investment in plant and machinery was in the last century.'[13] Economic success and full employment may well be the product of superior education and training, but other factors must be considered. For example, in international comparisons of educational standards and skilled workers, the children and young people of France and Germany frequently score higher than those of the United Kingdom and the United States of America do. The British workforce contains some 6.8 million employees whose highest qualification falls below grade C at GCSE.[14] Nevertheless, between 1992 and 1998 unemployment in France and Germany remained stubbornly above 10 per cent, while that in the United Kingdom and United States of America fell steadily to 5 per cent. Some 70 per cent of working-age Americans and Britons are in paid work, as compared to only 60 per cent in France.[15] These differences in unemployment rates do not necessarily reflect differences in educational standards and training skills. They may be attributed to a variety of factors, from the acceptance of an enterprise culture and the use of monetary policy to stimulate growth and employment on the one hand, to the decline of trade union power and restrictive practices and the lack of protection and consequent low pay afforded to many US and British workers on the other. History shows that there has been no consistent relationship between education, training and employment. In a recent paper reporting on longitudinal data from Germany and the United Kingdom over the last 170 years, Carpentier and Diebolt have stated that:

> Results indicate that human capital investment prior to 1945 was a response to economic growth. It was only from 1945 that human capital investment appears to have driven economic growth. A shift since 1973 leads to doubts as to whether the post-war human capital-driven growth is being sustained. The results raise the question of whether human capital investment might be as much a consequence as a cause of economic stability.[16]

Increased investment and direction in education and training and the raising of skill levels may be of value in many ways, but they do not of themselves guarantee either a reduction in unemployment or an improvement in the economy. Indeed, education and training may consume resources, both human and financial, which from an economic standpoint could be more effectively deployed.

Understanding of these issues may be enhanced by a further consideration of the comparative perspective. In the late 1980s and early 1990s much attention was focused on the educational and economic successes of some Pacific Rim countries. Viewed from an historical perspective, however, such success can be correctly interpreted for what it is: the modest clawing back of a former position which nevertheless began to run into difficulties in 1997. At the beginning of the nineteenth century 'Asia still accounted for about 58 per cent of the world's GDP. By 1920 this figure had been more than halved. Over the following 20 years, Asia's share fell further, to 19 per cent, though Asia was home to 60 per cent of the world's population.'[17]

Cultural issues facing the DfEE are of two kinds. The first concerns the production of a unified culture within the department. The very title of Department for Education and Employment enshrines the names of two antecedents which, as this book has shown, throughout the twentieth century have exhibited significant differences in terms of size, function and organization. The numbers of Employment department staff were commonly some 10 times greater than those of the Education department, and the Employment department had a local identity in the shape of employment exchanges and benefit offices. The Education department, on the other hand, was a policy department which had to rely on co-operation or coercion, both of the Local Education Authorities (LEAs) which owned most of the schools and of the teachers who were employed within them. The two departments operated within different legislative frameworks. Prior to the merger, the Employment department had wide powers to inter- vene and spend; the Education department did not. Divergent organiza- tional cultures arose from the different structures and relationships with their constituencies. Gillian Shephard acknowledged these differences, arguing that 'the two heritages of the Departments fit them to play different roles' and conceding that adjustment to a single culture 'won't have been entirely comfortable for everyone'. [18]

As yet, the potential changes in culture envisaged by the creation of the DfEE, namely the bridging of divides between education and training on the one hand and employment and industry on the other, have not been achieved. In one sense, this is understandable, given that a mere five years have elapsed. As David Blunkett has acknowledged, although in Opposition Labour had promised a merged programme of education and training at post-16 level:

A post-16 agenda is very difficult. We have greater difficulty in producing final policy proposals because I do not think the department is
geared in the same way to dealing with it ... there was no integrated
structure which pulled together further and higher education with the
wider skills perspective, the relationship to the world of work and to
new technologies. [19]

Nevertheless, it is apparent that of itself a merger of two departments at
central level, complemented by the introduction of private sector ethos
and methods and top-down managerialist intervention is unlikely to
achieve these ends. Substantial and effective change will depend upon
convergence and co-operation at three different levels. These are: the
administrative culture of the department and its agencies, those political
and organizational cultures which permeate Westminster and Whitehall
and the broad national culture.

There can be no doubt that since 1995 the DfEE has been a site of considerable change. For example, in 1998 Edward de Bono, the expert in
lateral thinking, was brought in to show its civil servants how to make
radical decisions. Sir Michael Bichard has argued that the aim of the
DfEE is 'not just bringing together two cultures' but the creation of 'a
different culture, a different kind of government department'. [20] He has
been strongly critical both of the former departments and of the attitudes
of senior civil servants across Whitehall. For example, in January 1998
in an interview with the authors of this book, he noted that 'When I came
here the department was very strong on administration and very strong
on the law of education ... but actually knew absolutely nothing about
teaching in the classroom.'[21] In September 1999 in an interview reported
in *The Stakeholder,* Sir Michael launched an unprecedented attack on
Civil Service colleagues who thought that 'if we keep our heads down
people like Bichard will bugger off':

If you were to put down the things that stifle creativity ... you would
have a good description of the way the Civil Service has worked: a
word-based culture, hierarchical, exclusive, doesn't work across
departments, doesn't involve outsiders. If we don't have a Civil Service

which is fast-moving, vibrant and creative, we've got real problems in this country.[22]

Sir Michael advocates a change in the 'gradist culture' typical of the Civil Service to one more focused on performance outcomes and merit. He believes that all permanent secretaries should have a mandatory 12–18 months 'operational management experience' in the private or public sector, and that they should be subject to regular assessment by the National Audit Office. He favours the devolution of more responsibility to junior staff, increased co-operation with external agencies in the private and public sectors, and with other government departments such as Health and Social Security.

In 1995 an administrative change occurred with the merging of two relatively second-ranking Whitehall departments. Even at the departmental level, it is clear that many of the traditional tensions in organization, culture and function remain at the centre, while others have been displaced to other levels of the system, both regional and local. As yet, it appears that cultural change has been confined largely to the general managerialist reforms common to many Whitehall departments. 'New Public Management' approaches to cultural change, however, especially if subject to traditional Civil Service modifications, will be insufficient to achieve the larger aims in respect of unification of education and training, the raising of standards and the promotion of a skilled workforce envisaged at the time of the creation of the DfEE and reflected in its statements of policy. Change must occur within a broader set of contexts, both within central government and in the country at large.

The second issue is how to provide a more integrated and productive administrative culture encompassing education and employment throughout the nation. Should restructuring at the centre be followed by restructuring at the local level? The Conservative governments of Margaret Thatcher and John Major contemplated the withering away of LEAs and the universal application of grant-maintained status to schools. Since 1997, the Labour government of Tony Blair has proclaimed a new era of partnership with LEAs. At the same time, however, it has introduced the Office for Standards in Education (OFSTED) inspections of LEAs on a five-year cycle, and has placed advertisements encouraging non-profit making private and public sector organizations to take over responsibilities from poorly performing LEAs. Provision has also been made for private companies to provide and run schools, including those in the Education Action Zones.

One particularly contentious issue has been the role of the TECs, a legacy from the Conservative era, which exemplified all of the historical tensions between centre and locality, training and employment. These tensions were compounded by uncertainties surrounding the precise roles of the TECs, their overlaps with other bodies, and increasing concerns about their financial viability and accountability. Proposals for the TECs to come under the aegis of the new Regional Development Agencies led to a new turf war with the Department of the Environment, Transport and the Regions (DETR).

Lifelong learning

The final conclusion takes up the theme of lifelong learning.

The DfEE's Business Plan for 1998–99 outlined three objectives:

1. Ensuring that all young people reach 16 with the skills, attitudes and personal qualities that will give them a secure foundation for lifelong learning, work and citizenship in a rapidly changing world.
2. Developing in everyone a commitment to lifelong learning, so as to enhance their lives, improve their employability in a changing labour market and create the skills that our economy and employers need.
3. To help people without a job into work.[23]

These are challenging and worthy objectives, which the faint-hearted might prefer to regard as aims. The third is both noticeably briefer and less confident than the others – an accurate reflection, perhaps, of the uncertainties that surround employment in the changing labour markets of a rapidly changing world.

The concept of lifelong learning is common to the first two objectives and is timely in at least two senses. It provides a link with the historic relationship between education and employment that preceded the introduction of compulsory age-specific schooling in the last quarter of the nineteenth century. It reflects the increasing opportunities for self-directed education afforded by the development of information and communications technology. The DfEE's place in history may well be bound up with the extent to which lifelong learning becomes a reality. For this is a key concept and goal for the twenty-first century, worthy to rank with those of national efficiency at the beginning of the twentieth century and national competitiveness at the end, and yet with the potential to surpass them both.

Notes

1. Pollitt, 1984, 128.
2. Letter from Sir Tim Lankester to Professor Richard Aldrich, 17 July 1998.
3. The Revised Code of 1862 introduced an annual inspection of children in six standards in the '3 Rs': reading, writing and arithmetic. The system subsequently underwent considerable modifications and was abolished in the 1890s.
4. Interview with David Blunkett, 23 April 1998.
5. Letter from Sir Tim Lankester to Professor Richard Aldrich, 17 July 1998.
6. Interview with David Blunkett, 23 April 1998.
7. Interview with Michael Bichard, 8 January 1998.
8. *The Times*, 28 May 1999.
9. Interview with Michael Bichard, 8 January 1998.
10. Interview with David Blunkett, 23 April 1998.
11. The employment figures cited in this section for the spring and summer of 1999 are taken from the Office for National Statistics as reported in *The Times*, 16 September 1999.
12. *DfEE News* 279/94, 9 November 1994.
13. *DfEE News* 97/99, 3 March 1999.
14. *TES*, 6 March 1998.
15. Handy, 1995, 27–28.
16. Carpentier and Diebolt, 1999, 1.
17. Patten, 1998, 130.
18. Ribbins and Sherratt, 1997, 212.

19. Interview with David Blunkett, 23 April 1998.
20. Interview with Michael Bichard, 8 January 1998.
21. Interview with Michael Bichard, 8 January 1998.
22. Reported in *The Times*, 14 September 1999.
23. http://ntweb1/DfEE Plan/DfEE Busplaan/dfeebp tasks.htm The Employment Service, which is the DfEE's 'Next Steps Agency', produces its own annual operational plan.

APPENDIX 1: Education department

Secretaries of State for Education*

Apr. 1900	Duke of Devonshire (Spencer Compton) (Con)
Aug. 1902	Marquess of Londonderry (Charles Stewart) (Con)
Dec. 1905	Augustine Birrell (Lib)
Jan. 1907	Reginald McKenna (Lib)
Apr. 1908	Walter Runciman (Lib)
Oct. 1911	Joseph Pease (Lib)
May 1915	Arthur Henderson (Coalition/Lab)
Aug. 1916	Marquess of Crewe (Coalition/Lab)
Dec. 1916	H.A.L. Fisher (Coalition/Lib)
Oct. 1922	Edward F.L. Wood (Con)
Jan. 1924	Charles P. Trevelyan (Lab)
Nov. 1924	Lord Eustace Percy (Con)
June 1929	Charles P. Trevelyan (Lab)
Mar. 1931	H.B. Lees-Smith (Lab)
Aug. 1931	Sir Donald Maclean (National/Lib)
July 1932	Lord Irwin (National/Con)
June 1935	Oliver F.G. Stanley (Con)
May 1937	Earl Stanhope (Con)
Oct. 1938	Earl de la Warr (Con)
May 1940	Herwald Ramsbotham (Coalition/Con)
July 1941	R.A. Butler (Coalition/Con)
May 1945	Richard K. Law (Caretaker government)
Aug. 1945	Ellen Wilkinson (Lab)
Feb. 1947	George Tomlinson (Lab)
Nov. 1951	Florence Horsbrugh (Con)
Oct. 1954	Sir David Eccles (Con)
Jan. 1957	Viscount Hailsham (Con)
Sept. 1957	Geoffrey Lloyd (Con)
Oct. 1959	Sir David Eccles (Con)
July 1962	Sir Edward Boyle (Con)
Apr. 1964	Quintin Hogg (Con)
Oct. 1964	Michael Stewart (Lab)
Jan. 1965	Anthony Crosland (Lab)
Aug. 1967	Patrick Gordon Walker (Lab)
Apr. 1968	Edward Short (Lab)
June 1970	Margaret Thatcher (Con)
Mar. 1974	Reginald Prentice (Lab)
June 1975	Frederick W. Mulley (Lab)
Sept. 1976	Shirley Williams (Lab)
May 1979	Mark Carlisle (Con)
Sept. 1981	Sir Keith Joseph (Con)
May 1986	Kenneth Baker (Con)
July 1989	John MacGregor (Con)
Nov. 1990	Kenneth Clarke (Con)
Apr. 1992	John Patten (Con)
July 1994	Gillian Shephard (Con)

Permanent Secretaries

1900	Sir George Kekewich
1903	Sir Robert Morant
1911	Sir Lewis Selby-Bigge
1925	Sir Aubrey Vere Symonds
1931	Sir Edward Pelham
1937	Sir Maurice Holmes
1945	Sir John Maud
1952	Sir Gilbert Flemming
1959	Dame Mary Smieton
1963	Sir Herbert Andrew
1970	Sir William Pile
1976	Sir James Hamilton
1983	Sir David Hancock
1989	Sir John Caines
1993	Sir Geoffrey Holland
1994	Sir Timothy Lankester

*Presidents 1900–44, Ministers 1944–64.

Source: DfEE Information Bureau & Library; *Education Information Sheet No. 3.*

APPENDIX 2: Employment department

Secretaries of State for Employment*

Dec. 1916	J. Hodge (Coalition/Lab)	
Aug. 1917	G.H. Roberts (Coalition/Lab)	
Jan. 1919	Sir R. Horne (Coalition/Con)	
Mar. 1920	T.J. Macnamara (Coalition/Lib)	
Oct. 1922	Sir C.A.M. Barlow (Con)	
Jan. 1924	T. Shaw (Lab)	
Nov. 1924	Sir A. Steel-Maitland (Con)	
June 1929	Margaret Bondfield (Lab)	
Aug. 1931	Sir H.B. Betterton (National/Con)	
June 1934	O. Stanley (National/Con)	
June 1935	E. Brown (Con)	
May 1940	E. Bevin (Coalition/Lab)	
May 1945	R.A. Butler (Caretaker gov.)	
Aug. 1945	George Isaacs (Lab)	
Jan. 1951	Aneurin Bevin (Lab)	
Apr. 1951	Alfred Robens (Lab)	
Oct. 1951	Sir Walter Monckton (Con)	
Dec. 1955	Iain Macleod (Con)	
Oct. 1959	Edward Heath (Con)	
July 1960	John Hare (Con)	
Oct. 1963	Joseph Godber (Con)	
Oct. 1964	Ray Gunter (Lab)	
Apr. 1968	Barbara Castle (Lab)	
June 1970	Robert Carr (Con)	
Apr. 1972	Maurice Macmillan (Con)	
Dec. 1973	William Whitelaw (Con)	
Mar. 1974	Michael Foot (Lab)	
Apr. 1976	Albert Booth (Lab)	
May 1979	James Prior (Con)	
Sept. 1981	Norman Tebbit (Con)	
Oct. 1983	Tom King (Con)	
Sept. 1985	Lord Young (Con)	
June 1987	Sir Norman Fowler (Con)	
Jan. 1990	Michael Howard (Con)	
Apr. 1992	Gillian Shephard (Con)	
May 1993	David Hunt (Con)	
July 1994	Michael Portillo (Con)	

Permanent Secretaries

1916	Sir D.J. Shackleton
1920	Sir J. Masterton-Smith
1921	Sir H.J. Wilson
1930	Sir F. Floud
1935	Sir T.W. Phillips
1944	Sir Godfrey Ince
1956	Sir Harold Emmerson
1960	Sir Laurence Helsby
1964	Sir James Dunnett
1967	Sir Denis Barnes
1975	Sir Conrad Heron
1977	Sir Kenneth Barnes
1983	Sir Michael Quinlan
1989	Sir Geoffrey Holland
1993	Sir Nicholas Monck
1995	Sir Michael Bichard

*Ministers 1916–68.

Sources: Lowe, R. (1986), *Adjusting to Democracy. The Role of the Ministry of Labour in British Politics, 1916–1939.* Oxford: Clarendon Press. Ince, Sir Godfrey (1960), *The Ministry of Labour and National Service.* London: Allen & Unwin. Cook, C. and Stevenson, J. (1996), *The Longman Companion to Britain since 1945.* London: Longman. *The British Imperial Calendar and Civil Service List.* London: HMSO, various dates. *The Civil Service Yearbook.* London: HMSO, various dates.

References

Addison, P. (1975), *The Road to 1945*. London: Quartet Books.

Ainley, P. (1988), *From School to YTS: Education and Training in England and Wales, 1944–1987*. Milton Keynes: Open University Press.

Ainley, P. (1995), 'Education without employment'. *Education Today and Tomorrow*, 47, 3, 8–9.

Ainley, P. and Corney, M. (1990), *Training for the Future: The Rise and Fall of the Manpower Services Commission*. London: Cassell.

Albu, A. (1963), 'Taboo on expertise'. *Encounter*, 21, 118, 45–50.

Aldrich, R. (1996), *Education for the Nation*. London: Cassell.

— and Leighton, P. (1985), *Education: Time for a New Act?* London: University of London Institute of Education.

Allaire, Y. and Firsirotu, M.E. (1984), 'Theories of organizational culture'. *Organization Studies*, 5, 193–226.

Anderson, R. and Haywood, R. (1996), 'Advancing GNVQs'. *Forum*, 38, 3, 81–83.

Anechiarico, F. (1998), 'Administrative culture and civil society: a comparative perspective'. *Administration and Society*, 30, 1, 13–34.

Ashton, D. and Green, F. (1996), *Education, Training and the Global Economy*. Cheltenham: Edward Elgar.

Avis, J., Bloomer, M., Esland, G., Gleeson, D. and Hodkinson, P. (1996), *Knowledge and Nationhood: Education, Politics and Work*. London: Cassell.

Ayer, J. (1994), *'The Great Jobs Crisis': Mobilising the UK's Education and Training Resources*. Cambridge: Tory Reform Group.

Baker, K. (1993), *The Turbulent Years: My Life in Politics*. London: Faber and Faber.

Baker, M. and Elias, P. (1992), 'Recent developments in vocational education and training in the UK'. In P. Townroe and R. Martin (eds), *Regional Development in the 1990s: The British Isles in Transition*. London: Jessica Kingsley, 237–250.

Balfour, A. (1927), *Factors in Industrial and Commercial Efficiency, being Part I of a survey of industries with an introduction by the Committee on Industry and Trade*. London: HMSO.

Ball, S. (1994), *Education Reform: A Critical and Post-Structural Approach*. Buckingham: Open University Press.

Barber, M. (1994), 'Power and control in education, 1944–2004'. *British Journal of Educational Studies*, XXXXII, 4, 348–362.

Barnett, C. (1963), 'The idea of leadership'. *Spectator*, 8 March, 210, 7028.

— (1978), 'Obsolescence and Dr. Arnold'. In P. Hutber (ed.), *What's Wrong with Britain?* London: Sphere, 29–34.

— (1986), *The Audit of War: The Illusion and Reality of Britain as a Great Nation*. London: Macmillan.

Beaumont, G. (1995), *Review of 100 NVQs and SVQs: A Report submitted to the Department for Education and Employment*. npp.

Benn, C. (1992), 'Common education and the radical tradition'. In A. Rattansi and D. Reeder (eds), *Rethinking Radical Education: Essays in Honour of Brian Simon*. London: Lawrence and Wishart, 142–165.

Bennett, R.J., Wicks, P. and McCoshan, A. (1994), *Local Empowerment and Business Services: Britain's Experiment with Training and Enterprise Councils*. London: UCL Press.

Bichard, M. (1996), 'Shake-up inspires new state of mind'. *People Management*, 8 February, 22–27.

Bishop, A.S. (1971), *The Rise of a Central Authority for English Education*. Cambridge: Cambridge University Press.

Blackman, S. and Evans, K. (1994), 'Comparative youth skill acquisition in Germany and England: training as a process not an outcome'. *Youth and Policy*, 43, 1–23.

Blakely, E.J. (1997), 'A new role for education in economic development: tomorrow's economy today'. *Education and Urban Society*, 29, 4, 509–523.

Board of Education (1930), *Education for Industry and Commerce: The West Midlands Metal Working Area* (Educational pamphlet 74). London: HMSO.

Bogdanor, V. (1979), 'Power and participation'. *Oxford Review of Education*, 5, 2, 157–168.

Bowe, R. and Whitty, G. (1989), 'The re-opening of the GCSE "settlement": recent developments in the politics of school examinations'. *British Journal of Sociology of Education*, 10, 4, 403–415.

Brennan, E. (ed.) (1975), *Education for National Efficiency: The Contribution of Sidney and Beatrice Webb*. London: Athlone Press.

Briar, C. (1997), *Working for Women? Gendered Work and Welfare Policies in Twentieth Century Britain*. London: UCL Press.

Brine, J. (1992), 'The European Social Fund and the vocational training of unemployed women: questions of gendering and re-gendering'. *Gender and Education*, 4, 1–2, 149–162.

Bullock, A. (1967), *The Life and Times of Ernest Bevin. Volume 2: Minister of Labour, 1940–45*. London: Heinemann.

Burgess, K. (1993), 'Education policy in relation to employment in Britain, 1935–45: a decade of "missed opportunities"?', *History of Education*, 22, 4, 365–390.

— (1995), 'Youth employment policy during the 1930s'. *Twentieth Century British History*, 6, 1, 23–55.

Burton, E. (1941), *What of the Women? A Study of Women in Wartime*. London: Frederick Muller.

Capey, J. (1995), *GNVQ Assessment Review*. London: National Council for Vocational Qualifications.

Carpentier, V. and Diebolt, C. (1999), 'Education and Economic Development: Germany and the United Kingdom in the 19th and 20th centuries'. Paper presented to the Oxford International Conference on Education and Development, September.

Carr, W. and Hartnett, A. (1996), *Education and the Struggle for Democracy: The Politics of Educational Ideas*. Buckingham: Open University Press.

Carter, M. (1966), *Into Work*. Harmondsworth: Penguin.

Chitty, C. (1989), *Towards a New Education System: The Victory of the New Right?* London: Falmer.

Chitty, C. (1992), *The Education System Transformed*. Manchester: Baseline Books.

Christoph, J.B. (1992), 'The remaking of British administrative culture: why Whitehall can't go home again'. *Administration and Society*, 24, 2, 163–181.

Cohen, P. (1984) 'Against the new vocationalism'. In I. Bates, J. Clarke, P. Cohen, D. Finn, R. Moore, and P. Willis (eds), *Schooling for the Dole? The new vocationalism*. London: Macmillan, 104–169.

Coles, B. and Maynard, M. (1990), 'Moving towards a fair start: equal gender opportunities and the careers service'. *Gender and Education*, 2, 3, 297–308.

Collini, S. (1993), 'Introduction'. In C.P. Snow, *The Two Cultures* (1993 edition). Cambridge: Cambridge University Press, vii–lxxi.

Collins, B. and Robbins, K. (eds) (1990), *British Culture and Economic Decline*. London: Weidenfeld and Nicolson.

Colls, R. (1986), 'Englishness and political culture'. In R. Colls and P. Dodd (eds), *Englishness, Politics and Culture, 1880–1920*. London: Croom Helm, 29–61.

Conservative Party Study Group on Youth Policy (1978), *A Time for Youth: The Report of a Conservative Party Study Group on Youth Policy*. London: Community Affairs Department, Conservative Central Office.

Crooks, C. (1993), *100 Not Out. The Centenary of the Employment Department, 1893–1993*. London: Employment Department.

Croucher, C. (1997), 'Skills-based full employment: the latest philosopher's stone', *British Journal of Industrial Relations*, 35, 3, 367–391.

Davis, G., Weller, P, Craswell, E. and Eggins, S. (1999), 'What drives machinery of government change? Australia, Canada and the United Kingdom, 1950–1997'. *Public Administration*, 77, 1, 7–50.

De la Mothe, J. (1992), *C.P Snow and the Struggle of Modernity*. Montreal: McGill-Queen's University Press.

Deakin, B.M. (1996), *The Youth Labour Market in Britain* (University of Cambridge Department of Applied Economics Occasional Paper no. 62). Cambridge: Cambridge University Press.

Dearing, R. (1996), *Review of Qualifications for 16 to 19-Year-Olds*. London: School Curriculum and Assessment Authority.

Department for Education and Employment (1995), *The English Education System. An Overview of Structure and Policy*. London: DfEE.

— (1997), *Learning and Working Together for the Future: A Consultation Document*. London: DfEE.

Department of Education and Science/Employment Department/Welsh Office (1991), *Education and Training for the 21st century,* 2 volumes, Cmnd 1536. London: HMSO.

Department of Employment (1986), *Working Together: Education and Training*. Cmnd 9823. London: HMSO.

Doyle, B. (1986), 'The invention of English'. In R. Colls and P. Dodd (eds), *Englishness, Politics and Culture, 1880–1920*. London: Croom Helm, 89–115.

Employment Policy Institute (1996), 'After the jobs ministry: options for running labour market policy'. *Economic Report*, January, 10, 1.

Evans, B. (1992), *The Politics of the Training Market: From Manpower Services Commission to Training and Enterprise Councils*. London: Routledge.

Evans, E.W. and Wiseman, N.C. (1984), 'Education, training and economic performance: British economists' views, 1868–1939', *Journal of European Economic History*, 13, 1, 129–148.

Fairlie, H. (1963), 'On the comforts of anger'. *Encounter*, 21, 118, 9–13.

Felstead, A. (1996), 'Identifying gender inequalities in the distribution of vocational qualifications in the UK'. *Gender, Work and Organization*, 3, 1, 38–50.

Finegold, D., Keep, E., Miliband, D., Raffe, D., Spours, K. and Young, M. (1990), *A British 'Baccalaureate': Ending the Division between Education and Training*. London: Institute for Public Policy Research.

Finegold, D. and Soskice, D. (1988), 'The failure of training in Britain: analysis and prescription'. *Oxford Review of Economic Policy*, 4, 3, 21–53.

Flecker, F., Meil, P. and Pollert, A. (1998), 'The sexual division of labour in process manufacturing: economic restructuring, training and "women's work"'. *European Journal of Industrial Relations*, 4, 1, 7–34.

Fletcher, J. (1995), 'Policy-making in DES/DfE via consensus and contention'. *Oxford Review of Education,* 21, 2, 133–148.

Foot, P. (1968), *The Politics of Harold Wilson.* Harmondsworth: Penguin.

Freedland, M. (1992), 'The role of the Department of Employment – twenty years of institutional change'. In W. McCarthy (ed.), *Legal Intervention in Industrial Relations: Gains and Losses.* Oxford: Blackwell, 274–295.

— (1996), 'Vocational training in EC law and policy – education, employment or welfare?'. *Industrial Law Journal*, 25, 2, 110–120.

Fry, G.K. (1993), *Reforming the Civil Service: The Fulton Committee on the British Home Civil Service of 1966–68.* Edinburgh: Edinburgh University Press.

Gewirtz, S. and Ozga, J. (1990), 'Partnership, pluralism and education policy: a reassessment'. *Journal of Education Policy*, 5, 1, 37–48.

Gibbon, Sir G. (1940), 'The organization of government'. *Public Administration*, 18, 1, 7–17.

Gordon, P., Aldrich, R. and Dean, D. (1991), *Education and Policy in England in the Twentieth Century.* London: Woburn Press.

Gosden, P. (1966), *The Development of Educational Administration in England and Wales.* Oxford: Blackwell.

— (1976), *Education in the Second World War: A Study in Policy and Administration.* London: Methuen.

— (1989), 'From Board to Ministry: the impact of the war on the Education department'. *History of Education*, 18, 3, 183–193.

Green, A. (1995), 'The role of the state and the social partners in VET systems'. In L. Bash and A. Green (eds), *World Yearbook of Education 1995: Youth, Education and Work.* London: Kogan Page, 92–108.

Green, F. (1997), 'Discussion'. *British Journal of Industrial Relations*, 35, 3, 392–398.

Haldane, R.B.H. (1918), *Report of the Machinery of Government Committee*, Cmnd 9230. London: HMSO.

Hamilton, Sir J. (1982), *Education, Industry and Society.* London: Council of Engineering Institutions.

Handy, C. (1995), *The Empty Raincoat.* London: Arrow Books.

— (1998), *The Hungry Spirit.* London: Arrow Books.

Harland, J. (1987), 'The TVEI experience: issues of control, response and the professional role of teachers'. In D. Gleeson (ed.), *TVEI and Secondary Education: A Critical Appraisal.* Milton Keynes: Open University Press, 38–54.

Harris, J. (1990), 'Economic knowledge and British social policy'. In M. Furner and B. Supple (eds), *The State and Economic Knowledge*. Cambridge: Cambridge University Press, 379–400.

— (1992), 'Political thought and the Welfare State, 1870–1940: an intellectual framework for British social policy'. *Past and Present*, 135, 116–141.

— (1994), *Private Lives, Public Spirit: A Social History of Britain, 1870–1914*. London: Penguin.

Heginbotham, H. (1951), *The Youth Employment Service*. London: Methuen.

Hennessy, P. (1989), *Whitehall*. London: Fontana.

Hickox, M. and Moore, R. (1995), 'Liberal-humanist education: the vocationalist challenge'. *Curriculum Studies*, 3, 1, 45–59.

Hinton, J. (1994), *Shop Floor Citizens: Engineering Democracy in 1940s Britain*. Aldershot: Edward Elgar.

Hodkinson, P. (1997), 'NVQs a way forward'. In R. Halsall and M. Cockett (eds), *Education and Training, 14–19: Chaos or Coherence*. Manchester: Manchester Metropolitan University, 17–32.

Howieson, C., Raffe, D., Spours, K. and Young, M. (1997), 'Unifying academic and vocational learning: the state of the debate in England and Scotland'. *Journal of Education and Work*, 10, 1, 5–35.

Hurrelman, K. and Roberts, K. (1991), 'Problems and solutions'. In J. Bynner and K. Roberts (eds) (1991), *Youth and Work: Transition to Employment in Germany and England*. London: Anglo-German Foundation, 229–250.

Hutber, P. (ed.) (1978), *What's Wrong with Britain?* London: Sphere.

Ince, Sir G. (1960), *The Ministry of Labour and National Service*. London: Allen and Unwin.

Jefferys, K. (ed.) (1987), *Labour and the Wartime Coalition: From the Diary of James Chuter Ede, 1941–45*. London: Historians' Press.

Jenkins, P. (1970), *The Battle of Downing Street*. London: Knight.

Jones, K. (1995), 'Across the great divide? Culture, economic life and the rethinking of education policy', *Curriculum Studies*, 3, 3, 227–243.

Jones, M. (1996), 'Full steam ahead to a workfare state? Analysing the UK Employment Department's abolition'. *Policy and Politics*, 24, 2, 137–153.

— (1997) 'Skills revolution? Sorry wrong number'. *Local Economy*, 11, 4, 290–298.

Jones, M. and Ward, K. (1998) 'The role of coalitions in urban economic development'. *Local Economy*, 31, 1, 28–38.

Joseph, K. (1978), 'Proclaim the message: Keynes is dead!'. In P. Hutber (ed.), *What's Wrong with Britain?* London: Sphere, 99–106.

Joseph, K. and Sumption, J. (1979), *Equality*. London: John Murray.

Kennedy, H. (1997), *Learning Works: Widening Participation in Further Education.* Coventry: Further Education Funding Council.

King, D. (1993), 'The Conservatives and training policy 1979–1992: from a tripartite to a neoliberal regime'. *Political Studies*, 41, 214–235.

— (1995), *Actively Seeking Work? The Politics of Unemployment and Welfare Policy in the United States and Great Britain.* Chicago: Chicago University Press.

Knight, C. (1990), *The Making of Tory Education Policy in Post-War Britain, 1950–1986.* Lewes: Falmer.

Koestler, A. (1963) 'Introduction'. *Encounter*, 21, 118, 5–8.

Kogan, M. (1978), *The Politics of Educational Change.* London: Fontana.

Labour Party (1967), *The Fulton Committee on the Civil Service: Labour Party Evidence.* London: The Labour Party.

Labour Party (1996), *Learn As You Earn: Labour's Plans For A Skills Revolution.* London: Labour Party.

Laski, H. (1942), 'Introduction'. In J.P.W. Mallalieu (ed.), *Passed to you Please. Britain's Red-Tape Machine at War.* London: Victor Gollancz.

Lawrence, I. (1992), *Power and Politics at the Department of Education and Science.* London: Cassell.

Lawton, D. (1994), *The Tory Mind on Education, 1979–1994.* London: Falmer.

Layard, R. (1997), *What Labour Can Do.* London: Warner Books.

Low, G. (1988), 'The MSC: a failure of democracy?'. In M. Morris and C. Griggs (eds) *Education: the Wasted Years? 1973–1986.* Brighton: Falmer.

Lowe, R. (1986), *Adjusting to Democracy: The Role of the Ministry of Labour in British Politics, 1916–1939.* Oxford: Clarendon Press.

— (1997), 'The core executive, modernization and the creation of the PESC, 1960–64'. *Public Administration*, 75, 601–615.

Maclure, S. (1969), *Educational Documents. England and Wales 1816–1968.* London: Methuen.

Malcolm, D. (1928), *Report of the Committee on Education and Industry (England and Wales).* London: HMSO.

Marsden, C. (1989), 'Why business should work with education'. *British Journal of Education and Work*, 2, 3, 79–89.

Marshall, G. (1995), *After 16. The Future for Education.* Cambridge: Tory Reform Group.

Mason, C. (1984), 'YTS and LEAs: a context'. *Local Government Studies*, 10, 1, 63–73.

— (1988), *Government Restructuring of Vocational Education and Training, 1981–87: Local Autonomy or Dependence?* (Occasional Paper 33). Bristol: University of Bristol School for Advanced Urban Studies.

Maxted, P. (1995), 'Together at last'. *Training Tomorrow*, 9, 6, 5–6.

McCarthy, W. (1997), *New Labour at Work. Reforming the Labour Market*. London: IPPR.

McCulloch, G. (1986), 'Policy, politics and education: the Technical and Vocational Education Initiative'. *Journal of Education Policy*, 1, 1, 35–57.

— (1994), *Educational Reconstruction: The 1944 Education Act and the Twenty-First Century*. London: Woburn.

McPherson, A. and Raab, C. (1988), *Governing Education: A Sociology of Policy since 1945*. Edinburgh: Edinburgh University Press.

Mercier, J. (1994), 'Looking at organizational culture, hermeneutically'. *Administration and Society*, 26, 1, 28–47.

Merson, M. (1995), 'Political explanations for economic decline in Britain and their relationship to policies for education and training'. *Journal of Education Policy*, 10, 3, 303–315.

Miles, S. and Middleton, C. (1990), 'Girls education in the balance: the ERA and inequality'. In M. Flude and M. Hammer (eds), *The Education Reform Act, 1988: Its Origins and Implications*. London: Falmer Press, 187–206.

Milne-Watson, Sir D. (1927), *Education and Industry* (Presidential address delivered at the Annual Conference of the Association for Education in Industry and Commerce). London: AEIC.

Ministry of Education (1951), *Education 1900–1950. The Report of the Ministry of Education and the Statistics of Public Education for the year 1950*, Cmd. 8244. London: HMSO.

Montgomery, R.J. (1965), *Examinations: An Account of Their Evolution as Administrative Devices in England*. London: Longmans.

Moon, J. and Richardson, J.J. (1984), 'Policy-making with a difference? The Technical and Vocational Education Initiative'. *Public Administration*, 62, 23–33.

Morgan, J.F. (1994), 'The Politics of Industrial Training in Britain, 1960–1990', unpublished PhD thesis, University of Leeds.

Morris, P. (1991), 'Freeing the spirit of enterprise: the genesis and development of the concept of enterprise culture'. In R. Keat and N. Abercrombie, *Enterprise Culture*. London: Routledge, 21–37.

Moser, C. (1999), *Improving Numeracy and Literacy: A Fresh Start*. London: DfEE.

National Commission on Education (1993), *Learning to Succeed: Report of the Paul Hamlyn Foundation National Commission on Education*. London: Heinemann.

— (1995), *Learning to Succeed: After Sixteen*. London: National Commission on Education.

National Joint Sub-Committee Report (1958), *Training for Skill: Recruitment and Training of Young Workers for Industry*. London: HMSO.

Newton, S. and Porter, D. (1988), *Modernization Frustrated: The Politics of Industrial Decline in Britain since 1900.* London: Unwin Hyman.

OECD (1975), *Education Development Strategy in England and Wales.* Paris: OECD.

Papadopoulos, G. (1994), *Education, 1960–1990: The OECD Perspective.* Paris: OECD.

Parker, D. (1995), ' "The talent at its command": the First World War and the vocational aspect of education, 1914–39'. *History of Education Quarterly*, 35, 3, 237–259.

Parker, H.M.D. (1957), *Manpower: A Study of War-time Policy and Administration.* London: HMSO.

Parkes, D. (1985) 'Competition and competence? Education, training and the role of the DES and MSC'. In I. McNay and J. Ozga (eds), *Policy-Making in Education: The Breakdown of Consensus.* Oxford: Pergammon Press, 159–172.

Patten, C. (1998), *East and West.* London: Macmillan.

Paz, D.G. (1976), 'The composition of the Education Committee of the Privy Council, 1839–1856'. *Journal of Educational Administration and History*, 8, 2, 1–8.

Percy, Lord Eustace (1928), 'Preface'. In: *Education for Industry and Commerce: A Survey of the Existing Arrangements for Cooperation between Industry, Commerce and the Professions and the Technical School System of England and Wales.* Board of Education Pamphlet no. 64 (Industry Series No. 1). London: HMSO.

Perkin, H. (1992), 'The enterprise culture in historical perspective: birth, life, death – and resurrection?'. In P. Heelas and P. Morris (eds), *The Values of the Enterprise Culture: The Moral Debate.* London: Routledge, 36–60.

Perkins, F.H. (1957), *Educational Problems of Industry. Address to the Annual Meeting of the Northern Counties Technical Examinations Council.* Bradford: Northern Counties Technical Examinations Council.

Perry, P.J.C. (1984), *Sand in the Sandwich and Other Editorials from the BACIE Journal, 1970–1984.* London: BACIE.

Pile, Sir W. (1979), *The Department of Education and Science.* London: Allen and Unwin.

Ploszajska, T. (1994), 'Training and enterprise in England and Wales: a critical review'. *British Journal of Education and Work*, 7, 3, 43–62.

Pollard, S. (1989), *Britain's Prime and Britain's Decline: The British Economy, 1870–1914.* London: Edward Arnold.

Pollitt, C. (1984), *Manipulating the Machine: Changing the Patterns of Ministerial Departments, 1960–83.* London: George Allen and Unwin.

Ranson, S. (1980), 'Changing relations between centre and locality in education'. *Local Government Studies*, 16, 6, 3–23.

— (1983), '16–19 policy: differentiated solidarity at the DES'. Paper presented to the seminar on the Decomposition of the DES, Cambridge, September.

Raven, J. (1989), 'British history and the enterprise culture'. *Past and Present*, 123, 178–204.

Reeder, D. (1979), 'A recurring debate: education and industry'. In G. Bernbaum (ed.), *Schooling in Decline*. London: Macmillan, 115–148.

Ribbins, P. and Sherratt, B. (1997), *Radical Educational Policies and Conservative Secretaries of State*. London: Cassell.

Richards, D. and Smith, M.J. (1997), 'How departments change: windows of opportunity and critical junctures in three departments'. *Public Policy and Administration*, 12, 2, 62–79.

Robinson, P. (1996), *Rhetoric and Reality: Britain's New Vocational Qualifications*. London: London School of Economics.

— (1997), *Literacy, Numeracy and Economic Performance*. London: London School of Economics.

— (1998), 'Tyranny of the league tables'. *Parliamentary Brief*, 5, 5, 59–61.

Royal Commission on Trade Unions and Employers' Associations (1965), *Written Evidence of the Ministry of Labour*. London: HMSO.

Savage, G. (1996), *The Social Construction of Expertise: The English Civil Service and its Influence, 1919–1939*. Pittsburgh: University of Pittsburgh Press.

Sheldrake, J. and Vickerstaff, S. (1987), *The History of Industrial Training in Britain*. Aldershot: Avebury.

Showler, B. (1976), *The Public Employment Service*. London: Longman.

Simon, B. (1974), *The Politics of Educational Reform, 1920–40*. London: Lawrence and Wishart.

Smircich, L. (1983), 'Concepts of culture and organizational analysis'. *Administrative Science Quarterly*, 28, 339–358.

Smith, H. (ed.) (1986), *War and Social Change: British Society in the Second World War*. Manchester: Manchester University Press.

Snow, C.P. (1959), *The Two Cultures and the Scientific Revolution*. Cambridge: Cambridge University Press.

Stacey, F. (1975), *British Government, 1966 to 1975: Years of Reform*. Oxford: Oxford University Press.

Taylor, S. and Henry, M. (1994), 'Equity and the new post-compulsory education and training policies in Australia: a progressive or repressive agenda?'. *Journal of Education Policy*, 9, 2, 105–127.

Thatcher, M. (1996), 'An advocate of change'. *People Management*, 8 February, 24–25.

Tomlinson, J. (1994), *Government and the Enterprise since 1900: The Changing Problem of Efficiency*. Oxford: Clarendon Press.

— (1998), *Decline as History, History as Decline. Is the notion of 'decline' helpful in understanding the last one hundred years of British economic history?* Brunel University, Department of Government, discussion paper series, 98/2.

Tonge, J. (1993), *Training and Enterprise Councils: The Privatisation of Britain's Unemployment Problem?* Bristol: University of the West of England, Faculty of Economics & Social Science.

Watson, D. (1998), 'Relations between the education and employment departments, 1921–45: an anti-industry culture versus industrial efficiency?', *History of Education*, 27, 3, 333–343.

Weiler, P. (1993), *Ernest Bevin.* Manchester: Manchester University Press.

Weiner, G. (1990), 'What price vocationalism: the feminist dilemma!'. *British Journal of Education and Work*, 4, 1, 23–30.

Wiener, M.J. (1981), *English Culture and the Decline of the Industrial Spirit, 1850–1980.* Cambridge: Cambridge University Press.

Williams, R. (1961), *Culture and Society, 1780–1950.* Harmondsworth: Penguin.

Wolf, A. (1997), 'Growth stocks and lemons: diplomas in the English market-place, 1976–96'. *Assessment in Education*, 4, 1, 33–49.

Wright, A. (1987), *R.H. Tawney.* Manchester: Manchester University Press.

Wright, I. (1979), 'F.R. Leavis, the 'Scrutiny' movement and the crisis'. In J. Clark, M. Heinemann, D. Margolies and C. Snee (eds), *Culture and Crisis in Britain in the Thirties.* London: Lawrence and Wishart, 37–65.

Young, Lord D. (1992), 'Enterprise regained'. In P. Heelas and P. Morris (eds), *The Values of the Enterprise Culture: The Moral Debate.* London: Routledge, 29–35.

Young, H. (1989), *One of Us: A Biography of Margaret Thatcher.* London: Macmillan.

Index